EDITED BY

David Madden

Tough Guy Writers
of the Thirties

WITH A PREFACE BY

Harry T. Moore

Carbondale and Edwardsville

SOUTHERN ILLINOIS UNIVERSITY PRESS

FEFFER & SIMONS, INC.

London and Amsterdam

43052

To James M. Cain,

twenty-minute egg of the hard-boiled writers

ACKNOWLEDGMENT:
The quotation from *The Rebel* by Albert Camus (Vintage
Books edition, pp. 265–66) is by permission of Alfred A.
Knopf, Inc.

Copyright © 1968 by Southern Illinois University Press
First published, March 1968
Second printing, July 1970
Printed in the United States of America
Designed by Andor Braun
ISBN 0–8093–0287–X
Library of Congress Catalog Card Number 68–10115

LITERATURE has from the first been full of violence. This applies even to literature of the highest type; indeed, the higher it is (Shakespeare, Dante, Greek tragedy), the fuller of violence.

But literature has not always been what we think of as tough. Yet there have been certain times which produced tough-guy writing: think of François Villon using thieves' argot in the fifteenth century.

Few periods of history, however, have seen tough writing flourish as it did in the American 1930's. James M. Cain, Dashiell Hammett, and others dealt with in the present book virtually established a new manner of expression. Of course there had earlier been literature, of various grades, in the American idiom, from Mark Twain through Ring Lardner's stories and George Ade's Fables in Slang, and although their books weren't, technically, tough-guy writing, they blazed the trail for it. (See also Kingsley Widmer's essay in the present book.)

As this volume attests, there was much gangsterism in tough-guy literature. Gangsters stood up large in the prohibition years, yet they had existed before the Volstead Act became the unpopular and often-broken law. One of the activities of the gangsters was participation in the wars between the newspaper circulation departments.

This was particularly intense in Chicago, with the street

battles between the thugs of the Tribune and those of William Randolph Hearst's papers. It is ironic that this great impetus to the gang wars came from the newspapers, whose primary function was the conveying of useful information!

The existence of gangsters—as this book again shows—made possible a special type of movie, often adapted from the tough-guy novels. As I remember those films of the early 1930's, it seems that Warner Brothers had a monopoly on them. Warner's nurtured a stock company whose actors appeared repeatedly as what were then called mobsters.

The big stars did their part, and often made their reputations, in gangster films. Paul Muni in Scarface, Edward G. Robinson in Little Caesar, and James Cagney in Public Enemy became symbols of the age.

Gangster films are of course only incidental to the tough-guy literature, but they do go with it. The literature itself, not only with the gangsters but the private eyes, was exciting to read, and in some cases taken quite seriously—by André Gide, for instance, who rated Dashiell Hammett among America's leading writers. In any event, to read the tough-guy writers in the 1930's was to be very much a part of the epoch. And now that epoch is of great historical interest.

Most of its writing wasn't up to the literature of the 1920's, but almost all of its writing (except the dreary extremes of what we called agitprop, or agitation-propaganda) was of intense interest, and it remains so.

That is why this particular book is both so absorbing and so valuable. It is, incidentally, a companion volume to Proletarian Writers of the Thirties, also edited by David Madden, and published simultaneously with the present book in the Crosscurrents / Modern Critiques series. For both volumes Mr. Madden has assembled star casts of critics who deal with their subjects excitingly. Because of the size of the books—and we couldn't bring ourselves to reduce Mr. Madden's superb collections—we have published these volumes as Crosscurrents "specials," which has made necessary an advance in price over most of the series.

The contributors to the tough-guy volume sometimes overlap in their discussions, when they talk about writers mentioned elsewhere in these pages. This multiple coverage is all to the good, for it deepens perspectives.

It would be hard to imagine two better introductions to our literature of the 1930's than these two volumes. Mr. Madden has also provided notes identifying his contributors, most of whom don't really need to be introduced, though the particulars of their careers are of importance and interest. Mr. Madden has further written an Introduction which will itself certainly prove to be of historical importance.

HARRY T. MOORE

Southern Illinois University
October 12, 1967

NOTES ON CONTRIBUTORS

DAVID MADDEN is the author of two literary studies, *James M. Cain* and *Wright Morris*, and of a novel, *The Beautiful Greed*. His literary essays have appeared in *Prairie Schooner, Antioch Review, Journal of Aesthetics, Modern Fiction Studies, Studies in Short Fiction,* and *The University Review*. Other articles and film criticism have appeared in *The Appalachian Review, Film Quarterly,* and *Film Heritage*. His stories and poems have been published in such journals as *The Kenyon Review, Botteghe Oscure, The Southwest Review,* and *Ante*. His prize-winning plays have had many productions and several have been published in *New Campus Writing #2* and *First Stage*. Former assistant editor of *The Kenyon Review*, he is associate editor of *Film Heritage*, and is Writer-in-Residence at Louisiana State University.

KINGSLEY WIDMER is the author of *The Art of Perversity: D. H. Lawrence, Henry Miller, The Literary Rebel,* and *Melville's Novellas;* he also writes essays of radical social criticism. A teacher, he lives in Southern California. His concern with the literature of outcasts derives in part from some of his own early experiences.

BENJAMIN APPEL graduated from Lafayette College at the beginning of the great Depression. His first novel, *Brain Guy,* was published in 1934. Since then he has published 13 novels. He is now working on the second in a series of six novels that will tell the story of two American families over the last sixty years. The first in the series, *A Time of Fortune,* was published in 1963.

SHELDON GREBSTEIN, Associate Professor of English at Harpur College, is the author of *Sinclair Lewis* and *John O'Hara*; he has edited a casebook on the Scopes trial and an anthology of contemporary criticism. His essays and reviews have appeared in numerous journals, and he is now at work on a book about Hemingway.

PHILIP YOUNG, Professor of English at Pennsylvania State, is the author of *Ernest Hemingway*, *Hemingway: A Reconsideration*, and numerous literary essays and reviews; a regular contributor to *The Kenyon Review*, his essays "Our Hemingway Man" and "Hemingway and Me" are particularly noteworthy.

PHILIP DURHAM, author of *Down These Mean Streets a Man Must Go: Raymond Chandler's Knight*, has received several fellowships and awards, including the Edgar Award from The Mystery Writers of America (1964). He is coauthor of *American Fiction in Finland* and of two books on the Negro cowboy. He is Professor of English at the University of California, Los Angeles.

ROBERT I. EDENBAUM, Associate Professor of English at Temple University, has published in *Journal of Aesthetics and Art Criticism*, *Art Journal*, *Texas Studies in Literature and Language*, and *The Massachusetts Review*. He is at work on a book dealing with recent American writers.

IRVING MALIN is the author of *William Faulkner: An Interpretation*, *New American Gothic*, and *Jews and Americans*; he edited *Psychoanalysis and American Fiction*, *Saul Bellow and the Critics* and *Breakthrough: A Treasury of Contemporary American-Jewish Literature* (with Irwin Stark). He teaches at City College of New York.

JOYCE CAROL OATES has published three collections of short stories, *By the North Gate*, *Upon the Sweeping Flood*, and *A Garden of Earthly Delights*, and a novel, *With Shuddering Fall*. Each year in the past three years, her stories have been reprinted in the O. Henry and Martha Foley collections. A teacher at the University of Windsor, she has also published criticism. In 1967 she was awarded a Guggenheim Fellowship.

MATTHEW J. BRUCCOLI, Professor of English at the University of South Carolina, is Director of Center for Editions of American Authors, and editor of *The Fitzgerald Newsletter.*

THOMAS STURAK's doctoral dissertation was a study of the life and writings of Horace McCoy, which he is preparing for publication. He has taught English at UCLA and is presently an editor for a West Coast research and development corporation.

E. R. HAGEMANN, director of graduate studies in English at the University of Louisville, has published nearly 30 articles in American literature, bibliography (on James M. Cain and B. Traven, among others), American history, and biography. With Robert W. Stallman, he is coeditor of two books on Stephen Crane.

HERBERT RUHM teaches in the Division of Literature and Philosophy at the State University of New York at New Paltz, and has published essays on Dashiell Hammett.

GEORGE GRELLA is mystery and thriller reviewer for *The Kansas City Star* and has published reviews and essays in *Life* and *The New Republic*. He is writing a literary study of the thriller. He teaches at the University of Rochester.

CAROLYN SEE's doctoral dissertation was a historical and critical survey of the Hollywood novel. She teaches extension courses at UCLA and is a free-lance writer. Her stories and essays have appeared in *The Arizona Quarterly, The Carolina Quarterly,* the *Bulletin of Bibliography,* and *West.*

CHARLES SHAPIRO, author of *Theodore Dreiser: Our Bitter Patriot,* has edited four volumes of critical essays on fiction. His work has appeared in such periodicals as *The Nation, New Republic, Saturday Review, Dissent, Mutiny,* and *The Chicago Review.* He teaches at Briarcliff College and is working on a study of Anthony Powell.

CHARLES ALVA HOYT, Associate Professor of English at Bennett College, wrote the signed article on contemporary British literature for *The Encyclopedia Americana*. He also contributed to two Crosscurrents volumes, *Contemporary American Novelists* and *Contemporary British Novelists*. His essays, reviews, poems, and stories have appeared in many periodicals.

R. V. CASSILL is the author of many works of fiction, including *The Eagle on the Coin, Clem Anderson, Pretty Leslie, The President,* and *The Father*. He is a frequent contributor to *Book Week,* and his essays and short stories have appeared in numerous publications. He teaches at Brown University.

CONTENTS

INTRODUCTION

ALTHOUGH THIS GROUP of original essays was underway before it became a cliché to note that we are into a vigorous revival of interest in the literature of the Thirties, this volume does spearhead a reevaluation of the place of one particular genre in American fiction: the tough or hard-boiled school. Though in his famous essay "The Boys in the Back Room" (1940–41), reprinted in *Classics and Commercials* (Vintage, 1962), Edmund Wilson assessed the place of James M. Cain, Horace McCoy, John O'Hara, and other tough guys, along with several who weren't tough guys, little serious criticism has ever been devoted to such writers. W. M. Frohock included a chapter on James M. Cain in his *The Novel of Violence in America* (Southern Methodist, 1953) but in the second edition submerged his commentary in an introduction, explaining that Cain was of *only* "retrospective" interest. Philip Durham's book on Raymond Chandler, which appeared in 1962, was the first full-length serious study of a tough guy writer. Albert Van Nostrand's *The Denatured Novel* (1960) surveys most of Cain's novels antagonistically in a chapter called "The Hollywood Payoff." My own essays, attempting to evaluate Cain more seriously, appeared in 1964. With the appearance of the present volume, perhaps a revival of critical interest may be said to exist.

The novels themselves are available: in the past few years, Knopf has published *The Raymond Chandler Om-*

nibus (*The Big Sleep, Farewell, My Lovely, The High Window, The Lady in the Lake*), *The Novels of Dashiell Hammett* (*Red Harvest, The Dain Curse, The Maltese Falcon, The Glass Key, The Thin Man*), and a collection of Hammett's stories and short novels from *Black Mask*, mostly about the Continental Op, with a moving introduction by Lillian Hellman; both Chandler and Hammett are now in Modern Library editions. One hopes that Knopf will do equal justice to Cain, with a volume consisting ideally of *The Postman Always Rings Twice, Serenade, Mildred Pierce, Double Indemnity*, and *The Butterfly*. Among Avon's many reprint achievements in both the tough and the proletarian genres of the literature of the Thirties are new editions of Horace McCoy's *They Shoot Horses, Don't They?* and *Kiss Tomorrow Goodbye*. What one cannot obtain in new editions, one can readily uncover wherever secondhand paperbacks gather dust.

The tough writers are interesting and important for the special way in which they simultaneously depicted and shaped certain aspects of the American character, dream, and scene. They created new types of novels, third-rate though their imitators often were: the new, peculiarly American detective novels of Hammett and Chandler and other *Black Mask* writers; the "pure" tough guy novels of Cain and McCoy; the tough guy proletarian novels of Traven (whose work is discussed in a fresh context in a companion volume of essays which deal with the proletarian writers of the Thirties). And they created a major type of American film: the gangster-private-detective-tough-lone-wolf movie. Smith and Miner in *Transatlantic Migration* (Duke, 1955) are only two of many critics, American and foreign, who testify to the direct and indirect influence of these writers during the late Thirties and early Forties upon French and Italian and, to lesser degrees, English and Scandinavian writers. Little known in America, McCoy, for instance, was hailed as "peer of Steinbeck and Hemingway" and regarded in France as the first American existentialist. "And if, as Camus elsewhere suggests," said Harry Levin in *Contexts of Criticism*, "the human condition is that of Sisyphus, going through his motions eternally and ineffectually, it is easy to understand French admiration for a novel about an American dance-marathon: Horace McCoy's *They Shoot Horses, Don't They?*" Camus himself used Cain's *The Postman Always Rings Twice* as a model for *The Stranger*. Despite the lack of serious attention from American critics, the tough guys also influenced in various ways certain important American writers.

What is a tough guy or hard-boiled novel? That label, as Benjamin Appel suggests in his essay, is as ineffectual as any other in literary criticism, and this book doesn't attempt to offer a definition that would make the term much more than serviceable. While a definition emerges from the essays themselves, a few observations are appropriate here. The lower social and economic levels provide the locale and characters of tough novels; it is mainly the private detective novels that penetrate to the underworld, and in those novels high society often completes the social picture—the poles meet, clash, merge, often prove essentially identical. An unusually tough era turns out the hard-boiled hero. A traumatic wrench like the Depression, its evils and despair touching all facets of human society, causes a violent reaction in these men as they find that they lay down in the great American dream-bed in the Twenties only to wake up screaming in the nightmare of the Thirties. Those hardest hit become the down-and-out, the disinherited, and soon develop a hard-boiled attitude that enables them to maintain a granite-like dignity against forces that chisel erratically at it. The tough guy hero is not very often a professional criminal or killer; such men are tough in any era. Except in the private detective novels, the tough novels depict less crime and mayhem than one might imagine. The characteristics of the tough vision are determined, of course, by the world it perceives, but it reflects that world in a way that is at once an objective description and an implicit judgment of it. Reacting in kind to the indifferent, violent, deceptive world that made him, the tough guy describes and responds objectively to a world that treats him like an object. "Not reason," says Leslie Fiedler in *Love and Death in the American Novel* (Criterion, 1960), "but only counter-violence can defeat decadence and corruption—counter-violence and dumb luck, which is to say, grace." In a society in which human events daily, on all levels, contradict the preachments of institutions, the tough guy is strategically placed to perceive lies and hypocrisy—he cannot live with or by them *now* as he might have under more congenial circumstances. He plays society's games—to win. In his actions more crucially than in his attitudes, he takes revenge on the forces that shaped him; however, they usually defeat him. The sentimentality that sometimes surprises us in the tough guy is partly a betrayal that the hard-boiled attitude is a willed stance, taken for daily occasions, that often gets set as self-delusion. Sometimes this streak of sentimentality or softness, especially in Cain, makes almost credible the incredible attitudes and behavior of the tough guy. It is also simply true that sentimentality is one of the things the tough exterior is created to conceal; a similar defensiveness is revealed in "serious" writers, who strive relentlessly to avoid lapsing from wit and irony into sentimentality.

A hostile world prompts the vocabulary of the tough hero. His is not a literary language, which may be appropriate to his creator (for instance, Chandler was educated in the classical English tradition). The tough guy does not analyze, he acts—even his attitudes seem acts of aggression; thus, he can dispense with all language that does not enable him to govern the immediate moment; and even as he tells his story in retrospect, it retains its original immediacy; he is not free of time-passing, for time now, as before, assaults him. To these men (and women), as for Frederick Henry, many words—"abstract words such as glory, honor, courage or hallow"—seem obscene beside the concrete words that control everyday realities: food, tobacco, drink, sex, money, shelter, sleep. Said one critic of *They Shoot Horses, Don't They?* "There's hardly a word tough enough to indicate how tough are these scenes and people." The forces in society so strongly opposing them must have seemed to these men like fate itself; caught up in the rush of such a force, they had neither the time nor inclination, if they were to keep their wits sharp for survival, for psychological analysis or lingering descriptions: "this I felt, this I saw, this I did at that moment" is the brutal formula of their language—style as action.

As my comments have suggested, the tough guy novel is usually told in the first person. The style is as terse and idiomatic as the news headlines, radio bulletins, and newsreels which reported the events of the Thirties: the St. Valentine's Day Massacre; labor strife; speakeasy raids; lynchings; the shooting of Legs Diamond; the Lindbergh kidnapping; the battle of Anacostia Flats; the Japanese in Manchuria, the Italians in Ethiopia, the fascists in Spain; the attempt to assassinate Roosevelt; the Scottsboro boys; the tactics of Hitler; the exploits and the street execution of Dillinger; the Dust Bowl and the great migrations; the shooting of Huey Long; the Harlem race riot; Dewey's war on crime; the Joe Louis fights; the Loeb-Leopold murder; the crash of the Hindenburg; the WPA workers' riots; the slaying of Trotsky; Ku Klux Klan activities; the Munich betrayal—events described in Henry Morton Robinson's *Fantastic Interim* (Harcourt, Brace, 1943) and, in relation to literary and other popular culture elements, in Leo Gurko's *Angry Decade* (Dodd, Mead, 1947). The tough style comes out of the mouths of the tough guy characters, who speak the language of the streets, the pool rooms, the union halls, the bull pens, the factories, the hobo jungles. In the third-person tough novels (Hammett's and Cain's) and especially in the proletarian novel, even in some of the first-person proletarian novels—whether written by men from authentic proletarian backgrounds or by middle-class men suddenly thrust down among the proletarians—the style is often literary, artificial. Cain's early, unpublished novels "faltered and stumbled" because, he discovered, they were written in the third person, and he didn't seem to have the least idea where he was going, while his short stories, "which were put into the mouth of some character, marched right along," and his characters "knew perfectly well what they had to say." Cain says that he reads comments on his style "with some surprise, for I make no conscious effort to be tough, or hard-boiled, or grim, or any of the things I am usually called. I merely try to write as the character would write, and I never forget that the average man, from the fields, the streets, the bars, the offices, and even the gutters of his country, has acquired a vividness of speech that goes beyond anything I could invent, and that if I stick to this heritage, this logos of the American countryside, I shall attain a maximum of effectiveness with very little effort." The narrating voice characteristically has little to say—after all, if only the present mattered, he is not likely to *dwell* upon past events. Hence, the pace for which these brief tough novels are famous.

The tough quality of these novels, then, is dictated by the social milieu, one in which norms, hollow to start with, are suddenly disrupted, and consequently by the narrating voice of the man mired in the milieu, reaching viciously for a straw. But what of the author? He may or may not be sinking in the same quicksand with his hero. Hammett was a Pinkerton detective; Cain was a Baltimore and New York newspaperman; McCoy was a sports writer, a bouncer, and a migrant worker—but Chandler was an oil company executive. In any case, none of these writers invested overtly his own subjective capital in his fictive ventures. They strove to be as objective toward their characters as their characters naturally were toward society and other men. In some of the popular writers, the tough sensibility is the manufactured product of a willed intention to present a salable object to a demanding public. In others, the choice and development of this extreme objectivity suggests a suppressed subjective life. The tough character, his objective style and brutal milieu may reflect the author's genuine attitude toward the world. Chandler, with less autobiographical involvement than the other three major tough writers, said "this elaborate, over-tooled civilization of ours just strikes me that way. The story of our time to me is not war, nor atomic energy but the marriage of an idealist to a gangster and how their home life and children turned out." Perhaps the capability of certain popular writers for creating expressive surfaces may be attributed to the very fact that they do *not* suffuse their material with their subjective life. Hemingway's objectivity is the result, in part, of the pressure of his subjective life and a special vision about it, and his recognition of the absolute necessity for developing a style to control it. If in writing for money and fame, some of the popular writers are divorced from self, they are often, in a unique way, at one with the world about which they write and the people for whom they re-create that world. In the case of the tough writers, this complicity with the audience results in a particularly revealing perspective on the life of the times—while it also raises special aesthetic questions.

In a time when exhaustive studies of major classic and modern writers have exhausted us, when books rapidly duplicate each other, one asks with increasing frequency, is there an urgent need for yet another study even of the major writers? Thus, the question naturally arises, how necessary is a book devoted to decidedly minor writers in a narrow genre? Just as studies of minor writers in the classic past not only provide a richer perspective on the giants but also lend detail to our picture of the times, on social, historical, and mass-cultural levels, a study of minor writers of the recent past serves the same function. Instead of poring solely over manuscripts in rare book rooms in Buffalo, Boston, New Haven, Los Angeles, and Austin, why not raid the dark, smelly secondhand bookstores in the same cities for dusty, greasy paperbacks? As more and more dissertations, and even trade studies, take popular writers as their subjects, this venturesome inclination does not necessarily indicate a desperate search for new raw material for the old academic mill. While I am convinced that the writers examined here are not meretricious, I do not argue that each of them deserves book-length study. Hammett, Chandler, Cain, O'Hara, and McCoy do. But for the others, one or two essays are certainly justified. The value of a critical journal dealing with these and other types of minor writers (not covered in the Twayne series, for instance) would be apparent, perhaps real.

That novels are written out of other novels, as movies spawn other movies, suggests that life is more persuasive when falsified into fiction's special truth. Movies come out of novels, but movies also inspire novels, as we've seen in recent years—for movies provided much of the "real" experience of the younger writers. In all arts, the second- and third-rate work contributes to the makeup, if not the heart, of the first-rate work; the first-rate work in turn, perhaps, in some later mutation, affects minor works. Of course, in an important sense, the best of the tough writers are not second-rate writers, but first-rate practitioners of a minor genre. Chandler suggests that if Hammett learned from Hemingway, perhaps Hemingway also learned from Hammett. Ideas and attitudes are "in the air" at any moment in history; independently, different writers, of varying calibre, hit on similar subjects and even similar styles. Thus, Cain may rightly deny Hemingway's influence upon his style, but the similarity remains. We need to understand this process, perhaps more urgently than we need yet another image-pattern study of Hemingway alone.

Every type of fiction has its own degree and special kind of relevance to the total body of literature and to the nature and composition of society, which it both reflects and affects. Although my own bias is aesthetic, I certainly do not minimize literature's function as metaphorical interpreter of society and culture. Every novel, directly (Upton Sinclair's *The Jungle*) or indirectly (Camus' *The Stranger*), makes its impact on the public mind and ultimately, in ways that remain a mystery, on human behavior. Perhaps we ought to assess more fully the consequences of the fact that popular writers, perhaps more than writers whom critics admire, affect the nerve centers of mass experience and shape the attitudes and predispositions of the mass of men. In terms of everyday reality, the tough novels, written off the headlines (*The Postman Always Rings Twice* was inspired by the Ruth Snyder case), are truer for the mass man than the finer novels written obliquely out of the same world. "Violence did not dismay them," Chandler said of Hammett's readers. "It was right down their street." If I doubt the direct influence of Hemingway's code upon the behavior of his midcult and highbrow readers, I little doubt, though I wish I more deeply understood, the effect of Cain's and Chandler's novels on the behavior of their mass readers, especially as their impact is made, vivified, through the movies. Perhaps it is in the so-called minor tough novels and movies, as they imitate Hemingway even to distortion, that the literate reader himself may be most affected by Hemingway's view of human conduct. Faulkner's art in *Sanctuary* stands between his raw material and the reader of true detective magazines (made immediate with photographs) who undergoes similar experiences in one official report after another. To him, Faulkner is unknown, Cain is real. It is Cain then who affects the popular imagination, which is so liable to translate its imaginative experiences if not into direct action, into real attitudes that have consequences in behavior. Perhaps it was a recognition of the dynamics of this process, and not intemperance alone, that moved Kenneth Rexroth to declare that "the only significant fiction in America is popular fiction. . . . It is from Chandler and Hammett and Hemingway that the best modern fiction derives."

Tough literature was not only one reflection of the times, but one way to live in them. Whether with the gangster or the private detective or other less affiliated outsiders and loners, the disinherited man of the Thirties revolted briefly against the universe itself, or so it must have seemed in the absence of any central figure of authority in a time when all agencies of society were disrupted, disoriented. The private detective offered a public gutter's-eye-view of a world in which gangster and civic leaders took advantage of this disruption; if this view explained little, it showed everything, in a coldly neutral light. Robert Warshow, in "The Gangster as Tragic Hero" (*The Immediate Experience*, Anchor, 1964), analyzes the appeal of the gangster. He is an idealization and stylization of the criminal, whose meaning inheres in the armor of his style. His actions are pessimistic protests against the forced optimism of society. "In ways that we do not easily or willingly define, the gangster speaks for us, expressing that part of the American psyche which rejects the qualities and the demands of modern life, which rejects 'Americanism' itself." In the jungle of the Thirties, "every attempt to succeed is an act of aggression." "The effect of the gangster film is to embody that dilemma in the person of the gangster and resolve it by his death. The dilemma is resolved because it is *his* death, not ours. We are safe; for the moment, we can acquiesce in our failure, we can choose to fail." Though the popularity of the cowboy as a folk hero of the past is more sustained, the conventions of the gangster film "have imposed themselves upon the general consciousness and become the accepted vehicles of a particular set of attitudes and a particular aesthetic effect . . . the experience of the gangster *as an experience of art* is universal to Americans." Warshow's insights apply, with appropriate variations, to all types of tough guy novels and movies.

Not only do the implications of the tough novels have a social relevance that transcends their entertainment value, their authors sometimes wrote directly against the evils of their times and even engaged in political activities. Hammett's *Red Harvest* is an attack on corruption in small-town politics; his real life activities resulted in his going to jail for refusing to reveal the names of contributors to the bail bond fund of the Civil Rights Congress of which he was a trustee; McCoy's *No Pockets in a Shroud* and *Kiss Tomorrow Goodbye* also attack corruption in municipal government; Cain's *Our Government* is a collection of his many satirical dialogues exposing the idiocies of government on all levels; and this sort of criticism is implicit in all of Chandler's fiction. But essentially, these writers explore beneath the surfaces of society only to present

other, but uniquely expressive, surfaces. And the lingering appeal of these writers to all levels of readers may
be due in part to our common desire to deal with our lives
in terms of these expressive surfaces rather than to plunge
into murky depths. Leslie Fiedler, looking at another dimension of this appeal, warns that these novels, at worst,
"run the risk of becoming horror-pornography: the extor-
tion of a shudder for its own sake, the submission to
reveries of violence for the sake of their voluptuous appeal." But there remains the danger of dismissing superficially the superficial images of our mass culture, without
exploring deeply the nature of their operation and effect.

What the man in the street—and in the Thirties he
spent more time there than he wished—believed or
wanted to believe was not necessarily what he experienced
in mass entertainment. The image of himself, in the past
and in the present, to which he turned is just as important
as social history, if not as literature, as the more literary
works of James T. Farrell, Faulkner, Hemingway,
Fitzgerald, Steinbeck, James Gould Cozzens, Katherine
Anne Porter, Walter Van Tilburg Clark, Thomas Wolfe.
In "The Detective Story as a Historical Source," (*Yale
Review*, 1949–50) William O. Aydelotte articulates this
value: "A knowledge of people's day-dreams may enable
us to progress to an understanding of their desires. In this
way, a careful study of literature of this kind may reveal
popular attitudes which shed a flood of light on the motivation behind political, social, and economic history." A
people aren't only what they apparently are, and do, but
what they think they are, wish they were, dream, and hope
to be. For instance, the perfectly wretched plays put on in
churches are perhaps appropriate indicators of the religious experiences that the performers and audiences actually have. If what is going on in *Playboy* began as the
manufactured erotic daydreams of a few, it is going on
now in the heads of millions of college students—and
their professors. The writer who caters to the preconcep-
tions, prejudices, tastes, cliché attitudes, stereotypes, so-
called baser interests and appetites of mass readers must

study those elements carefully (and uncritically, perhaps) if he is to capture images representative of their real and imagined world, and shape them in terms acceptable to mass readers. (Often the writer is not so far removed himself from the mass reader that this task requires of *him* a "suspension of disbelief.") Thus, his novels project *one* picture of his society, valid *because* it is distorted, and valuable if we understand how and why. Those subjects and locutions that get dropped in the dialogue between the special sensibilities of the "serious" writer and his readers, the popular writer often picks up for the consumption of an audience that craves them. If the popular writer works on the assumption that the view he offers his readers is the one they want (though not necessarily the one he prefers himself), the serious writer (despite his personal commitment), serves *his* readers as well—with yet another antihero, yet another note from underground, yet another supine posture of alienation. The popular and the serious writer offer two different kinds of distortion—the one sometimes deliberately, cynically manipulated, the other sometimes unconsciously or faddishly indulged in.

The popular writer, like the serious writer, tells "lies like truth." The tough guy is a stylized exaggeration of very real traits in the American character, his life of action is the nightmare version of the American Dream, and he is quite as perversely attractive, to both author and reader, as Satan in Books I, II, and III of *Paradise Lost*. The French cherished the impression, projected by American tough movies and novels, that in America gangsters waited in every shadow, that each citizen carried a gun and beat up a dame daily. Decades later, the image of the Thirties lingers on. A few years ago a young Frenchman, just in from Paris, stopped off to see me en route to Hollywood; he carried a gun in a shoulder holster and planned to "make out" with movie stars. Was he less impressionable than Gide, who said, in *Imaginary Interviews*, that "the American cities and countryside must offer a foretaste of hell"? In giving himself up in his imagination to what he

considers a harmless lie, doesn't the general reader perpet-
uate the actualities that inspired the exaggeration, and
mightn't he scale back down to a quotidian level in his
own behavior and attitudes the postures and dialogue of
that fictional experience? Such are the risks a popular
culture lightly takes. Turning the pages of almost any
American family album, one is not startled to discover a
photograph of a man posing with a gun—unless one recalls the picture of Lee Harvey Oswald in his harmless
back yard. The tough novel's source of appeal, Chandler
said, was "the smell of fear which these stories managed to
generate. Their characters lived in a world gone wrong, a
world in which long before the atom bomb, civilization
had created the machinery for its own destruction, and
was learning to use it with all the moronic delight of a
gangster trying out his first machine gun." That this tough
guy attitude was not confined to books was still evident in
1944. Saul Bellow opens *Dangling Man* with the statement that "this is an era of hardboiled-dom."

> Today, the code of the athlete, of the tough boy . . .
> that curious mixture of striving, asceticism, and rigor, the
> origins of which some trace back to Alexander the Great—
> is stronger than ever. Do you have feelings? There are cor-
> rect and incorrect ways of indicating them. Do you have an
> inner life? It is nobody's business but your own. Do you
> have emotions? Strangle them. To a degree, everyone obeys
> this code. And it does admit of a limited kind of candor, a
> closemouthed straightforwardness. But on the truest can-
> dor, it has an inhibitory effect. Most serious matters are
> closed to the hard-boiled. They are unpracticed in introspec-
> tion, and therefore badly equipped to deal with opponents
> whom they cannot shoot like big game or outdo in daring.
> If you have difficulties, grapple with them silently, goes
> one of their commandments.

Life—as anyone knows who taught freshmen in the days
when Salinger's Holden Caulfield set the style for adolescent attitudes—imitates literature. Huckleberry Finn is a
true-to-life, though nonetheless fictional, idealization of
thousands of boys of Twain's childhood; but it is the

fictional character who, up until 1940, say, set the style for boys who may never have even read the book. This is not, of course, a one-way process; it is a dynamic interplay. When Marlon Brando in *A Streetcar Named Desire* (and later in *The Wild One* and *On the Waterfront*, in roles that even more powerfully encourage clichés) stripped away the clichés of the stage portrayal of the American tough guy, he was responding to a truer model which he had observed in real life; but it was *his* image that transformed that range of new life details into a lifelike style (modified by the two somewhat different kinds of sullen lyricism of James Dean and Montgomery Clift) that captivated two generations and inspired an endless procession of grotesque imitations. Noting the admixtures of Holden and of the beats, we have observed over twenty years the evolution of this style into the mongrel version we now observe in the cool behavior of the young. But the Brando style was foreshadowed in the movies of Cagney and Bogart. Stanley's clearing of the table in *Streetcar* is reminiscent of Cagney's shoving the grapefruit in Mae Clark's face in *Public Enemy* (1931).

We go back, out of a special, nonliterary compulsion, to the tough vision, among other escapist visions, because it is "truer" of what actually happened in the public mind than are the subjectively distorted private worlds of individual "serious" writers. Of course, some popular visions are more compelling than others. During the years in which the tough novels appeared, novels reliving the romantic, historical past became a million-dollar industry: *Gone with the Wind* (which still lives on the screen); Edna Ferber's *Cimarron*; Kenneth Roberts' and Walter Edmonds' novels; and Hervey Allen's *Anthony Adverse*—in a present of victims, the heroes of the past. Many novels, such as Louis Bromfield's *The Rains Came*, dealt with exotic, foreign worlds. Pearl Buck in *The Good Earth* reminded us that a whole race was worse off than we, and *had been* for centuries. Erskine Caldwell in *Tobacco Road* (not so remote, but equally exotic) reminded us that long before the Depression, men like Jeeter Lester rooted and competed with the hogs. At a time when the present was unbearable, different sorts of writers satisfied a different sort of audience with novels whose function perished with the times that needed them. Though perhaps a backward look now might find those novels also somehow relevant. But the urge to violence that is the Siamese twin of the American urge to peace and tranquility is still with us—in an affluent society, our crime rate rises, reaching for the gratification of a perverse craving produced by consumer satiation no less than by deprivation. The tough novel shows us not only how we were, but how we always have been, and now are. Hammett's world, Chandler insisted, is "the world you live in."

Removed in time, these novels appear to project a kind of expressionistic image or metaphor of the decade that was. There is a mythic world of difference in responding to the freshness of a living Bogart on the screen in the late Thirties and responding in the late Sixties to a dead Bogart on the late show. With his picture, like an icon, on the nation's walls, he is a mythic figure, along with the Tramp, Mae West, W. C. Fields, Gatsby, Laurel and Hardy, Dick Tracy, Superman, Lindbergh, Al Jolson, Huck Finn, FDR, Will Rogers, Joe Louis, The Lone Ranger, Clark Gable, Jean Harlow, "Papa" Hemingway, Robert Frost, Jesse James, Scarlett O'Hara, Sergeant York (whose counterpart in World War ii, Audie Murphy, was not portrayed by a Gary Cooper, but went to Hollywood himself, thus combining the old-style mythic figure with the new). These tough novels are epiphanized in our common consciousness into poetic images: as on an electronic-age urn, the gang leader stands forever in the night-club doorway, his henchmen behind him. The face may change from Muni's to Robinson's to Cagney's to Bogart's, but the stance is unaltered. And scholars explicating Joyce are no less affected than the janitor sweeping out the offices of university presses all over the American dreamscape.

In response to a vague nostalgic pull, I wrote an essay on James M. Cain, the twenty-minute egg of the hard-boiled school, for Norman Holmes Pearson's course in American literature. Five years later, I gave a speech on Cain, in fear and trembling, to a group of Ohio English professors; to my surprise, that lecture conjured up in them a latent literary interest, mingled with a passionate nostalgia. I discovered that while a professor of medieval literature may not have found time to read William Styron, Wright Morris, John Hawkes, Walker Percy, Flannery O'Connor, Saul Bellow, John Barth, he has read and remembered fondly *The Postman Always Rings Twice*, and certainly the novels of Hammett and Raymond Chandler, and speaks of them in tones echoing truck drivers I overheard in Santa Fe. Literary people seem to live a double life, thumbing through *The Kenyon Review* in the library, poring over *Playboy* at home. The tough novels have, it seems, an impact that transcends mere entertainment; one may set out to "kill a few hours" reading Chandler, but, testimony reveals, one undergoes an experience so vivid that its peculiar authenticity lingers over the years. I asked some of our finest, and busiest, critics to contribute to this volume of essays; unmistakable regret made the refusals of those who were *too* busy almost poignant. A kind of terrible nostalgia, caused perhaps by the movies made from the novels as much as by the novels themselves, it seems, keeps these novels alive, just as a feeling of obligation keeps the dust thin on proletarian novels.

This volume appears at a time when the question might naturally be asked, are we concerned here with camp criticism on camp writers? These essays were undertaken before Susan Sontag set up camp in the marketplace, but of course the situation was real before she articulated it. One must admit that there is a certain amount of camp involved in any interest in the popular experience of the past, but one must also admit that the mysteries of taste among men of high cultural judgment are even more paradoxical than Miss Sontag's analysis can reveal. However, if camp is one dimension, there are other dimensions to a revival of interest in the tough novels: the social and aesthetic realities that transcend camp and similar "low" levels of experience. It would be a mistake then to dismiss an interest in tough fiction, even in Bogart himself, as merely camp, high or low.

Most of the essays in this book are, at least implicitly, as much concerned with the aesthetic as with the social veracity of the tough novel. In "The Guilty Vicarage" (*The Dyer's Hand,* Random House, 1962), W. H. Auden speaks of Chandler's social and aesthetic achievements in the same breath: "Mr. Chandler is interested in writing, not detective stories, but serious studies of a criminal milieu, the Great Wrong Place, and his powerful but extremely depressing books should be read and judged, not as escape literature, but as works of art." Chandler himself made a similar claim for most tough fiction: "The mystery story grew hard and cynical about motive and character, but it was not cynical about the effects it tried to produce nor about its technique of producing them. A few unusual critics recognized this at the time." The craft of the popular novel deserves study. Here one may see in bold relief some of the techniques used more subtly in more literary novels. Students of literature and young writers particularly may see the mysteries of creativity mechanically at work, and sometimes sublimely. While there is, perhaps, no great task here, it is one worth doing.

On the value of the contribution of the tough guy writers to American and foreign literature, critics, writing in the Thirties and since, are somewhat divided, though few discuss them at any length. Herbert J. Muller, in 1937, said, in the course of a discussion of Hemingway, "this 'cult of the simple' appears in various forms in the modern world: the 'hard-boiled school,' the movement back to the farm, the interest in primitive people, the craze for primitive art. It is usually a symptom of surface restlessness, a craving for novelty or thrill—the popularity among the sophisticated readers of novelists like Dashiell Hammett is more a fad than a portent. But it also represents a serious effort by some intellectuals to find happiness in the mere being or doing of the great mass of common people; and as a means of salvation, a cult, its futility is obvious. . . ." (*Modern Fiction*, McGraw-Hill). Some critics rejected the tough novels on moral, some on aesthetic grounds, some on both. Raymond Chandler noted the problem: "It takes a very open mind indeed . . . to recognize the authentic power of a kind of writing that, even at its most mannered and artificial, made most of the fiction of the time taste like a cup of luke-warm consommé at a spinster-ish tearoom." Wallace Fowlie reminds us that French critics "paid earlier and more sophisticated attention to contributions of American art than American critics."

Frederick J. Hoffman and other critics see the tough guy novel as a development of the European naturalism of Zola, the Americanized naturalism of Norris and Dreiser, and the selective realism of Crane, London, and Dos Passos (*The Modern Novel in America*, Regnery, 1951). Though Alfred Kazin, in 1942, rejected the tough guys as exploiting Hemingway's "nihilism" to produce titillation in the depiction of forbidden subjects, thus avoiding the common problems of experience, he saw a correlation between the tough and the proletarian writers: "The violence of the left-wing writing all through the Thirties, its need of demonstrative terror and brutality, relates that writing to the slick, hard-boiled novel"—which "became a distinctive contemporary fashion" (*On Native Grounds*, Anchor, 1956). Indeed, the tough and proletarian novels had common social and political origins and causes, and depicted similar elements: violence, poverty, lawlessness, disenchantment, and a certain sentimentality.

Both the tough and the proletarian hero were outsiders, often against the law, though the proletarian joined forces with others like himself in an effort to make his revolt ideologically meaningful. This sometimes made him more dangerous than the tough criminal, even the gangster. The union or the band of radicals is reduced in the hard-boiled novel to the private eye, who sees in his pursuit of the criminal the same social injustices as the young proletarian. But what the radical observes and describes passion-ately, the tough guy merely reports objectively. An essay relating the tough to the proletarian novel was suggested for this volume; the responses were so numerous and interesting that a companion volume devoted to that genre came into being. In the proletarian volume the relationship is often remarked; the presence of a commentary on Ira Wolfert's *Tucker's People*, which one might call a gangster novel, in that book instead of this one, suggests this relationship. In the present volume, Kingsley Widmer draws on firsthand experience to examine some "life-style sources of proletarian and tough heroes."

The essays in this volume deal with several types of tough guy novels. Philip Durham surveys the writers of the *Black Mask* school: Carroll John Daly, Frederick Nebel, Hammett, George Harmon Coxe, Paul Cain (Peter Ruric), Chandler. A number of the hard-boiled detective novelists are *not* discussed in the course of this volume, but the ones included are representative. One may find stories by Norbert Davis, John K. Butler, Frederick Nebel, Raoul Whitfield, Frank Gruber, Richard Sale, Lester Dent, and Erle Stanley Gardner in *The Hard-boiled Dicks*, an anthology of detective fiction from the pulp magazines, edited by science fiction writer Ron Goulart (Sherbourne Press, 1965). Earlier, Joseph T. Shaw, the Maxwell Perkins of *Black Mask*, offered an anthology of early *Black Mask* stories in *The Hard-boiled Omnibus* (Simon and Schuster, 1946; Pocket Books, 1952).

Newsweek, in an article called "The Murder Business," explained the popularity of the old-fashioned detective story. It offered "a form of resolution in a time of unresolved conflicts." The reader felt the "soothing certainty that whatever the violence, whatever the problem, it is going to be unraveled, the obscure made clear, the issue settled, the crime avenged, the guilty person punished. This, in our time, is a solace not to be taken lightly." Hammett was the serpent in this paradise. "Our essential contribution to the form in the twentieth century," says Fiedler, "is a strange off-shoot of the '30's novel of urban violence: a 'realistic' exposé of corruption in the big city, presided over by the private eye. But the private eye is not the dandy turned sleuth; he is the cowboy adapted to life on the city streets, the embodiment of innocence moving untouched through universal guilt. As created by Dashiell Hammett, the blameless shamus is also the honest proletarian, illuminating by contrast the decadent society of the rich." Further analysis of the distinction between the old-style detective mystery and the new-style Hammett private eye stories comes up in the course of the essays. Some good books on the subject are *Murder for Pleasure* (Appleton-Century, 1941) by Howard Haycraft; *The Art of the Mystery Story*, essays by various hands (Universal Library, 1947); and *The Development of the Detective Novel* (Philosophical Library, 1958) by A. E. Murch.

Following Robert I. Edenbaum's analysis of the poetics of the private eye in the novels of Hammett, Irving Malin focuses on one of the classics: *The Maltese Falcon*. Some may argue that when critics see metaphysical implications in such a novel, as Malin does, the revival has gone too far, but one may as well set the limits quickly, and such a so-called extreme approach may allow certain insights which would elude a more cautious approach. Herbert Ruhm examines the curious life, writing career, and works of Raymond Chandler, who moved from Bloomsbury into the jungle of L. A. (no writer has described an American city more hauntingly). He concentrates on two of Chandler's last, least-celebrated and least-discussed novels, *The Long Goodbye* and *The Little Sister*.

What distinguishes the hard-boiled detective from the "pure" tough novels of Cain and McCoy? Despite the violence done to the form of the detective novel, mainly English in pattern, by Hammett's stories, there lingers over his and over Chandler's novels the excuse for toughness which lies in the fact that the private detective's world is violent, brutal, horrible, dark, and melodramatic as a matter of course. Though Hammett exaggerated, his world was more authentic than that of the old-fashioned detective story, and the reader's interest was less in tracking down and evaluating clues and solving the crime than in being exposed to and shocked by the criminal world of his own morning headlines; he enjoyed moving through this world with a man who was *not* shocked by what he saw, but who suffered the malaise of one for whom nothing was extraordinary (Hammett's first case as a detective was to track down a stolen ferris wheel). But the pure tough novels of Cain and McCoy had nothing to do with detectives, seldom with gangsters, although Cain wrote one of the worst and McCoy one of the best gangster novels. In *The Postman,* Frank Chambers' tough response, almost totally unconscious (while it is rather melodramatically self-conscious in Hammett and ironically and wittily self-conscious in Chandler) synchronizes more closely with the reader's own attitudes. In *They Shoot Horses, Don't They?* the two young marathon dance contestants represent two poles in the American character—the optimism of Robert clashes with the suicidal disillusionment of Gloria; unprepared for the shock, Robert, nurtured on Hollywood dreams and happy endings, surrenders his will and feelings to a stronger though more destructive will, and acts on Gloria's cue. His telling of the story is all the more powerful since he is describing in tough style those fiery events which forged that style. The "pure" tough novel is a rather rare type. Joyce Carol Oates looks at Cain's major novels as depicting "man under sentence of death" (That happens to be the burden of her own novels). Thomas Sturak analyzes the objective lyricism of Horace McCoy, looking closely at that minor classic, *They Shoot Horses, Don't They?*

One finds tough guy elements in the work of "serious" American writers: Dos Passos, whose *U.S.A.* came out during the Thirties; Steinbeck; Faulkner; Farrell; Caldwell; Ring Lardner; London (*The Sea Wolf*); Algren; Richard Wright; Nathanael West. For instance, it is curious that Jack Burden in Robert Penn Warren's *All the King's Men* speaks like Humphrey Bogart or Philip Marlowe out of one side of his mouth and like Faulkner out of the other. Sheldon Grebstein discusses Hemingway's role as father of the hard-boiled writers, and he joins Philip Young in arguing that *To Have and Have Not* was

Hemingway's only tough novel, and perhaps the best of the genre. Another serious writer whose work occasionally shows elements of the tough is John O'Hara, whose *Appointment in Samarra*, Matthew Bruccoli shows, reveals a characteristic of all tough writers: the importance in a tough world of knowing what you're talking about.

In a style somewhat similar to the one used in the novel itself, E. R. Hagemann discusses Richard Hallas' (Eric Knight's) *You Play the Black and the Red Comes Up*—one of the many novels by non-Americans which imitate the tough strain and achieve a perverse authenticity of their own. George Grella examines *No Orchids for Miss Blandish* by another Britisher, James Hadley Chase (had Chase been reading Faulkner's *Sanctuary* and *The Big Sleep*, side by side?).

This book cannot examine all the types of tough novels. But in his essay, Kingsley Widmer looks at one type—the hobo—in London's *The Road*, Jim Tully's *Beggars of Life*, and others. (Frederick Feied's book *No Pie in the Sky* is also recommended.) The gangster movie developed simultaneously with the gangster novel. Though Sternberg's *Underworld* (curious, a soundless gangster movie) appeared in 1927, it was *Little Caesar* (1930) which set a style in both novel and film. Examining the gangster type novel as an urban pastoral, George Grella discusses W. R. Burnett's *Little Caesar*, Donald Henderson Clarke's *Louis Beretti*, and Benjamin Appel's *Brain Guy*. Related to the gangster novel is the juvenile delinquent novel, so prevalent in the late Forties: Willard Motley's *Knock on Any Door*, Charles Gorham's *The Future of Mr. Dolan*, Shulberg's *The Amboy Dukes*.

Parker Tyler offers some fascinating observations on the gangster movies ("Good Villain and the Bad Hero," in the *Hollywood Hallucination*, Creative Age, 1944) and on movies made from Cain's novels (*Magic and Myth of the Movies*, Henry Holt, 1947). Hammett, Chandler, McCoy, and Cain worked for Hollywood, and some of the best tough guy movies came from their novels. (See my essay in *Film Heritage*, Fall, 1967.) It is interesting to note that

Faulkner worked on Hemingway's *To Have and Have Not* and on Chandler's *The Big Sleep,* while Chandler worked on Cain's *Double Indemnity.* With many of the tough guy writers working in Hollywood, it is not surprising that one type would be the Hollywood tough novel. Carolyn See examines this type as the "American Dream Cheat": Paul Cain's *Fast One,* Raoul Whitfield's *Death in a Bowl,* Richard Sale's *Lazarus #7,* Chandler's *The Little Sister* (compared with Mailer's *The Deer Park*), O'Hara's *Hope of Heaven,* Hallas' *You Play the Black and the Red Comes Up,* McCoy's *I Should Have Stayed Home,* West's *The Day of the Locust.* Charles Shapiro deals with another type in the world of entertainment: the carnival novel, focussing on *Nightmare Alley,* by William Lindsay Gresham, one descendant in the Forties of the tough novelists. One of the many descendants we might have discussed is Walter Tevis, whose hero in *The Hustler* is somewhat like Gresham's Stanley in *Nightmare Alley.* Some of the writers discussed in this volume are being examined seriously for the first time. Many readers will be introduced to Jim Thompson's fiction in R. V. Cassill's focus essay on *The Killer Inside Me,* a descendant in the Fifties. A third descendant is John D. MacDonald; Charles Alva Hoyt examines the tough guy as hero and villain in *The Damned.*

Finally, this genre would have been well-served by a long, annotated bibliography, but obviously, one volume cannot begin to exhaust the work to be done in the field, although I've tried to suggest, along the way, some of the tasks that remain. The following is a list of such other essays on the genre:

Charles J. Rolo, "Simenon and Spillane: The Metaphysics of Murder for the Millions" (*New World Writing,* No. 1, New American Library, 1952).

George P. Elliott, "Country Full of Blondes" (*The Nation,* April 23, 1960) —on Chandler.

Raymond Chandler, "The Simple Art of Murder" (*Atlantic,* December, 1944) —source of Chandler passages quoted earlier.

John Paterson, "A Cosmic View of the Private Eye" (*The Saturday Review*, August 22, 1953).

James M. Cain's prefaces to *Three of a Kind* (Knopf, 1943) and *The Butterfly* (Knopf, 1947).

Frank Gruber's introduction to a collection of his stories, "The Life and Times of the Pulp Story," *Brass Knuckles* (Sherbourne, 1966).

Edmund Wilson, "Why Do People Read Detective Stories?" and "Who Cares Who Killed Roger Ackroyd?" *Classics and Commercials* (Vintage, 1962).

D. C. Russell, "The Chandler Books" (*Atlantic*, March, 1945).

Ben Ray Redman, "The Decline and Fall of the Whodunit" (*The Saturday Review*, May 31, 1952).

George Orwell, "Raffles and Miss Blandish," *A Collection of Essays* (Anchor, 1954).

Milton Klonsky, "Along the Midway of Mass Culture," *The New Partisan Reader* (Harcourt, Brace, 1953).

Clement Greenberg, "Avant-Garde and Kitsch," *Art and Culture* (Beacon, 1961).

Penelope Houston, "The Private Eye" (*Sight and Sound*, Summer, 1956).

James D. Hart, *The Popular Book: A History of America's Literary Taste* (Oxford, 1950).

Kingsley Amis, *The James Bond Dossier* (New American Library, 1965).

Up to the Chandler piece, the essays in this volume are arranged chronologically. Following each general essay is a brief focus essay, dealing either with a novel by the author discussed in the preceding piece or by a writer who resembles that figure in some manner. After the Chandler, come essays on two types: the gangster and the Hollywood novels. We then focus on three descendants into the Forties and Fifties of the tough novel. Though each essayist wrote with some knowledge of what the others were doing, no pretense to careful unity is made here. Perhaps ideally the first general examination of tough fiction should have been undertaken by a single (and singular) critic, but the multiple approach enables the reader to make his own discoveries, not dreamt of here, to fill in the lacunae, and thus to shape his own total vision of a still fertile field of literature.

For financial assistance in the preparation of this book and for allowing me time to work on it, I wish to thank Bruce Haywood and Robert Daniel of Kenyon College and Edgar Whan and Arvin Wells of Ohio University. My wife Robbie, Margaret Myers, and Lorraine Howard struggled with me in the preparation of the manuscript. For their encouragement, suggestions, advice, I wish to thank Harry Levin, Robie Macauley, George Lanning, George Bluestone, Pauline Kael, Robert Creeley, George P. Elliott, Brock Brower, Jonathan Baumbach, Brook Whiting, Sheridan Baker, Sylvia Bowman, Stephen Taylor, Alan Casty, John W. Aldridge, Peter Shaw (whose essay on the tough guy intellectuals got by me), Ernest Callenbach, Germaine Brée, Mark Schorer, James M. Cox, Wayne C. Booth, Frederic I. Carpenter, Malcolm Cowley, John Hagopian, Isidore Haiblum, Granville Hicks, Martin Light, Austin Wright.

DAVID MADDEN

Athens, Ohio
April 9, 1967

Tough Guy Writers of the Thirties

The Way Out
Some Life-Style Sources of the Literary Tough Guy and the Proletarian Hero

KINGSLEY WIDMER

THE TOUGHENING of the American, from the colonial forest frontiers to the megalopolitan margins, usually includes a stylization of wandering defiance. Take an historic image of the "hard-boiled" character: an isolato with sneering side-of-mouth cigarette, bruised felt hat, off-beat dress (e.g., suit jacket with dark colored shirt), stubbly and fist-like face, and defensively terse gestures. His hard drinking, laconically derisive speech, and hard travelling provide other marks of the kind. Violent, he also expects violence and endures it with stoicism and the mocking faith that "God is guts." He displays a connoisseurship of harsh sensations, the grace of "being his own man," and the pride of losing well. Such an outcast understates an heroic effort, however narrow, for resisting an essentially hostile and cheating world.

This sketch does not derive from the tough guy and proletarian writers of the Thirties but from portrayals of hobos of some decades earlier. The narrow-brimmed felt hat—by the Thirties a cliché identifying the movie "gun"—was favored by the hobo as a distinction over the usual workingman's cap. "God is guts"—a pre-Hemingway and pre-Hammett apothegm of toughness—is from the hobo ballad *The Little Red God*. The many similar details, available in documents as well as in literature, suggest the hobo as both a source for the tough guy and the proletarian hero and himself an archetype.

The toughness of style and spirit projects an alienation beyond classical wariness and romantic pathos: life is amorally hostile. To confront it and yet endure requires a controlled rage, or, in a later version, the "hipster cool." Defiant attitudes, of course, are partly inversion, and portrayals of toughness almost always reveal some reverse sentimentality. Certainly the tough hobo displaced virility into his fists and humane values into a sardonically grim self-sufficiency. But these are hardly violations in America. The man on the way out finds that our competitive order leads to no Enlightenment harmony. So all he can do is toughen up, and follow the road beyond any easy acceptance.

The more aggressive hobo seems continuous with the explorers, frontiersmen, Forty-niners, cowboys, mariners, and others of our puritanically energetic, lonely and violent vagabond-rogues. The hobo has a special relevance; not only were there some millions of them in the "second frontier"—the period of cruelly expansive industrialization from the 1870's to 1920's—they also contributed to a mythos (though it has received less attention than the other he-man legends) which found literary and subliterary expression. Fictional figures on the outside in twentieth century literature, from the dispossessed to the picaresque, often draw heavily on the style of hobo toughness.

One source, and a literary tradition in itself, may be found in the autobiographies of life on the road, from Jack London to Jack Kerouac. In London's sketches of his hoboing in the Nineties, *The Road* (1907), his bumming, working and fighting across the country are treated as an initiation into virile identity. He translates hardiness and hostility into "zest for living"; and endless flight and punishment become affirmative, even gay, because of the rebellious sense of freedom and hard distinction of the man on the road. The hobo's wisdom, says London, comes from his living fully in the present and accepting "the futility of telic endeavour." (The existential picaresque will rediscover this dark immediacy of the man outside, which also traces back through rogues and goliards, holy vagabonds and cynics.) As with most of the hobo writers, London scorns the usual American exploitative labors, narrow communities and arbitrary powers; his hobos insist on a lively "antagonism to organized authority." A rough camaraderie of the road, and some fraternal feeling for the outcast, provide the only community. Most of his account consists of the jocund documentation of adventitious drifting and endless defiances of cops and other authorities. For London, "the hobo defies society" and thus intensely creates a manly self-hood.

This certainly draws on a romantic heroism, despite the anecdotal realism of the writing. As with Gorki, a heightened individuality underlies the naturalistic description of vagrancy and the critical social perception. But this has often been a poetic side of the naturalistic mode—recall the exceptional development, and almost surreal responsiveness, of Zola's hero in *Germinal*, who begins and ends as an apocalyptic vagabond. Here literature provides a parallel motivation with life. A once famous American hobo-tramp, Harry Kemp, acknowledges in his autobiography, *Tramping On Life* (1922), that his hard life as a "bindle stiff" was partly an idealization derived from London and Gorki's images of the rebellious wanderer.

Hobo memoirs have been a fairly persistent sub-genre in our literature. From Josiah Flint (who hoboed in the 1880's and later turned private detective and then joined the literati) and London, they slide through the troubadorism of Vachel Lindsay (A *Handy Guide for Beggars*, 1916) and W. H. Davies (*Autobiography of a Super-Tramp*, 1917), then into the journalist-hobos and descriptive sociologists of the Twenties and the "protest" writers of Thirties migrancy, continuing in Clancy Sigal's *Going Away* (1962) and the Beat memorialists of dharma bums and angelic delinquents on roads out of contemporary American life.

A middling, representative and once well-known hobo

writer was Jim Tully. Though he wrote much in the obvious tough guy forms—sentimental reportage and fictions about prize fighters, criminals and drug addicts—his better writing was hobo autobiography, as in *Beggars of Life* (1924). The "man's code" of the road, he explains, represented a way of sophistication as well as an escape from the meaningless labors and puritanic rigidities of the midwestern small town. As with Sherwood Anderson's wandering populist intellectuals, life on the road is seen not only as authentic experience but as the way to social and moral awareness. Tully argues that outcast state and intellectual responsiveness go together. Also, he writes (*Shadows of Men*, 1930), hobos, cons, and other self-aware victims reveal a distinctive ethos; their "iron code" includes "asking no quarter," resistance to pervasive injustice, and sardonic endurance of fate. They wear a sacred penumbra: Jesus was one of the first hobos (an image taken up again by Jack Kerouac in *Lonesome Traveller*). It would be hard to separate the exalted "man's code" of so many of the hobo writers from the later stoic-hedonist saintliness of the Hemingwayesque.

Whatever the mixed realities of American vagrancy, moral iconoclasm as well as hyper-masculine assertion characterize its self-consciousness. It also seems relevant that Tully was a literary protégé of H. L. Mencken, one of his documentors in the *American Mercury* of the undersides of American society. There the zestful exposure of non-genteel realms was itself viewed as satiric of the parochial and the bigoted. With some practical reason, violence, sex, liquor, the vulgate idiom and death were taken as giving the lie to the morals and manners of the middle-class boob and booster. In spirit as well as in practitioners, the sentimental-cynical newspaper reporter lies fist-close to this exposé disenchantment. Tough styles probably owe much (including some superficial contempt and a-politics) to Menckenism. The academic hall rather than the newspaper office is now the refuge of belles-lettres, but we should not forget that journalism in the past—as de Tocqueville insisted—powerfully influenced both subject and style. The creators of the tough guy and the proletarian hero were figuratively as well as literally the wandering disillusioned reporters of the American scene.

The hoboing memoirs are less important in themselves—none of the several dozen I know are exceptional works of literature—than as openings to several kinds of reality. A continuing rebelliousness linked to the road is one. From the memoirs (and other documents) the hobos appear as exemplars of positive alienation. Mostly northern Europeans, generally sane and competent, engaged in exceptionally arduous though intermittent labors in a peculiarly atomized male migration, American hobos were not the European-style defeated tramps. They were assertive, achieving considerable pride, bravado and, at times, social militancy. Some of the first to "March on Washington"—"Coxey's Army" in 1894—they were imitated by the Veterans of the Thirties and the Negroes of the Sixties. As the memoirs insist, there developed "hobo intellectuals" with both literary and political lineages. The latter helped create the anarcho-syndicalism of the Wobblies prior to World War I. This tough protest was direct, antidecorous, individualistic, egalitarian, Luddite, sometimes violent, and based on radical-utopian social perceptions. The more rugged or anarchistic defiers in the protest and proletarian literature—as in Traven and Dos Passos—are indebted to them. So are later "movement" politics, tough in desperation at American authorities and culture that counterfeitingly absorb and exploit most usual forms of dissent. Thus we can find a serious nostalgia for Wobbly styles in the "direct action," antibureaucratic and pro-outcast protests of the declassed "new radicals" of the 1960's.

Since parts of hoboing were also in the tradition of romantic wandering, they furthered the "masterless man" individuality and scornful vitality of the vagabond adventurer. In the somewhat mobile American social order, hoboing could be a temporary and positive state, an initiation for the young—later including college students—into a rebellious fraternity and perspective. For perhaps three generations there was a lore passed on from father to son and ex-hobo to adolescent about taking to the road. It presupposed the familial estrangement and moral revolt of sons in the American protestant ethos. Our versions of the *Bildungsroman*, therefore, draw upon the hobo experiences. His placelessness and hyper-manly assertiveness — fighting, drinking, varied labors, covert homoeroticism — pervade our novels about youth, and provide a hard and amoral cast in comparison with European fictions about the young man's education into life.

This was also appropriate in that the more perceptive awareness and art of the road make much of a distinctive consciousness. The separateness from other men's parochial loyalties and securities creates its own clarity. Or, as a Céline character comments on his American travels (*Journey to the End of the Night*), "That's what . . . travelling is . . . this inexorable glimpse of existence as it really is during those few lucid hours" when one leaves one order behind and is not yet encompassed by another. There are some unique truths to be found outside.

The inner experience of the wanderer includes feverish dissatisfaction, free-floating fantasy, and guilty catharsis. He can also hardly avoid being an *enragé*. Especially bitter at hypocrisy, the outsider sees many of our social and cultural arrangements as overwhelmingly mean and arbitrary. George Orwell noted (*Down and Out in Paris and London*) that the outcast persistently recognizes the aggressive "enclosure of the respectable against the rest." The man on the road naturally senses the hostile order and anxious pretenses of the society and, in America, often responds with a counter-hostility—that is what makes him "tough"—to the solid citizens and their fraudulent civilization.

Thus "social protest" literature, as in the Thirties, almost inevitably will give a considerable place to the wandering consciousness, though it may also attenuate the tough vitality and sense of freedom for purposes of didactic pathos. The denuded drifters of Dahlberg (*Bottom Dogs*), the sententious migrants of Steinbeck (*In Dubious Battle*), the defeated radicals of Dos Passos

(*U.S.A.*), the ornate underdogs of Algren (*Somebody in Boots*, and its poeticized rewriting twenty years later in *A Walk on the Wild Side*), and many of the figures in the works of the proletarian allegorists, include stylizations of the tough hobo experiences. The décor of the social novel in the past needed the violently defeated figure such as the anonymous "Vag" in Dos Passos' *The Big Money* for a penultimate image of indignation at the injustice and alienation of America.

The didactic social style, of course, sacrifices some of the rebellious and humorous freedom of the hobo. That found other forms in the communal imagination: the comic-tragic gestures of Chaplin's tramp, the mordant comments of the cartoon bums, the surreal buffoonery of Henry Miller's bohemian vagrants, the still proliferating folksong figures going down the road feeling both sad and glad, etc.

But the probably dominant image of the tough hobo in our literature takes a different shape. Drawing broadly on the writers' modification of the reality, I suggest a mythic figure who might be called the "American Joe." His rough pattern goes something like this: he has fled the Protestant ethos of sanctified labor, ascetic conscience and respectable competition. Hobo (or tramp, hitch-hiking worker, jalopy drifter), he frenziedly pursues a loser's road, ending where he began. His herculean labors provide no sense of accomplishment other than hardnosed endurance. Since he both labors and flees, his identity remains uncertain in a land where what you do tells who you are. His vivid moments with booze, whores, jails, crimes and fights assert an anxious virility. Despite violence and bitterness, he remains the pathetic innocent yearning for the geography of opportunity and a new land of release. His wanderings after community in a hostile society may be given rationale in the guilty juvenile fantasy of being an orphan of dubious parentage—our ambiguous father-killing heritage. Like the anonymous "Joe" of American folk speech (the "good Joe," the "square Joe," the omnipresent "GI Joe" of World War II) he is seen both as representative and as a bit degraded. This tough guy ends in some apparently longed-for castration by sexual and social forces he does not comprehend, though he goes down fighting. His open but fatal quest, and manliness, permit no grail, only membership in the fraternity of harsh experience as the one real communion.

Though drawn from the actual hobo, the American Joe of our literature considerably reverses the reality. Part of our culture's concern with him seems to go beyond the obvious obsession with violence and outcast pathos to an inversion of the pathological American insistence on "success." Dramatized as more victim than rebel, the American Joe serves to confirm American freedom—the openness of the road—but then reveals that it is really compulsive and destructive, thus re-enforcing our refusal of freedom. This mythos of the hoboing experience, which variously appears in a far wider range of fictions than so-cial-naturalism, often oddly uses the man down-and-out in apologetics for the way in-and-up.

Faulkner's Joe Christmas in *Light in August* almost exactly fits the mythic template given above and epitomizes its ritualistic gestures of toughness, except for the parodistic Christian gloss which serves as part of the author's mockery of the Protestant crucifying spirit. (The ex-Christian Everyman pursuing the folk girl and her bastard up the road at the end provides the balancing affirmation that the road must lead to an earthy order.) James Jones' hero of the army stockade in *From Here to Eternity*, an ex-hobo who has turned toughness into a Jesuitical masochism, provides only a variation in self-punitive fatality which confirms the novel's theme of the necessary martyrdom of all manliness. In such fictions there is a puzzling fear of freedom and an assertion of value as its negation, as also in the destructive exaltation of vigilante law in the "Private Eye" tough guy tales. The apotheosis given the rebel who turns self-destroyer apparently aims to redeem the amoral toughness.

In more recent novels, the hobo experiences and amorality still remain important—the ritualistic trips down the road, the immersion in violent sensations, and the cool defiances—but the resolutions are most often fideistic confirmations of the given social order. Thus, to take some examples from the Fifties, the protagonists of Gold's *The Man Who Was Not With It*, Bellow's *Adventures of Augie March*, and Malamud's *The Assistant* come out of a flight down the road and disenchanted toughness into baroquely pyrrhic affirmations of ordinary settled life. Such ironic conversion of the man from the road requires a style of ornately synthetic self-consciousness. A more pertinent extension of the tough hobo is Ken Kesey's hero in *One Flew Over the Cuckoo's Nest* (1962) who "growed up so wild all over the country, batting around from one place to another . . . travelling lightfooted and fast, keeping on the move so much" that he never did learn to soften and submit. This brawling Irish bum and wit, this boozer, con-man and vagabond lover, returns us to the heroic tough guy from the road. With the outcast's vital amorality, he mockingly "acted out his hostilities against authority figures"—as the authorities disapprovingly note—instead of desublimating them into a repressively bland social order. Kesey also gives his roughneck rebel, now appropriately trapped by a shrewdly vicious psychiatric bureaucracy, an apotheosis as sacrificial figure for the weakly decent who lack the tough élan of the eternal savior on the outside.

There are other sophisticated developments from the nuclear tough hobo, especially in the current revival of the sardonic picaresque, for the figure explores fundamental American responses. Often perplexing, to be sure, since such tough guys variously combine the idealization and degradation appropriate to the prophetic stranger and his wisdom of extremity. Polite literary moralists may bemoan that harsh sensations and amoral toughness provide so much of the significant initiation into American reality. But adequate awareness of the society and affirmation of the self come hard. The imaginative violations and violence have their sources in our most basic life-styles. The torturings of freedom and of virility in the mythos of a hostile society and a hostile resistance to it may also twist deeper—into revenge on the man down and out. For our fascinated repulsion with the tough guy proletarian on the road may also suggest an expiation for belonging at all to our civilization, from which at times we must all yearn to find a way out.

Labels

BENJAMIN APPEL

LITERARY LABELS, like any other kind, are convenient. But over the years they don't hold up. The glue dries. The label drops off.

Back in the Thirties, the Tough Guy novel and the Proletarian novel were both à la mode. And although styles have long changed, the best of the tough guy novels will endure because the vice was genuine and not simply a device. In fact, some of the best of the tough guy novels were also among the best of the proletarian novels. I can illustrate this idea with an anecdote. Away back in 1934 when the Great Depression had turned America into a breadline, when the Soviet Union seemed like pie-in-the-sky—a splendiferous Red Pie—there was a party in New York for the various delegates and guests who had come from all over the country to attend the first League of American Writers' Congress. The late Kyle Crichton, somewhat drunk, embraced or tried to embrace James T. Farrell, Nelson Algren, and the author of this essay. Clutching at all three of us, he proclaimed loudly: "Here are the three toughest and best writers in America!"

Hastily, let me say I'm not disinterring this merely to drench my little ego with some belated perfume. Crichton was over-enthusiastic, and after all it *was* a cocktail party. What he really meant was that the three of us, each in his own way and with varying degrees of success, had tried to write about the America we knew. The *tough* label was just convenient.

Farrell had just published the first *Studs Lonigan;* Algren his *Somebody In Boots;* and I, *Brain Guy.* Farrell's shanty Irish, Algren's hoboes and Wobblies, the Hell's Kitchen kids in my novel, had this much in common. They were not minted out of the headlines, the movies, the novels of other writers.

For almost three decades, beginning in the Thirties, the tough guy novel would become a literary staple. Most were three-dollar bills forged to sell for hard cash. Just as today the Alienated novel, for example, is being produced by all sorts of cozy hands who really aren't alienated from this Affluent Society—except when they walk out of their handsome houses, passing the two cars in the driveway, to step inside the studio where, gritting their teeth, they mutter: "I'm alienated alienated ALIENATED . . ."

One thing is sure. The conveyor belt from studio to publishing house has never stopped operating. Only the product changes. Yesterday's cornflakes is no longer soaked in killer-diller bathroom gin but in a distillate supplied by *Sartre, Genet et Cie.*

But there are also fine novels by men and women who are truly alienated and who write out of their hearts, that most authentic of inkwells.

The proletarian novel had a shorter vogue. Their authors, unlike most of the tough guys, were in earnest. Shaken by the Depression, horrified by Hitler, enamored of Stalin, many conducted private little seances with themselves: "What I ought to do is write about the working class or maybe the sharecroppers!"

Often, it didn't really matter whether they ended up in smoky Pittsburgh or sunny Alabama. They were bemused (and so was this writer) by a vision of the Noble Worker, exploited by the Wicked Capitalists in Silk Hats, toiling away somewhere in Sweatballs County. And, it was all true. In the Depression years, the whole country was full of "Negroes." Millions and millions of white workingmen and farmers were no better off than Negroes today. Most writers were literary sharecroppers, scratching out a living, or else employed by the Federal Government's Writers' Projects.

President Franklin Roosevelt's New Deal saved the Wicked Capitalists (as they belatedly realized). The Affluent Society was on its way . . .

But back in the Thirties, labor and management slugged it out on the picket line. The proletarian novelists—mostly middle-class college graduates—were entranced. The Noble Worker, beaten around the ears, hungry in the belly, somehow would become the savior of America: another Christ in blue overalls. So, from the best of motives, the prolet novelists, like the cash-and-carry tough guys, produced their own formula fiction.

> *Prolet*   The union is trying to organize the steel mill / textile / cotton field, the filthy boss is hiring finks / vigilantes, but the strike is won in the last chapter / UP THE REVOLUTION!

> *Tough*   The bastard (who? who! never mind, somebody!) gets kicked down the stairs / one rape or seduction every 50 pages / one murder every 100 pages / make it 75 / BE TOUGH!

But there were also fine proletarian novels. Some were by "real proletarians" like Jack Conroy; others by writers like William Rollins, Jr., no miner's son like Conroy, but of an ivy-league family.

Now with all this said, maybe the reader is wondering what I meant by my statement: "some of the best of the tough guy novels were also among the best of the proletarian novels."

It seems to me that novelists, no matter how labeled, have always had the dual task of writing about man and man's society: the individual and the mighty package that encloses us all. Alas, we are all a part of the package whether we call ourselves Republicans or Democrats—and with a hasty secret-op look around the corner—Socialists or Communists. Squares or lefty-louies, pot hounds or teetotallers, black laughter boys or black power advocates—we are all inside society.

True, the fish can be described, the ocean omitted.

The best of the tough guy novelists, in this sense, were oceanographers. And to wind up this little essay, let me quote from some old book reviews of mine to illustrate what I mean. In 1935, I reviewed John O'Hara's *Butterfield 8* for a little magazine called *Literary America*.

> He differs from the I'm-tough-as-hell school in one important respect. He is interested in people, if superficially . . . O'Hara mobilizes . . . Gloria Wandrous, the speakeasy gal de luxe, her ex-Yale ex-crew man lover, Malloy the reporter . . . other drunks, damechasers, potential rapists, powerful boozers and marches them through a succession of scenes familiar to all Hammett-Cain fans; waking up in bedrooms wearing men's pajamas, naked and waiting for boy friends, heisting mink coats, getting socked around by tough guys. . . . But there is an important difference. There are scenes where O'Hara is trying and succeeding to get to the bedrock of reality, where his brutality is not phony but genuine because it springs from the conflict of character and not the manipulation of a knock-'em-dizzy yarn spinner. Jimmy Malloy's talk on the Irish and their racial uniqueness that Brooks clothes and Yale degrees cannot camouflage . . . Leggett's love affair with his wife's best friend has a brutality that reminds one of the decadence of Proust.

In short, O'Hara was a real writer who wrote about people he knew and the society that had shaped them. This was equally true of Nelson Algren, another *tough guy writer* (I promise to stop using labels myself!) whose *Never Come Morning* I reviewed for the *Saturday Review of Literature* in 1942. Algren's novel was tough and it was also proletarian or rather lumpen-proletarian (to paste on all the labels!). The Polish streets of Chicago housed the thugs, the finks, the poor. Like O'Hara, Algren's knowledge was first-hand. His pages are full of the hard bitter poetry of the street argot: "Don't gimme that hustle, Bicek. Don't gimme that executive hustle."

Algren had heard living people talk a living language. The ersatz tough guy writers had only heard James Cagney and Edward G. Robinson. Algren's superbly done world of gang and street, cop and jail, whore and jukebox, couldn't be imitated.

Bruno Lefty Bicek, his central character, was talented with his fists. And the prize-fighting ring (the baseball diamond too) has always been a port-of-call for the dispossessed at different times in American history. That is, if they had the physiques and the abilities. First, the Irish, then the Jews, Italians, Poles, and today the Negroes. But Bicek doesn't make it. He becomes a pimp, a worker, so to speak, in another industry: the crime racket. Back in the Thirties as today in the Sixties, this industry has remained the same although its public image has changed. No more big diamonds and gangster wars: *cool it, man, look respectable.* At the center there are the millionaire receivers of the take. Revolving around them are the important satellites, the brokers, politicians, corrupt judges and police, a host of little-shot big shots. "And way out in the darkness of a hundred American cities," I wrote, "a million million dollars away from the center are the bread and butter employees."

Never Come Morning tells the story of some of these bread and butter people, and the particular corner they occupied inside the mighty package we call modern society. Bruno Lefty Bicek, his pals and enemies, become unforgettable and terrifying—these tough guys and rum-dum (to use a phrase of Algren's) prolets.

Tough guy fiction? Proletarian fiction?

Enough of labels!

Critics, particularly the young critics to whom the depression decade is only a chapter in a book, have the responsibility critics have always had—to open the books.

The Tough Hemingway and His Hard-Boiled Children

SHELDON NORMAN GREBSTEIN

THAT WE AMERICANS are a peace-loving people who are fascinated by violence, a democratic people who worship superior men, a sentimental people who admire emotional control, and a garrulous and demonstrative people who favor short speech and guarded action are propositions as self-evident as they are paradoxical. Among our culture heroes and demi-gods are Paul Bunyan and Mike Fink, Daniel Boone and Davy Crockett, Jesse James and Buffalo Bill; and among our most vivid literary characters are Cooper's Natty Bumppo, Melville's Ahab, and London's Wolf Larsen. As various as these figures are, and whether of life or of the imagination, all are, in Jefferson's phrase, Natural Aristocrats. All are physically hard and emotionally tough. All are supremely adept at their crafts. All espouse objectives which frequently do not square with conventional moral norms but which are admirable nevertheless. All are pragmatists who employ questionable means toward desirable ends. In the Darwinian terminology, they are superbly equipped in the struggle for existence; in the Nietzschean, they practice a Master rather than a Slave morality. Such is the cosmic condition that they are ultimately destroyed: Natty Bumppo by the natural decay of time, Ahab by his animistic foe, Larsen by a brain cancer; but their courage persists so long as there is life in them. They are, in short, the splendid ancestors and prototypes of the tough guy hero who emerged in the popular fiction of the Twenties and Thirties and who is still very much with us in more ways than we can possibly discern.

The writer who provided the mode of transmittal from cultural prototype to popular type, the writer who more than any other transformed the Superman into the tough guy, and thus fathered the hard-boiled heroes who populate the tough novels of the Thirties and after, was Ernest Hemingway. As Philip Young and others have said, from Hemingway's novels and stories were derived the manner, the world view, and the qualities of character which defined the tough guy. Furthermore, in *To Have and Have Not* Hemingway wrote what is probably the best tough novel of the Thirties and certainly that which best depicts both the moral pragmatism of the hard-boiled hero and the class conflict which is a subtle but recurrent factor in the work of the tough guy writers. I therefore intend to trace those aspects of Hemingway's early work which were immediately and significantly influential on the tough guy school, and I will conclude with an analysis of *To Have and Have Not* and its protagonist Harry Morgan as they relate to the tough guy tradition. As bases of comparison with Hemingway I will employ Dashiell Hammett's *Red Harvest* and Raymond Chandler's *The Big Sleep*, which I take to be representative works by two of the ablest practitioners of the tough school.

We begin with a world view and a scenario. "Gangsters, killers, executions, murders—all these abound both in Hemingway's early stories and in his later novels such as *To Have and Have Not* and *For Whom the Bell Tolls*," wrote the Russian critic Ivan Kashkeen in 1956. But only a quick survey is required to conclude that, strictly speaking, Kashkeen's observation is incorrect. Aside from *To Have and Have Not*, gangsters and killers appear in only two Hemingway stories, directly and centrally in "The Killers," briefly and obliquely in "Fifty Grand." There is but one "execution"—other than those in time of war or civil war—and this appears in "Chapter xv" of *In Our Time*. Murders, to be precise, occur in but two places in Hemingway's work: "Chapter viii" of *In Our Time*, in which the murderer is a policeman who kills cold-bloodedly but under official sanction, and again in *To Have and Have Not.* Quantitatively, then, gangsters, killers, executions, and murders, which are the basic materials of tough fiction, are a relatively minor part of the whole range of Hemingway's writing.

Kashkeen's statement does, however, represent a kind of figurative truth. Despite the fact that a surprising amount of Hemingway's work is social commentary and satire, that much of it has to do with the peace-time relationships of men and women, children and parents, or friend and friend, and that a good deal of it partakes of the comic, the overwhelming impression derived by the reader of Hemingway is that of a violent world, a world at war, a world in which anarchy prevails. Hemingway's depiction of violence, although it is in frequency by no means his major concern, is nevertheless perhaps the most vivid and memorable aspect of his art. And even where there is little or no violence, as in *The Sun Also Rises*, we are given the sense of breakdown, fragmentation, disintegration. In such a world, toughness seems the only means of survival.

Throughout Hemingway's early work, and despite the keen social consciousness of much of it, law neither guides human conduct nor seemingly has much relevance to it. No characters in modern fiction exercise greater moral awareness than Hemingway's; none struggle harder for moral certainties, and almost none achieve such little success. Witness Jake Barnes' continuing, agonized, but ultimately futile attempts to find some durable meaning in his suffering and make some useful philosophy from it. Each of these attempts concludes only in Jake's recognition of the emptiness of his endeavor, culminating in his final, stark, tough comment "Isn't it pretty to think so?"

Frederick Henry's struggles to achieve a satisfactory moral resolution in *A Farewell to Arms* have equally unsatisfactory results. The brutal actualities of war have taught him to distrust such shibboleths and abstractions as glory and honor, and Catherine's agonies in childbirth lead him to conclude that men's sufferings in life are as pathetically frantic and meaningless as the scrambling of ants on a burning log. Society is partner to this cruel deception because it insists in promulgating a mock order and respectability which ignore the harsh reality of the human condition. Once he has discovered its vicious sham, the Hemingway protagonist can no longer count himself one of its members.

This bleakness and despair, this exacerbated awareness of the betrayal of what had once been a precious innocence, and the grimly distrustful and corrosively ironic response which follow inevitably from the betrayal, compose the nucleus of the tough *Weltanschauung*. Perhaps the most succinct statement of the whole situation occurs in a little poem by Stephen Crane, one of Hemingway's tough predecessors (recall, too, that Crane's *Maggie: A Girl of the Streets* contains the earliest depiction in American literature of tough characters in their social environment): "A man said to the universe: / 'Sir, I exist!' / 'However,' replied the universe, / 'The fact has not created in me / 'A sense of obligation.' " Although the tough guy writers avoid philosophical excursions even more strenuously than their master Hemingway, it is exactly this bitter sense of cosmic indifference which they share with him and which their work indirectly reflects. Appropriate to its different intentions and audience, however, there are important alterations and substitutions.

Hemingway's scenario of a world at war, or of a landscape ruined and its inhabitants crippled by war, is replaced in the tough novel by the scenario of a society beset and corrupted by crime. Crime is the specific social equivalent of war, and its prevalence signifies that no watchful deity and no meaningful pattern of order rules over man. Just as the Hemingway hero in making his "separate peace" must abnegate his former idealism and establish his own pragmatic terms for survival, so the characters of the tough school must adjust their values and behavior to the specific conditions in which they find themselves. In Hammett's *Red Harvest* the Continental Op reminds one

of his colleagues, who has questioned the destructiveness
of his method of carrying out his assignment, that "it's
right enough for the agency to have rules and regulations,
but when you're out on a job you've got to do it the best
way you can. And anybody that brings any ethics to
Poisonville [sic] is going to get them all dirty." Furthermore, the city to which the Continental Op has come,
Personville (the very name is significant), created by a
pioneer entrepreneur but now dominated by gangsters, is
the exact counterpart of the social wasteland which is the
milieu of much of Hemingway's early work. Personville is,
simply, a synecdoche for a ruined America.

Under such extreme conditions, what replaces the
hero's commitment to causes (there can be no heroism
without a cause)? Both Hemingway's protagonists and
those of the tough guy writers replace abstract loyalties
with personal loyalties: Hemingway's characters bind
themselves to their craft, their friends, and their loved
ones; the tough hero to his work, his employer, and his
subjective sense of decency. Jake Barnes' devotion to Brett
serves to bring him to her side, no matter what her tres-
passes, and in the same novel Pedro Romero's devotion to
his profession as a matador becomes an exemplum for the
dignity and meaning to be found in craft—regardless of
the condition of the society in which it is practiced. Precisely the same sort of personal commitment, although
necessarily framed in a different dimension and context, is
voiced by Philip Marlowe in *The Big Sleep*, as Marlowe
rebuffs his employer's attempt to dictate conditions:
"When you hire a boy in my line of work it isn't like
hiring a window-washer and showing him eight windows
and saying: 'Wash those and you're through.' *You* don't
know what I have to go through or over or under to do
your job for you. I do it my way. I do my best to protect
you and I may break a few rules, but I break them in your
favor. The client comes first, unless he's crooked. Even
then all I do is hand his job back to him and keep my
mouth shut." Actually, there lies behind this hard-boiled
statement and its seeming disregard for "rules" a still

unblemished idealism. In Marlowe's assertion "I do my best to protect you," in his unspoken but nevertheless firm conception of a straightness against which crookedness can be measured, in his persistent attempt to preserve what little honor remains to the lives of his clients, and in his capacity for silence, Marlowe practices a creed taken directly from the celebrated Hemingway Code, which simultaneously rejects social convention, cleanly respectability, and the rule of law, and affirms love, courage, dignity, comradeship, and professional integrity.

From such a world view and social stance derive the manner of conduct, the character configuration, and the style which manifest the "toughness" that gives this entire mode of writing its name. It seems to me that the crucial psychological element of toughness is that of control and self-discipline won at enormous expense from a series of violent and painful experiences. This control partakes, all at once, of the battle-hardness of the seasoned soldier, the stoicism and coolness of the accomplished professional (accomplished both at staying alive and getting his work done), and the numbness of the man who has witnessed more horror than he can absorb. We can trace the evolution of this control through the experiences of the various Hemingway protagonists, from the first childhood encounter with death in "Indian Camp," through the betrayals and disappointments of love in "Ten Indians" and "The End of Something," through the struggle to overcome the trauma of war wounds in "Now I Lay Me" and *The Sun Also Rises*, through the debasement of patriotism and idealism in *A Farewell to Arms*, to the hard sardonic detachment of "A Natural History of the Dead."

In Hemingway, as in his followers, there are three tests or criteria for toughness. The first and most obvious of these is sheer physical stamina and the ability—a synthesis of physical stamina and iron will—to keep functioning despite pain and bodily damage. Although Hemingway's protagonists are never supermen, they are distinguished by their power to rise to the crisis. Frederick Henry, seriously wounded by the explosion of a heavy mortar shell, retains sufficient control over himself to attempt to care for another soldier mangled by the same explosion. Later, despite his shrapnel-riddled legs, Henry makes love to Catherine in the hospital. Manuel Garcia, "the undefeated," his body torn by a severe and perhaps fatal *cornada,* summons sufficient strength to kill the bull which has gored him. Jack Doyle of "Fifty Grand" withstands a smash to his groin and outwits a double-cross by crumpling his opponent with the same kind of blow—to fall would mean the loss of his bet. Similarly, in "Today Is Friday" Hemingway portrays an utterly manly and physically courageous Christ who sustains the tortures of crucifixion bravely enough to win the admiration of the hard-bitten Roman soldiers. "He was pretty good in there today," one of the soldiers compulsively repeats over and over.

Parallels abound among the tough writers. Whether the hero be Hammett's Sam Spade or Continental Op, Chandler's Marlowe, Frederick Nebel's Captain Steve Macbride, John K. Butler's Steve Midnight, or almost any other of a host of hard-boiled dicks, and regardless of differences in physique or personality, all have in common the ability to take punishment. To be drugged, beaten, or shot only slows them temporarily; after the traumatic moment itself all are able to resume activity. Even when their physical strength is impaired, their keenness of wit and aptness of movement are not. For example, in *The Big Sleep* Philip Marlowe, despite handcuffs and a recent beating, decoys his assailant (an exceedingly expert killer) into a vulnerable position and then dispatches him with several well-placed shots.

The second standard for toughness is that of control over personal feeling and natural appetites, especially in a professional situation. The epitome of sloppy sentimentality and self-indulgence, and thus at the furthest remove from the tough hero, is the character of Robert Cohn in *The Sun Also Rises.* But on this point we encounter a paradox. As weak and childish as Cohn is made to seem in his predilection for sentiment and public displays of emotion, no Hemingway protagonist and few of the protagonists of his disciples, is wholly successful in the restraint of emotion. All strive for coolness and freedom from passion, but all are subject to it. Frederick Henry begins his courtship of Catherine with no loftier intention than to secure a clean and attractive girl he need share with no one. His earliest words and kisses are merely moves in a sexual game. But before he knows it or can help it, he finds himself in love with her. Manuel Garcia commits the cardinal error of losing his temper both at the jeering crowd and the bull who stubbornly resists his sword thrusts, and his rage leads directly to his goring. The single crack in the icily hard front Jack Doyle shows to the world is his devotion to his family and his loneliness away from them. The Roman soldiers who have attended dozens, perhaps hundreds of crucifixions, are nevertheless not sufficiently immune to suffering not to be moved by that of Christ.

Likewise, in *Red Harvest* Hammett's Continental Op, the apotheosis of toughness, develops a tenderness almost of love for Dinah Brand, blowzy, vital, greedy ex-mistress of a gangster. Philip Marlowe conceives so strong a filial admiration and affection for his elderly client, General Sternwood, that he is able to resist the sexual advances of both the General's luscious daughters. Although the protagonists of Hammett, Chandler, and others lead far from ascetic lives, it must be remarked that they will not take to bed a woman who is merely desirable and available. At minimum there must be affection, need, and emotional rapport to exalt the sexual drive.

Indeed, the tough hero's capacity for emotion constitutes the essence of his humanity. It is this quality which renders him most humanly attractive and credible to the reader and which provides the most important means of distinguishing him from his antagonists, the gangsters and thugs. Quite aside from the inalienable situation in which we approve the hero because he stands for Right and the villain for Wrong, we identify with him because, in his power to *feel*, the tough hero is fundamentally normal. In contrast, the criminal's inveterate choice of things or money over people, his immunity to love, guilt, or remorse (the criminal's prime emotions are greed, fear, anger, and hatred), his total callousness to the pain endured by others, and his incapacity for compassion or empathy, all mark him as less than human and consequently deserving of destruction.

That is, in achieving perfect toughness, the criminal also achieves complete isolation from mankind, whereas the tough hero, regardless of his frequent departure from social norms and his frequent ruthlessness, even cruelty, never abandons his humanity. His toughness, therefore, most truly consists not in the total conquest of feeling, but in the conquest of his tendency to *show* his feelings. Jake Barnes can cry about his shattered manhood and as the expression of his frustrated desire for Brett, because he cries in private, as Hemingway's protagonists often weep and sometimes plead or pray—in private. What the tough protagonist can never permit himself is the open exhibition of feeling, the spilling over of one's emotions upon others.

The inhumanity of the criminal is nowhere more vividly portrayed than in Hemingway's "The Killers." With their identical black costumes and white faces, the studied repetitiousness of their speech, and the casualness of the announcement of their deadly mission, the two gunmen are depicted as wholly inhuman, or, one might say, antihuman. They are not only the instruments of death, they embody the very mood of death. Because their talk and movements convey such intense menace and utter indifference to the three men in the lunchroom, George, Nick, and Sam submissively obey the thugs' orders long before any weapons are shown or murderous intent is revealed. Though as subsequent events prove, neither Nick nor George lack courage, Nick and the others are subdued simply by words and an instinct of dread. Furthermore, when the killers depart, their decision to let these men live seems to be entirely a matter of whim, of chance. There is not the slightest element of mercy in the decision. Al's parting statement makes this plain: " 'So long, bright boy,' he said to George. 'You got a lot of luck.' 'That's the truth,' Max said. 'You ought to play the races, bright boy.' " Lash Canino, the hardened killer in *The Big Sleep,* and the great majority of the hoodlums who throng the pages of the tough writers, are the direct descendants of the prototypes Hemingway created in this story.

Finally, we observe that toughness in Hemingway and his hard-boiled followers is defined not only by physical durability and the maintenance of the stoic pose, but also and ultimately the power to confront death without morbid pessimism or specious piety. A representative statement of the tough confrontation of death appears in the opening pages of "The Undefeated": "Manuel looked up at the stuffed bull. He had seen it often before. He felt a certain family interest in it. It had killed his brother, the promising one, about nine years ago. Manuel remembered the day. There was a brass plate on the oak shield the bull's head was mounted on. Manuel could not read it, but he imagined it was in memory of his brother. Well, he had been a good kid." This passage, with its laconic references to the loss of a loved one and the scrupulous avoidance of pathos, is part of a consistent attempt in Hemingway's early work not to deny death but to deglamorize and de-romanticize it. The Hemingway hero attains a secular grace when in the very presence and full consciousness of death he behaves as though he would live forever. The point is made emphatic by the white hunter Wilson, in "The Short Happy Life of Francis Macomber," who quotes Shakespeare on the matter: " 'By my troth, I care not; a man can die but once; we owe God a death and let it go which way it will he that dies this year is quit for the next.' " Wilson's genuine toughness and habitually stoic composure make the expression of this sentiment the instance of profound embarrassment to him; it could have been elicited only by so special an occasion as the coming to manhood of Francis Macomber, i.e., Macomber's attainment of the highest degree of toughness, the ability to confront death. Now, facing the buffalo, "Macomber felt his heart pounding and his mouth was dry again, but it was excitement, not fear."

To Hemingway death provides the most severe and intense test of character, the sharpest lens through which to study life. As he explains it in the opening chapter of *Death in the Afternoon,* it is for these reasons he assigns it so prominent a place in his work. It is also the prime reason why Hemingway recurrently returns to the bullring as the locale for his fiction, and why he professes such admiration for the brave matador. At first glance the tough hero and the matador would seem to have little in common, so far removed are they in locale and circumstance, yet only a little reflection serves to emphasize their fundamental likenesses: notably their professional devotion to craft, their physical toughness, and above all, their coolness in the presence of death. Indeed, Hemingway's description of his friend Maera (one of the originals for the brave protagonist of "The Undefeated") could well apply to the prototypal tough guy: "He was generous, humorous, proud, bitter, foulmouthed and a great drinker. He neither sucked after intellectuals nor married money." A major source of these attributes is Maera's disdain for death, his capacity to live with "much passion and enjoyment" despite his knowledge that he was dying of tuberculosis.

Hemingway's most consistently hard-bitten treatment of death, at least in its manner, is his curious little essay-story "A Natural History of the Dead," first published in 1932 as part of *Death in the Afternoon* and later printed as a self-contained work in his volume of collected stories *The Fifth Column and the First Forty-Nine* (1938). Heavily ironic in tone, in style a deliberate parody of the objective and dispassionate report of the field naturalist, and in overt statement a sardonic reply to the New Humanists' insistence that literature avoid the sordid and vulgar, "A Natural History of the Dead" really has as its basic theme and purpose the attempt to stare unblinkingly into the face of death, and by so doing to dispel its mystery and its terror. The following passage illustrates Hemingway's intention.

> The first thing that you found about the dead was that, hit badly enough, they died like animals. Some quickly from a little wound you would not think would kill a rabbit. They died from little wounds as rabbits die sometimes from three or four small grains of shot that hardly seem to break the skin. Others would die like cats; a skull broken in and iron in the brain, they lie alive two days like cats that crawl into a coalbin with a bullet in the brain and will not die until you cut their heads off. Maybe cats do not die then, they say they have nine lives, I do not know, but most men die like animals, not men.

This reductionist view of death and the seemingly objective reporting of it, the note of contempt for death, has had pervasive influence on tough writers. Compare this passage from Chandler's *The Big Sleep*, "What did it matter where you lay once you were dead? In a dirty sump or in a marble tower on top of a high hill? You were dead, you were sleeping the big sleep, you were not bothered by things like that. Oil and water were the same as wind and air to you. You just slept the big sleep, not caring about the nastiness of how you died or where you fell."

The great danger in such an attitude is that the contempt for death should not insidiously develop into contempt for life, that stoicism become callousness, that the tough hero become exactly the sort of psychopathic non-human he combats. We find an awareness of this danger expressed by the Continental Op in *Red Harvest* when the Op becomes concerned over the excitement he has begun to feel in the violence around him, most of which he has provoked, "I've got a hard skin all over what's left of my soul, and after twenty years of messing around with crime I can look at any sort of murder without seeing anything in it but my bread and butter, the day's work. But this getting a rear out of planning deaths is not natural to me. It's what this place has done to me." As we consider the tough hero from Hammett to Mickey Spillane and beyond, we realize (and this correlates with what has been said about the tough hero's capacity for feeling) that only the hero who is tough enough to stare death down, but not so tough as to be wholly immune to its grim appearance, is indeed *heroic*; only such a man engages our imagination without also provoking our incredulity or disdain. To attain the proper relationship with death is therefore the most difficult, the final, test of toughness, and to pass the test is, in Hemingway's phrase from *For Whom the Bell Tolls*, "like having immortality while you were still alive."

The tough style is not the only style at Hemingway's command, nor is it even typical of the greater body of his work, but, to recall Kashkeen's remark about the prevalence of criminals and murders, Hemingway's tough style is so highly visible, was in its first appearance so original, and has been so widely imitated (and parodied), that in our literary imaginations it has assumed far larger significance than it actually possesses for Hemingway himself. As Richard Bridgman has recently demonstrated in his book *The Colloquial Style in America*, the tough style is a form of colloquial style which descends most directly from Mark Twain. It employs a simplified diction, limited vocabulary, and seemingly basic but subtly varied grammatical and sentence constructions. It also stresses the concrete noun and verb, and conveys a sense of objectivity through the avoidance of adjectives and adverbs. When Hemingway wishes to portray characters of little formal education and/or low class origin, he will also make use of the vulgate, e.g., slang, profanity, broken grammar, fragmented constructions. Although the simplicity, clarity, concreteness, and objectivity which characterize the various Hemingway styles were lessons learned only after hard study with Mark Twain, Gertrude Stein, Ezra Pound, Sherwood Anderson, and an arduous apprenticeship in journalism, Hemingway's native voice is that of a Midwestern American whose manner of expression seems drawn from living speech rather than books.

To be specific, Hemingway's tough style depends on three dominant elements: first, short and simple sentence constructions, with heavy use of parallelism, which convey the effect of control, terseness, and blunt honesty; second, purged diction which above all eschews the use of bookish, latinate, or abstract words and thus achieves the effect of being heard or spoken or transcribed from reality rather than appearing as a construct of the imagination (in brief, verisimilitude); and third, skillful use of repetition and a kind of verbal counterpoint, which operate either by pairing or juxtaposing opposites, or else by running the same word or phrase through a series of shifting meanings and inflections. The following passage from "The Battler," a story in Hemingway's first collection *In Our Time* (1925), exhibits all the characteristics I have noted (Nick Adams has just been thrown from a freight train and now approaches a campfire).

> The man sat there looking into the fire. When Nick stopped quite close to him he did not move.
> "Hello!" Nick said.
> The man looked up.
> "Where did you get the shiner?" he said.
> "A brakeman busted me."
> "Off the through freight?"
> "Yes."
> "I saw the bastard," the man said. "He went through here about an hour and a half ago. He was walking along the top of the cars slapping his arms and singing."
> "The bastard!"
> "It must have made him feel good to bust you," the man said seriously.
> "I'll bust him."
> "Get him with a rock sometime when he's going through," the man advised.
> "I'll get him."
> "You're a tough one, aren't you?"
> "No," Nick answered.
> "All you kids are tough."
> "You got to be tough," Nick said.
> The man looked at Nick and smiled. In the firelight Nick saw that his face was misshapen. His nose was sunken, his eyes were slits, he had queer-shaped lips. Nick did not perceive all this at once, he only saw the man's face was

queerly formed and mutilated. It was like putty in color. Dead looking in the firelight.

The tough qualities conveyed by terse, abrupt sentences, the clipped interchanges of dialogue, and harshness of the diction are so self-evident in this passage they require little comment. I would only point out that in the paragraph which describes the man's face Hemingway has deliberately used a number of terms which are not appropriate to colloquial speech: *misshapen, perceive, mutilated,* so that he may "distance" from the scene in order to distinguish sharply between what Nick sees as a physical fact and the intellectual-evaluative processes immediately following his actual visual perception. Hemingway's shift in diction from the vulgate of the dialogue to the standard-informal of the exposition combines with the skillful use of narrative perspective (selective omniscience) to permit the writer to attain the immediacy of the I-narrator and yet the flexibility and objectivity of the outside narrator. That is, Hemingway simultaneously hovers above the scene, controlling all its elements, and at the same time renders what Nick sees and thinks as though Nick's voice told the story. I should add that this expertise in the management of narrative perspective is one of the dominant qualitative differences between Hemingway and his tough pupils, who tend almost invariably toward the I-narrator approach. Indeed, Walker Gibson in *Tough, Sweet, and Stuffy* characterizes the Tough style as essentially that of "I-talk," in which the persona "is a man dramatized as centrally concerned with himself."

The special effect of toughness conveyed explicitly by such words as *shiner* and *bastard* is enhanced and made resonant by a series of repetitions, variations, and juxtapositions. Notice the repetition and subtle variation in the connection of *man* and *looked*: "The man sat there looking into the fire." "The man looked up." "The man looked at Nick and smiled." And at last the subtle inversion and juxtaposition in which *looking* assumes another, more sinister level of meaning: "Dead looking in the firelight." Notice the play and slight shift of inflection in *busted, bust, bust.* There is a similar play and movement in the repetitions of *bastard, get him, tough.* What Hemingway is creating in this scene and these linguistic interplays is an undertone of danger and portent echoing beneath a seemingly good-natured exchange, a portent of the story's later show of violence. In this function the repetitions work like muted, ominous drum-beats, so faint as to be almost subliminal; it is precisely the technique of the opening of "The Killers."

> The door of Henry's lunch-room opened and two men came in. They sat down at the counter.
> "What's yours?" George asked them.
> "I don't know," one of the men said. "What do you want to eat, Al?"
> "I don't know," said Al. "I don't know what I want to eat."
> Outside it was getting dark.

With such a beginning we sense, without knowing exactly why, that nothing cheerful or pleasant will transpire.

Another way of understanding or explaining the effect of this technique of repetition-variation-juxaposition is to ground it in life. We know from empirical observation that the speech of the tough, the unlettered, the low caste is heavily repetitious, depending on varying inflections of the same words to achieve the emphasis which the educated man achieves through amplification, restatement, analogy. Furthermore, in its use of repetition, in the curt response, in the stripped diction, the tough style manifests its disdain for abstractions, flights of imagination, and the effete joy in language for its own sake. In the tough style, we have the evidence of the implicit American belief that doing is more important than saying, that breath should be spent in working, not gabbling, and that long-windedness and elegance of expression are *de facto* proof of one's incapacity for truth, accomplishment, reality, life. The tough style is thus the attempt to give organic form to a world view: muscular, functional, and deliberately unbeautiful.

Hemingway's most extensive work in the tough tradition is his 1937 novel *To Have and Have Not*. Not only does it bear out the definition of toughness we have established, it also exhibits an important but often neglected dimension of the tough guy school, and a dimension which has so far not been explored in this essay. I speak of the socio-economic dimension, which involves both class conflict and social injustice. And here we encounter a curious ambiguity: the employers of the tough hero, who is almost always a private detective, are the rich and the aristocratic (since only they can afford his fees), and his antagonists are the criminals who are almost invariably the poor or who once had their origins in poverty; yet the tough hero's own origins and sympathies belong more to the poor than the rich. Furthermore, because the tough hero is usually engaged to keep the rich from suffering the consequences of their misdeeds, he is obliged in the very nature of his mission to make certain that the poor (criminal) do not escape the consequences of *their* misdeeds. Finally, as vicious, brutal, and treacherous as the thugs, hoodlums, conmen, blackmailers, etc., who threaten the rich, the rich often prove themselves capable of equal if not greater depravity, all the more despicable because it is carried on under the guise of elegant manners and respectability.

The situations of both *Red Harvest* and *The Big Sleep* illustrate these points. In both novels the tough hero is called in to protect the rich against the results of their earlier sins. In *Red Harvest* the Continental Op comes to clean up Personville, a city which has fallen into the hands of gangsters and a crooked police chief who were originally brought in by the town's leading capitalist to break the power of organized labor. Once the hoodlums had performed their service and crushed the union, they had taken over the city themselves; and their erstwhile employer, guilty by his connection with them and now aging and ailing (no doubt Hammett's metaphor for a decaying capitalistic system), was helpless against them. Enter Continental Op, who disinfects Personville almost literally with blood, that is, by playing off one gangster against the other; so much slaughter results that he begins to fear for his sanity.

Similarly, Philip Marlowe's employer in *The Big Sleep* is a once splendid aristocrat, now very old and frail, who has bred two beautiful but corrupt daughters whose transgressions make them the prey of blackmailers and gamblers. One daughter is merely a snob, a liar, and an accessory to murder; the other is a psychopathic murderer and nymphomaniac. Such are the people Marlowe must protect. The irony of the situation is further emphasized by the fact that even among the criminals Marlowe encounters, only those of the lower order are vulnerable. The successful crook, by virtue of the money, power, political connections, and appearance of respectability his success has brought him, is almost immune to punishment. Chandler squarely confronts the social injustice in all this when he has one of the minor characters in *The Big Sleep*, a police captain, say to Marlowe,

> "I'm a copper. . . . Just a plain ordinary copper. Reasonably honest. As honest as you could expect a man to be in a world where it's out of style. . . . I'd like you to believe that. Being a copper I like to see the law win. I'd like to see the flashy well-dressed muggs . . . spoiling their manicures in the rock quarry at Folsom, alongside of the poor little slum-bred hard guys that got knocked over on their first caper and never had a break since. That's what I'd like. You and me both lived too long to think I'm likely to see it happen. Not in this town, not in any town half this size, in any part of this wide, green and beautiful U. S. A. We just don't run our country that way."

Although such explicit statements are rare in the tough novel, which is neither a proper medium for social reform nor a suitable forum for the exchange of ideas, the elements of class conflict and social injustice I have outlined do often provide a substructure for the strenuous action and hard-boiled manner of tough writing. It could also be said that social conflict operates as the motivation and the context for the action and manner.

The case in point is Hemingway's *To Have and Have Not*. While no critic in possession of his faculties could call it a great novel and while it certainly falls far short of Hemingway's own best work, it is nevertheless an interesting, vividly written, and memorable book. Furthermore, although its structure is episodic, in part resembling that of a story-cycle (such as the Nick Adams stories) and in part that of a conventional novel, there exists through much of the work a closer relationship between the saga of the tough protagonist, Harry Morgan, and the portrayal of a number of minor characters, the rich, than most critics have perceived. One could summarize the relationship by saying that it is the rich who drive Harry to those extreme acts of toughness which produce his death. First and most directly, two rich men damage his capacity to earn a living: the rich tourist Johnson sneaks away without paying Harry for the charter of his boat and the loss of his equipment, thereby compelling Harry to go outside the law in order to support his family; during one of these episodes (smuggling whiskey) Harry is seen and reported by a pompous rich official, thus losing the boat which is his only source of income. Secondly, and this is as true of the other "conches" and of the veterans we observe in Freddy's bar as it is of Harry Morgan, the poor have been victimized by the Depression, itself the fault of the "economic royalists," to apply Roosevelt's once-potent phrase. Indeed, although Harry Morgan's crimes lead swiftly to his annihilation, his moral character is no worse, and in some cases better, than that of the rich who are above retribution.

The world Hemingway portrays in *To Have and Have Not* is, then, the essential milieu of all tough novels, a society so dominated by crime and injustice that law and order have become viciously hypocritical terms. Only power, money, and indomitable individual action make for survival, and if one must survive at the expense of others, so be it. Consequently, Harry Morgan, tough hero that he is, adopts a personal and pragmatic standard of behavior, a Darwinian-Nietzschean morality at the furthest remove from the official morality of our Judaeo-Christian culture, a morality in which a man must sometimes act as a "criminal" in order to win decency and dignity as a man. To Morgan, no man worthy of the name would work for seven dollars and fifty cents a week digging sewers on a government project, especially not a man who has been a police officer and who has known the independence of owning a charter fishing boat. For Harry Morgan, impelled by destiny, character, and the social condition, there can be no alternatives. His toughness is both necessitated and justified by the social jungle he inhabits.

But the personal pride typical of the tough hero is only one of Morgan's motivations. As ruthlessly pragmatic as is his moral code, he is not without human sympathies. What he undertakes is determined in considerable measure by the attempt to provide for his family, not out of any gratuitous impulse toward brutality. If it becomes necessary for Harry to kill, as he does with cold skill in two of the novel's episodes—Mr. Sing, the smuggler of Chinese, and the Cuban revolutionaries who rob the bank—he neither initiates the killing nor the situation which demands it. Because Sing demonstrates himself to be a creature wholly without humanity, suggesting to Harry that the twelve men who have paid to be brought into the United States may be merely murdered or abandoned to die (as scores of others have doubtless been), Sing can be dispatched with no greater compunction than one would destroy a rattlesnake. As for the Cubans, although some of them profess to rob and kill in the service of their political cause, they in fact care nothing for the life of anyone but members of their own group. One of them now kills for the sheer joy of it, as he cuts down the lawyer Simmons and then Albert. Harry is spared only so long as he is useful; therefore, when he has the chance to shoot first, there is no reason to hesitate. In short, just as the tough writer always marks out an often narrow but nevertheless sharp line which distinguishes his heroes from their antagonists, so Hemingway in *To Have and Have*

Not clearly differentiates between Harry Morgan, who kills to survive, and the others who kill either for profit, politics, or out of bloodlust.

Another prime characteristic of the tough hero exhibited by Harry Morgan is the capacity to withstand physical punishment and pain. In the whiskey-running incident, Harry's arm is so badly mangled it must later be amputated, yet he still musters sufficient stamina and self-discipline first to make the crossing from Cuba to Florida and then to lift the heavy sacks of whiskey and drop them overboard. Meanwhile, his Negro helper, much less severely wounded, marshals sufficient strength only to lie on the floor of the boat and whine about his wound. Harry, in contrast, permits not a syllable of complaint to pass through his clenched teeth. The same stamina and courage are in evidence in Harry's last adventure. Shot in the stomach at almost point-blank range, Harry (now one-armed) manages to put away his assailant, switch off the boat's motor, and then stay alive for a day and half. Were it not for a small error in judgment, or, to say it another way, were Harry truly a Superman, he would emerge from the slaughter unscathed. In fact, Harry's vulnerability to severe wounds and fatal mistakes provide an important counterweight of credibility to his heroic traits; as superior as he is to ordinary men, Hemingway's protagonist remains a frail mortal who commits errors, sustains grievous injury, and then dies.

If Harry's values and character have been hardened by circumstance (Albert, a very ordinary man, says of him: "He was mean talking now, all right, and since he was a boy he never had no pity for nobody. But he never had no pity for himself either."), his exceptional physical vitality, strength, and stamina are largely natural endowments. These also encompass his sexuality. To other males Harry is homely, but to his wife Marie and to Mrs. Laughton, a tourist, he is "beautiful." His beauty, of course, is that of utter masculinity, a virility so intense that it elicits the adoration of his wife, once a prostitute, and presumably an experienced judge of such matters. In his sexuality Harry is again the prototypal tough hero.

As many critics have noted, Hemingway undoubtedly intended Harry's courage, independence, and masculinity to contrast with the decadence of two segments of the upper class depicted late in the novel: the idle rich and the time-serving intellectuals who make literary capital out of social conflict. However, it has not recently been emphasized that Hemingway also projects a no less significant contrast between Harry and the lower classes. Harry's capacity both to deal out and withstand punishment has its ironic counterpart in the meaningless "toughness" of the group of veterans who congregate in Freddy's bar. Although these men are tough enough casually to beat one another bloody and at the same time boast of their capacity to "take it," their toughness is not admirable but revolting because their physical stamina has no point or purpose. The very fact of such violence and toughness indicates a disease both of body and spirit: bodily it is a symptom of the blunting of nerves and sensibilities; spiritually it reveals that the energy and vitality once valuable to society in war has been reduced by society's neglect into brutal sado-masochism.

The Marxist critics of the Thirties who had chastised Hemingway for the lack of ideological content in his work were cheered by the new social consciousness reflected in *To Have and Have Not.* Yet the more sensitive of them were rightfully given pause by the novel. That Hemingway was at last specifically concerned with social injustice was manifest, but where was he going? The portraits of the filthy rich and the diseased intellectuals were admirably sharp, but in whose cause was Harry Morgan enlisted? And did Hemingway intend these battered and boozing veterans to represent the working class who would build a new world?

It is largely because Hemingway raises these questions of ideology without fully or satisfactorily answering them that *To Have and Have Not* aspires to be simultaneously a tough novel and a proletarian novel, with the result that it is never wholly either. The first eighteen chapters of the novel, or approximately three-fourths of its length, are essentially the story of Harry Morgan, tough protagonist,

who loses first an arm and then his life trying to make a
living in the only way his pride as a man will let him. His
refusal to abide by rule of law and his hatred for the rich
are justified and dramatized by what actually happens to
him, victimized both in his direct encounters with the rich
and by the economic system dominated by the rich. However, in the later portion of the book, when the weight of
the narrative shifts from Harry to the depraved poor and
the decadent rich of Key West, the novel loses its true
center of gravity. In other words, when the social conflict
which I earlier described as a substructure for the tough
novel becomes its façade as well, the result is inevitably a
confusion of purpose and design. Harry Morgan is hardly
a loveable character and the actions which center around
him are savage and gory, but they are credible in their own
terms and they provide the atavistic release which is for
the reader the ultimate function of the tough novel. We
can believe in Harry Morgan only when he behaves as he
is, a tough hero, not when he repudiates his identity in
order to convey a social message. He has been too much
and too successfully a man alone for us to believe the
dying words Hemingway has given him to utter for our
socio-political edification: "No matter how a man alone
ain't got no bloody f——ing chance."

With all its flaws, and regardless of its success as a social
document, *To Have and Have Not* remains the best of
the tough novels of its decade and perhaps the best yet written in America, as Hemingway, despite almost a half century of imitation, remains unsurpassed as a tough writer.
His total artistic achievement amounts to a great deal
more than that, of course, and in the estimation of many,
he belongs in the front rank of the fiction writers of our
language. Considering his stature and originality, there is
small wonder he has given rise to so many different kinds
of progeny, among them two generations of hard-boiled
children, from Dashiell Hammett to Ian Fleming. No
doubt each new decade will see the emergence of other
varieties of tough writers whose work we will continue
reading to satisfy our vicarious desire for the strenuous

life, to participate in the adventures of the strong, stoical heroes who can take it and hand it out, to become in our imaginations the tough guys who transcend the fear of softness, of old age, and of dying.

Focus on *To Have and Have Not*
To Have Not: Tough Luck

PHILIP YOUNG

> KENT. Vex not his ghost; O, let him pass! He hates him
> That would upon the rack of this tough world
> Stretch him out longer.
> —*King Lear*, v, 3

IT IS SOMEWHERE recorded that long ago a broker named
Chapman approached a man sitting peacefully in a club
and said "So you're Hemingway . . . tough guy, huh?"
and pushed him in the face. The assailant lived to regret
having been right on both counts. A foolish one, Mr.
Chapman, or at any rate a drinking man. But he was only
one among many who did not believe Hemingway was as
tough as he sounded. The doubt was, ironically, a
simple-minded perception of a basic truth. The writer was
quite tough enough to take care of belligerent drunks and
all threats that a man exposed to lions, bulls, and bombs
may encounter. And yet as a very young man, he had
managed, through his prose, to suggest to a few readers at
least that his "primitivism" was actually the product of a
sophistication and delicacy that called the masculinity of
his fiction and his press into question. The masculinity
was no pose, however, nor the artistry a delusion. An old
New Yorker cartoon of the hairy-chested writer clutching
a single rose in a big fist expressed the incongruous truth.
Fist and rose, both were real.

But it will still come as a surprise to many that *To Have
and Have Not* is the only hard-boiled book Hemingway
ever wrote; further, that there are almost no tough guys
among the leading characters in his fiction, and only a few

in minor roles. The most important single fact about his central, recurrent and loosely autobiographical protagonist—Nick Adams, Jake Barnes, Frederick Henry, Robert Jordan, Richard Cantwell—is that he is *not* tough. The front looks solid enough, at least from a distance, but it was built by will and courage to protect what is damaged inside. "No," said Nick, rejecting a reference to his bravery under fire. "I know how I am and I prefer to get stinking."

Hemingway does stand, however, in some sort of relation to the Hard-Boiled School of fiction—more of an influence on it than anything else. If the genre really got started in the magazine called the *Black Mask*, which was founded in 1919, then Hemingway could have learned something from it. But if, as alleged, "the first full-fledged example of the hard-boiled method was Dashiell Hammett's story 'Fly Paper,' " then the method got started too late to have much influence on him, since that story did not appear in the magazine until 1929, by which time Hemingway was almost completely established in manner and method both. Two parts of *To Have and Have Not* (1937)—the fight in the bar and Marie Morgan's final soliloquy—are obviously indebted to Joyce's *Ulysses*. But the hunch is that Hemingway's "tough" owes a lot less to his contemporaries than to a few forebears, and his own imagination. The similarity of some of his work to the Tough Detective School (particularly to the novels of Raymond Chandler, the only member of it Hemingway once said he could read) is the result of his effect on them. "The Killers," surely one source for the American gangster movie,[1] was published in 1927, and so was "Fifty Grand," which features his first real tough guy, a prizefighter named Jack, who is a clear forecast of Harry Morgan, protagonist of *To Have and Have Not*. Like Jack, Harry has no sons, only daughters;[2] like Jack he can think very fast in a pinch. If not entirely amoral, both men are highly illegal; both are pitiless and both *very* tough.

A remoter precedent for Harry is more obvious: his namesake, Henry Morgan the pirate, who once ravaged the coasts off which Harry works, who like Harry was really hard, but brave and resourceful too. Where the parallel breaks down, we get what may be the main point of it: following his capture by the law Henry was knighted; Harry was killed. A closer precedent is more obscure: a minor Hemingway story called "After the Storm" (1932), which also features a fight in a Key West bar, and also deals with a self-reliant, tough, modern pirate (an exact working-sketch for Harry), who takes off in his boat and discovers a sunken ocean liner he is unable to loot.

A real curiosity, however, lies in the fact that if Hemingway's book does not have origins in the nearly-forgotten, turn-of-the-century, primitive branch of American naturalism, then the coincidences are astonishing. Frank Norris's *Moran of the Lady Letty* (1898) —a rather ridiculous novel—is built around a Have and Have Not Contrast (again the rich arc effcte, the poor robust); there is brutality, as in Hemingway, for the Chinese, and a lot of deep-sea fishing. Further, the Moran of the title is the image of one Morgan, Harry's wife Marie: a great blond woman, too big and strong to be pretty but a wonderful mate. And as if that were not enough there is Jack London's *The Sea Wolf* (1904), which comes directly out of *Moran,* and presents another original for Harry himself in the person of Wolf Larsen, a virile, hard, amoral loner whose survival-of-the-fittest ethic seems, like Harry's, the central concern of the plot. The novel is again a sea story, full of violence and cruelty, and even the apparent "message" is the same: no matter how potent and pitiless, a man has no chance alone.

That is the instruction that Harry Morgan provides, and it is always taken to be the message of *To Have and Have Not.* Also taken to be the book's climax, when Henry speaks his last words, "No man alone now. . . . No matter how a man alone ain't got no bloody f——ing chance." But the trouble is that these words do not seem as they should to put a finishing touch on the novel's structure. Indeed, it is hard to see how any lesson could, so faulty is the book's architecture. The story of how it got built and then knocked apart is the story of how Hemingway's tough novel became Hemingway's tough luck.

Kidding around one day some years after publication of the book, Hemingway described it as a "frail volume . . . devoted to adultery, sodomy, masturbation, rape, mayhem, mass murder, frigidity, alcoholism, prostitution, impotency, anarchy, rum-running, chink-smuggling, nymphomania and abortion." That may be too many things for a relatively short volume to devote itself to. But when the author agreed with those of his critics (not this one) who regarded the novel as his weakest effort, he gave a different reason: "The thing wrong . . . is that it is made up of short stories. I wrote one, then another when I was in Spain, then I came back and saw Harry Morgan again and that gave me the idea for a third. It came out as a new novel, but it was short stories, and there is a hell of a lot of difference." [3]

That was an explanation which the "publishing history" of the book more or less bears out, and not an excuse. Hemingway didn't make excuses, but if he had wanted to, he had a good one: his deep involvement in the Spanish Civil War. He didn't make speeches, either; even his own Nobel Prize address was delivered by someone else. And he didn't believe that writers should have political affiliations. But so committed was he to the Republic that he did make one speech, his only one and a good one, to the Second American Writer's Conference in Carnegie Hall in June of 1937. And so it was that *To Have and Have Not* became the only book he ever published that he did not care much about at the time.

It was after publishing the second of the three stories that he made the unlucky decision to build a novel, and arrived at the equally unfortunate decision to put a theme to it. The theme, he wrote his friend and editor Max Perkins, was to be "the decline of the individual" (which hasn't come through to many readers as what the book is about). The first idea, of writing a full-scale novel, was an unhappy one because if he had kept within the good old

Unities, and restricted himself to the three Morgan stories, he might have had a successful "novelette." Instead,
however, he tried to flesh out the stories with the portraits
of some contrasting Haves—particularly with the story of
a well-to-do pseudo-proletarian novelist, Richard Gordon.
Presumably to point up Morgan's masculinity, he also
provided him with a wife. But neither the emptiness of
Morgan's pocket nor his curious virility needed emphasis,
and anyway Gordon is treated so sketchily that he cannot
possibly stand up to a contrast. The brevity of his role is
one result of yet another mistake.

Until quite recently, readers had no way of knowing
why it is that there is such an imbalance between the
considerable space devoted to the Have Nots in this book
and the small room given the Haves (which is one reason
for its failure—if it can truly be said to fail). But now we
know that the disproportion springs from a very bad guess
on Hemingway's part as to just how much he could print
about certain living Haves and get away with it. In the
end he had to dump a good deal of material, and didn't
bother to put anything in its place.

We have this information from Arnold Gingrich,
publisher of *Esquire*. He reports that when the book was
done he was flown to Key West and handed the "finished
script." He read it, and out of his own experience of such
matters came up with the opinion that three people in it
were "libelled right up to the eyeballs. They were Dos
Passos, and Janie,[4] and her then husband, Grant Mason."
Hemingway protested a good deal, particularly that Dos
Passos would sign a "release," but in the end, Gingrich
says, he "mutilated . . . large portions of the *Have* sec-
tions . . . without any sort of replacement of the deleted
elements. I thought the least he might have done would
have been to change the title, because, as the book appeared, the title applied about like the 'fifty-fifty' recipe
for hamburger: one horse, one rabbit. It was a little disillu-
sioning."

It was worse than that. Beyond inequity, here was a
perfect case where the whole amounts to less than the sum

of its parts—for the simple reason that the parts don't appear to "add up." Though not vintage Hemingway, many of the fragments are good. The Morgan stories are vivid, mostly convincing, and occasionally exciting. If Hemingway had struck objectively to Harry, they could have had power. There are good things, furthermore, beyond Morgan. Gordon breaking up with his wife is one; the portrait of Professor MacWalsey (a little reminiscent of "Owl Eyes" in *The Great Gatsby*) is another; the vets' fight in the bar (toughness become positively sickening, as the author intended it should) is a third. But the ex-soldiers are made to contrast with some corrupt yacht owners, and the relationship is too obvious. So is the contrast between the real Marie and Gordon's fatuously ignorant thoughts about her; so, later, her equally unknowing glimpse of him. So too the dragged-in comparison between a rich bachelor's depleted income (still plenty) with that of a fisherman and his family (insufficient). Hemingway was underlining with a crayon what at his best he would have felt no need to remark at all. An elaborate rationale for all the switches in point of view the novel undergoes does exist, and it may reveal Hemingway's intentions quite accurately. But the changes actually accomplish very little beyond momentary confusion, and they increase the sense of fragmentation.

These are minor difficulties. A major one is that the book's ostensible message, a man alone has no chance anymore, seems inserted by Hemingway rather than extracted from Harry—perhaps to fit that "decline of the individual" business. Now this is one place where the tough guy fiction of the Thirties more or less crosses with the depression novel. As Carlos Baker has pointed out, Hemingway clearly intended us to see his Key West as America in small—or at its worst—in that grim decade; and meant us to see that Morgan, in the foreground, showed that the age of the gutty, self-reliant American pioneer was over and done. Minor figures representing capitalism, communism, and fascism meet with Harry's bitter disapproval and the reader's. All right, a plague on all your houses. But what's wrong is that the social cooperation implied by the "no man alone now" message has nowhere to go and just stalls.

Another impediment to implementing this "moral" is that a sensitive reading of the book will show some of the Haves, whom we expect to despise as the villains, to have been drawn with considerable sympathy. The result is a temporary emotional confusion, which is not straightened out by the perception that in practically everything but money, sex for instance, it is Hemingway's Haves who have not and his Have Nots who have. On first meeting Richard Gordon, for example, it is easy to dislike him, as expected. He is clearly an ass. "A writer," he says, "has got to know about everything. He can't restrict his experience to conform to Bourgeois standards." But after his wife decides to leave him, and has denounced him in the most spectacularly abusive speech in American literature, it is hard not to feel sorry for the man, particularly as we learn how much he loves her, and as the delusion that he had been good to her in bed crashes about him. Similarly, it first appears that we are supposed to deplore Professor MacWalsey as a professor, a useless drunk, and—far worse in Hemingway's scheme of things—a tourist to boot. But this man is really a very good person, and the author quickly brings us to like him a lot. In like wise, the evocation of the recent Haves who lost their money, particularly the capitalist "who shot himself early one morning before breakfast," brings little but sympathy. Conversely, Hemingway does not permit us to like some of his Have Nots.

In the end many of the things that once seemed clear about this novel have blurred extraordinarily. Harry Morgan, for instance. He is usually thought of as one of Hemingway's "code heroes" (and never more confidently than by the present writer). As defined, however, this figure in Hemingway is a man who makes a basic moral compromise and then sticks to his bargain come what can. He may throw a fight, play crooked cards, guide the unlikable rich on safari and service their women. But after the first compromise there is no other. Morgan, on the other hand, makes his bargain (chink-smuggling instead of rum-running) and then betrays it quickly as he is able, having intended to all along. As a matter of fact it is not even certain that he may legitimately be called "tough," though he can surely take it, as we say, and dish it out. But following his planned, cold-blooded, bare-handed murder of the Chinese Mr. Sing rather early in the book, the question is whether he is tough or simply brutal, which is not at all the same thing. Even Eddy, Harry's rummy companion (whom he was going to kill too until chance made it unnecessary), is shaken by that one, and asks the reader's question for him, "What did you kill him for?" Harry's answer, "To keep from killing twelve other chinks," is not completely convincing.

If then we have misgivings about Morgan as a tough hero, if his dying words do not function well as a "moral," if the announced theme is seldom felt to be one, and if our sympathies extend to several of the Haves but are withheld from a few Have Nots, then we are caught up in some sort of maze. But there is a way out. And, good news: it leads to the discovery that this just might be a better novel—more meaningful, more nearly unified— than Hemingway or his readers have believed. Despite the title, here is surely not another of those books about the well against the badly off, where allegiance is easy to pledge and the point easily got. What the novel really says, most steadily and conclusively, is what Hemingway had been expressing all through the Thirties, and it didn't have anything much to do with depressions or tough guys. It was simpler: a profound loss of hope for the lot of man. A savage civil war was going to bring him back, but that was later. *To Have and Have Not* comes in the darkest night of the soul, not the dubious dawn of social pronouncement. Its real message is not cooperation, it's desperation. It is not expressed by Harry but by Marie. It is not forced, but grows naturally out of all that's happened, and arrives with an air of finality at the finish of the novel in the last sentence of the following passage. Harry is dead, his wife widowed, and she is wondering what it's going to be like for her now: "How do you get through nights if you can't sleep? I guess you find out like you find out how it feels to lose your husband. I guess you find out all right. I guess you find out everything in this goddamned life."

Though not at its very best, *that* is the authentic voice of Hemingway, speaking through one who has survived to learn the lesson. It hasn't a lot to do with having or not having things—nor primarily with losing things you had, though that is much of it. What Marie has epitomized is the anguish that pervades the book. Rich or poor makes no difference in the very end; disparate elements are gathered into a unity brought about by nothing but Hemingway's unflagging awareness of mental and physical pain, his memorable sense of what a beating people take from life. The world he saw this time is a very rough place indeed, and the feeling that stays with you is of pity for anyone who is stretched out and racked up on it.

The *Black Mask* School

PHILIP DURHAM

WHEN HENRY L. MENCKEN and George Jean Nathan began publishing, in the early spring of 1920, the *Black Mask* — one of their three pulp magazines — they could not have known that they were creating a medium which became a vehicle for the "hard-boiled" writers, those writers whose heroes acted as rugged individualists while they brought justice to the deserving. The heroes were violent, but their violence was not merely that of sensationalism. It was rather a kind of meaningful violence, sometimes symbolic of a special ethical code or attitude, sometimes an explicit description and implicit criticism of a corrupt society. Thus, in one of America's unique magazines, the *Black Mask* School was created.

The early *Black Mask*, featuring "mystery, detective, adventure, western, horror, and novelty," was patterned along the lines of such first rate pulps as *Argosy*, but the original contributors rarely measured up to the stature of those writers found in the better-known *Argosy*. In those days, however, pulps were money makers, and editors Mencken and Nathan sold *Black Mask* after six months for a nice profit. Under the subsequent editorship of such capable men as Phil Cody and Harry North, *Black Mask* began to take on a specific character, and within two or three years a version of the heroic knight emerged; the Private Investigator was poised and indestructably ready to clean up the cesspools of crime in New York City.

The two heroes who played a major role in the development of *Black Mask* were Race Williams and the Continental Op in tales by Carroll John Daly and Dashiell Hammett. In November 1926, the *Black Mask* acquired a new editor, Captain Joseph T. Shaw, who during a full decade molded the magazine into a medium which made a unique contribution to American literature. Characteristics of daring, courage, egotism, artistry, and appealing personality combined to place the new editor in a position where his stable of writers began to look to his approval as a panegyric.

A descendant of Roger Shaw, one of the New England immigrants of the 1630's, Joseph Shaw graduated from Bowdoin College, where he specialized in athletics, and then went to work for the American Woolen Company. When he published *From Wool to Cloth* (1904), Shaw was destined to become a literary man. His next work, *Spain of To-day; A Narrative Guide to the Country of the Dons, with Suggestions for Travellers* (1909), indicated broader interests. In the meantime he had begun to specialize in the handling of the sword, eventually winning the national championship in sabers and the president's medal for the championship in all three weapons, foil, epée, and saber. After World War 1 the captain stayed in Europe to serve for five years with the Hoover mission in Czechoslovakia, completing the experiences he was to find useful for an editorial and literary career. That Joe Shaw had writing ambitions can be inferred from his numerous short stories and half dozen novels in the field of mystery, detection, and adventure. It was not in fiction, however, that his talent lay. His novel *Danger Ahead*, for example, begins with the hero executing "graceful motions" with the saber; but the story is a stilted Jamesian imitation without grace of style. Cap Shaw was an editor, as his magazine and many of its contributors will testify.

From the vantage point of twenty years, Shaw looked back, in 1946, to the time when he first came to *Black Mask*. He had meditated then, he later wrote, on the possibility of creating a new type of detective story, different from the one established by Poe in 1841 and so consistently followed right down to the 1920's: the tale of ratiocination, of clues, of puzzles, the locked closet had-I-but-known sort of thing. In the pages of the *Black Mask* he singled out the stories of Dashiell Hammett as approximating what he had in mind: "simplicity for the sake of clarity, plausibility, and belief." Shaw wanted action, but he "held that action is meaningless unless it involves recognizable human character in three-dimensional form." With the work of Hammett as the model, the editor began to search for the stories of those men who wrote in a similar vein; the July 1927 issue carried the statement "We are constantly looking for new writers who have the *Black Mask* spirit and the *Black Mask* idea of what a short story should be." The result became known as the Hard-Boiled School or the *Black Mask School* of Detective Fiction, with such chief practitioners as Dashiell Hammett, Raymond Chandler, Raoul Whitfield, Paul Cain, Lester Dent. The characters which the writers created were, admitted Shaw, hard-boiled, but the authors' "style and treatment were something else again." Modern critics identify the style and treatment as objective realism. Shaw was explicit in pointing out that his writers observed a cardinal principle—"in creating the illusion of reality"—by allowing their characters to act and talk tough rather than by making them do it. Instead of telling the reader how infallible the actors were, the authors allowed their heroes to demonstrate their abilities. By achieving ever greater restraint and by carefully avoiding incredibility, the *Black Mask* boys, thought Shaw, "wrote convincingly."

Eventually the cover of the *Black Mask* dropped such previously used terms as mystery, adventure, western, horror, and novelty; and over the objections of some of the authors but with the approval of many, the magazine retained only one exciting challenge—SMASHING DETECTIVE STORIES.

Those writers who did not agree with the literary theories of Joe Shaw drifted away, or at least their stories did, to other pulp magazines. Some of those who remained, however, confused him with George Bernard. One of the latter was Lester Dent, who after thirty-five years of publishing fiction still thought Shaw the "finest coachwhip I ever met in an editor's chair." Cap convinced his boys that they were not pulp hacks, but rather he inspired them to believe in themselves as writers with great futures. *Black Mask* in Cap Shaw's hands, said Dent, "was akin to a writer's shrine." That was in the twenties and thirties, that "brief and wonderful time when American literature was endowed with the most effective training ground in all history—the pulp magazine." The writers whom Shaw published, continued Dent, "were sort of automatically endowed with a hair shirt that they wore with pride and some dubiousness, because where writers got together you were pointed out as a *Black Mask* man; not a *Post* writer, a *Colliers* writer, or *Doc Savage* writer, but a *Black Mask* writer."

Joseph Shaw gave dignity to *Black Mask* magazine by his constant reference to it as "the book." He refused, also, ever to use the word "pulp." One wrote either for his "rough paper book" or for a "smooth paper" magazine. There was a difference. Raymond Chandler once wrote a story, "I'll Be Waiting," for the *Saturday Evening Post* and was sorry about it until his death twenty years later because in the smooth paper attempt he felt he had given in to slickness. It was Chandler's work, incidentally, which Shaw frequently used as a model to illustrate what could be done with style. A writer sitting across the desk from the editor would suddenly find in one hand a paragraph from Chandler and in the other a blue pencil and the Captain would be saying, "Would you cut that somewhere. Just cut a few words." The idea, of course, was that there was no wordage fat. One could not cut. Every word had to be there.

When Shaw became the editor of *Black Mask* it contained, as Erle Stanley Gardner has pointed out, a type and a style. The type was well known through the stories of Daly, but it was left to Hammett to combine the type and style. Short on style though Daly was, one would have a difficult time finding a more effective hard-boiled hero

than was his Race Williams, whom the readers did not
examine but merely swallowed in great quantities. One of
the earliest, latest, and most prolific of the *Black Mask*
contributors, Daly turned out Race Williams stories and
novels by the score. According to Gardner, editor Harry
North once said that when he put Race Williams on the
cover, the *Black Mask* sales jumped fifteen per cent.

In both the June, 1923, and April, 1927, issues of *Black
Mask* the editors reported interviews with contributor
Carroll John Daly, an assured and somewhat flippant
writer, who described his hero, Race Williams, as thirty,
five feet eleven and one half inches, one hundred eighty-
three pounds, with dark brown hair and black eyes. There
was nothing "soft-boiled" about the man who admired a
clever woman and respected a good one—"when he finds
her." He was a Private Investigator, in the business for
thrills and money. Here was the original hard-boiled detective, the private eye who, during the next forty years,
moved in fiction across the country—from New York to
Chicago to San Francisco to Los Angeles. At times he
changed into the clothes of a police detective, newspaper
man, camera man, undercover man for the Racing Com-
mission, insurance investigator, good-guy gambler, or just
plain knight, but he was always, essentially, the same
hard-boiled hero. Some of these men were more attractive
than Race Williams, although they were like him: indes-
tructible, fearless, courageous; he was violent, often brutal,
a dead-shot, killing when he thought it necessary; he was a
celibate admired by women and feared by men; he had his
own sense of right and wrong by which he lived, meting
out his individual concept of justice that more often than
not was contrary to the accepted mores or to the law,
which was restrictive and too slow. With supreme confidence in his own judgment, this individualist did not
think it necessary to play by the book—one who did was
often thought naive. In addition to what he said and did,
he frequently administered justice by what he did not do:
letting a murderer go free if he exhibited an extra measure
of guts, or allowing a girl—who had just put a bullet from

a small Colt automatic through a two-timing skunk—to escape because she had been victimized, had a good heart, and meant well. The private eye was always on the side of right, but it was his own personal interpretation and definition of "right."

In "Knights of the Open Palm" Race Williams, always the first person narrator, stated his position: "I'm what you might call the middle-man—just a halfway house between the dicks and the crooks. . . . But my conscience is clear; I never bumped off a guy who didn't need it." This credo was elaborated on throughout his heroic career. In *The Snarl of the Beast*, for example, Race restated his position, adding that "right and wrong are not written on the statutes for me, nor do I find my code of morals in the essays of long-winded professors. My ethics are my own. I'm not saying they're good and I'm not admitting they're bad, and what's more I'm not interested in the opinions of others on that subject." Williams, in "The Amateur Murderer," promised the readers that if anything happened to the girl he would "pop" off the offender, and he followed the assurance with his philosophy: "Not good ethics? Not right thinking? Maybe not. We won't go into that." The fact that he was on the side of right in the spirit of individualism justified almost any act. As he threw terror into all evil-thinking men, Williams' reputation became a symbol which allowed his problems to remain comparatively simple as long as he followed his slogan: "I trusted myself. That was what counted."

Opinions on patriotism, nativism, altruism, communism, and politics were all within the scope of Carroll John Daly. With an eye to public sentiment in the 1920's, Daly had Williams speak on the uselessness of senators, from whom one gets nothing at all. A congressman was a little better, for one can at least get garden seeds from him. When in *The Third Murderer* Florence Drummond—The Flame, the good girl with the criminal mind—complained to Race of the state of society by saying "Honesty—the one thing that the rich leave for the poor to fatten on," Race replied, "You didn't bring me here to fill me up on Communism." "No," Flame said,

"Communism is a hatred of the poor for the rich—not simply an envy." Appealing to Williams as a "staunch citizen" was the wrong approach, for he did his work only at the right price. Like the big shoe manufacturer and Henry Ford and John D. Rockefeller, with Race Williams it was a business. They did not give away shoes, cars, or oil, but they gave generously to charity. Foreigners from all of Asia and most of Europe were villains per se, and because they were so frequently arch criminals they made excellent antagonists for Race. He favored patriotic Americans, born and raised, unlike Count Jehdo, on American soil. Yet in "Murder Book" when Race acquired the document which might have saved our country and prevented a war, he returned it for the life of The Flame who was being tortured after having been caught acting as an agent of the government. Williams' personal sense of justice, integrity, and loyalty came first.

Daly was not one to miss the value of "reckless courage" even in the villains; he could say admiringly of Mark Yarrow—the number two bad man of "Murder Book"—"He passed out tough." And there was Purdy Young in *Tainted Power* who represented the "new school" of racketeering because he wore a hundred and fifty dollar gray business suit instead of a sweater and cap—"Purdy Young had guts." Daly saved his unstinted praise, however, for the show of guts in the good guys, including one cop: "Good old Sergeant O'Rourke. He had the guts to live no matter what the consequences." The guttiest of them all was, of course, Race Williams himself, admirably summed up by The Flame.

> "You made use of just what you always make use of. It's not your head; it's the animal in you. The courage in you; the thing that drives you on. You're licked—licked a dozen times, over and over. Everybody knows it but you! No, it's not your head."
> "If it isn't my head, what is it?"
> "Just guts, I guess," she said. "Just guts."

Clichés and sloppy writing characterized Daly's work. He was a "he don't" writer who had Williams say, "I shoved a butt into my face, gave it heat." Williams identified a bad guy on a foggy, dark night by his bloodshot eyes and yellow teeth. Daly employed brutal death in the tough manner: "Joe Gorgon jumped sort of in the air, half spun, fired wildly, and I laid my next bullet smack between his eyes. Just a little round hole, ever growing larger. Joe Gorgon waved his hands once. His right foot came slowly up, like a lad in the slow motion pictures. Then he pitched forward on his face." Some of his most extravagant prose Daly saved for Williams in "I'll Tell the World": "Both my guns had spoken—both roared out their message of death—and, so help me God, but a single hole appeared in Lutz's forehead. I've done a deal of shooting in my day—mighty fine shooting, but never anything like that." Mr. Daly had been reading Dime Novels.

Carroll John Daly was a careless writer and a muddy thinker who created the hard-boiled detective, the prototype for numberless writers to follow. Race Williams was a popular literary hero in the 1920's and 1930's, but no different from the rugged individualists of any other decade who could say with Race,

> "I'm a man of action but I can think occasionally."
> "I'm sorry if I appear hard boiled or cold blooded . . .
> but them that live by the gun should die by the gun."
> "I'm all for justice and fair play."

Within a few months after the stereotyped, single-minded Race Williams first appeared in *Black Mask*, a relatively complex hard-boiled hero began his career in the pages of "the book": The Continental Op, a far more imaginative character than Race Williams, was created by Dashiell Hammett, who became one of the most successful of all *Black Mask* contributors. After a varied career which included a period of several years with the Pinkerton Detective Agency, Hammett—who knew a man who once stole a Ferris-wheel—began to turn his experiences into stories. With an eye to style and literary effectiveness, he experimented with techniques. Although he was credited with being the leader of the hard-boiled school of detective fiction, and although his hero had the basic characteristics found in the traditionally tough hero, it is no good trying to make Hammett all of a piece; the idea is too simple and his writing is too subtle. The good writers of Hammett's group, as do good writers in any group, experimented with writing techniques in order to determine what was most useful and effective for their own individual expression. They worked with plot, trying to keep it from becoming too obviously stereotyped; they created a character in their developing short stories who would later stand up in longer works of fiction; they agreed on the theme of the rugged individualist righting the social wrongs; they tried both the first and third person to see which would make the style more objective; and they concentrated on their hard-boiled style, hoping to make it as action-packed as possible. Hammett did all of these things and a bit more. Although he may not have been the smoothest and most consistent stylist, throughout his decade of prolific writing, he changed viewpoint and modified his hero several different times in trying for maximum literary results.

Nicely written though it is, there is but little in such an early Hammett story as "The Green Elephant," which appeared in *The Smart Set* in 1923, to draw unusual attention to the writer. Joe Shupe, whose fault was "that he was an unskilled laborer in the world of crime, and therefore had to content himself with stealing whatever came to hand," was suddenly and accidentally the possessor of a quarter of a million stolen dollars. Unable to cope with so much money, Joe walked the streets, couldn't sleep nights, and changed hotels every day. Only after his suspicious actions caused him to be picked up and jailed by prohibition officers could Joe become "his normal self again, both physically and mentally." There was no hero, let alone a hard-boiled one, in this story without even any tough writing, and tales of this kind did not bring for Hammett the acclaim he later received.

Dashiell Hammett soon, however, acquired a reputation, and among the many who eventually gave him un-

stinted praise for his writing ability, few were more succinct in expressing praise than Raymond Chandler. He
realized that Hammett continually viewed violence as an
act of human courage, and therefore admirable. Violence,
according to Chandler, did not dismay the Hammett characters, "it was right down their street." Furthermore,
Hammett was writing for "people with a sharp, aggressive
attitude to life." It was in the matter of style, however,
that Chandler was most critically aware. Hammett had a
style, "but his audience didn't know it, because it was in a
language not supposed to be capable of such refinements."
The "style," which Chandler held did not belong to Hammett or to any particular individual because it is "the
American language," could say things that Hammett did
not know or feel the need of saying. Hammett "was spare,
frugal, hard-boiled, but he did over and over again what
only the best writers can ever do at all. He wrote scenes
that seemed never to have been written before." The idea
that style is the American language—discovered independently by several writers in the hard-boiled genre—is un-
questionably one of the most significant aspects of the
evolving, hard-boiled tradition. Style, then, is where you
find it: not restricted to the drawing room or study, but
equally discoverable in the alleys. Stephen Crane went
down into Rum Alley, and in *Maggie* produced a first-rate
novel; but "tattered gamins" making a "furious assault"
on their "antagonist," while they were "swearing in bar-
baric trebles," is neither alley style nor American style.
Hammett went to the American alleys and came out with
an authentic expression of the people who live in and by
violence.

Although the early *Black Mask* story "House Dick"
contained brutality and four killings, it was only a
warm-up for what was to come in later works. The Continental Op did not figure in much of the violence, being
rather just simply a thoughtful, fearless man, doing his
job. As his creator had done before him, the Op carefully
and thoroughly checked his evidence, for "from any crime
to its author there is a trail. It may be—as in this case—

obscure [but] finding and following such trails is what a detective is paid to do." There was in this story, however, early evidence of clipped prose, that which was to become a Hammett trademark: "Picked him up when he got his mail yesterday afternoon." "Got an apartment on Van Ness Avenue." "Packing a gun under his left arm." The statements imply—although the economy of expression purposely controls—action, violence, and excitement. Perhaps the most important contribution of an early *Black Mask* story such as this was the presentation of the nameless fat man with an age varying between thirty-five and forty (based, said Hammett later, on James Wright, Assistant Superintendent of Pinkerton's Baltimore Agency, under whom Hammett worked); the detective performed through dozens of Hammett's pieces for the Continental Detective Agency's San Francisco office. In these short stories Hammett developed his style and prepared his character, the Op, for the novels which were to come.

In "The Tenth Clue," at the beginning of 1924, the Op continued his patient pursuit of evidence and details, but he threw in a little detection hint: "There are many, many murders with never a woman in them anywhere; but seldom a very conspicuous killing." An unusual Hammett story for these years appeared in the middle of January, unusual because of the setting and the switch to third person. In "The Man Who Killed Dan Odams" the Montana scene was vital, and the Odams woman and her son were like the determined, worn, brutal West of which they were a part. The people and the landscape were immeasurably strong, but the strongest of all was Silence. By the spring of 1924 in "Zigzags of Treachery" the Op was an efficient, dependable detective, but as yet not much given to heroics. He did not like eloquence because "if it isn't effective enough to pierce your hide, it's tiresome; and if it is effective enough then it muddles your thoughts." He was not "a brilliant thinker," yet he had "flashes of intelligence." He was a man of action, really, who liked his jobs to be "simply jobs—emotions are nuisances during business hours." Not yet legendary, he accounted for some of his feats after shooting a gun out of Jake Ledwich's hand: it "looks like a great stunt," the Op told the reader, "but it's a thing that happens now and then. A man who is a fair shot (and that is exactly what I am—no more, no less), naturally and automatically shoots pretty close to the spot upon which his eyes are focused." Unlike Race Williams, whose shooting was calculated to overshadow that of Davy Crockett, the Op simply maintained that when a man goes for his gun you shoot at *him* and if you are looking at his gun you might hit that; if you do, it looks impressive.

It was not long, however, before an accent on violence became pronounced in Hammett's stories, although at first the hero observed it with detachment and only later performed it with virtuous reflection. In "The Golden Horseshoe" the story started slowly with "thumbnail gouging into eye," and a head hanging "crookedly, dangling from a neck that had been cut clean through to the bone." The tempo stepped up when Gooseneck fired at Kewpie at the moment she threw a knife at him. Kewpie "spun back across the room—hammered back by the bullets that tore through her chest. Her back hit the wall. She pitched forward to the floor." Gooseneck was in similar trouble as he stopped shooting and tried to speak, while the haft of the girl's knife protruded from his throat. "He couldn't get his words past the blade. He dropped one gun and tried to take hold of the protruding haft. Halfway up to it his hand came, and dropped. He went down slowly—to his knees—rolled over on his side—and lay still." Hammett was beginning to succumb to the literary tricks used by writers trying to squeeze out the full value of violence but who resorted to artificial means for the effect. The knife in the throat, along with the ice pick in the chest, became a common device for increasing the intensity of the narrative, restricting natural movement, and hindering speech. Although it was not dwelt upon with as much pleasure, it was hardly more ingenious than hand-stomping in the Western story.

The Continental Op soon became physically and personally involved in violence, getting smashed up thoroughly in "One Hour." It was not long, as in "Women, Politics and Murder," before he thought violence was sheer pleasure, "I began to throw my right fist into him. I liked that. His belly was flabby, and it got softer every time I hit it. I hit it often." And the mood continued in "Dead Yellow Women" where the Op observed Dummy Uhl, who with "all the middle of him gone — slid down to the floor and made more of a puddle than a pile there." As the Op continued down a hall, "cracking everything" that got in his way and being "cracked" back, he began to enjoy the violence which was technically accentuated by one sentence paragraphs.

> "When he crouched above me I let him have it.
> My bullet cut the gullet out of him.
> I patted his face with my gun as he tumbled down past me."

The violence-is-fun technique which Hammett so thoroughly explored in his short stories of the middle 1920's was soon to reach its apex in his first novel.

In the meantime, however, Hammett had not forgotten the complete role his hero was playing in the tradition. In "The Gutting of Couffignal," for instance, the Op's intelligence was questioned because he refused to cut himself in on a big take. He stopped long enough to explain his role and concept of right and wrong: in addition to his honesty and sense of loyalty, he was a detective because he wanted to be one and because he liked the work. He knew he could make a great deal more money doing something else, but "liking work makes you want to do it as well as you can. Otherwise there'd be no sense to it." But being loyal to himself and his employer did not obviate his commenting on social situations. Couffignal was an island owned and ruled by "well-fed old gentlemen who, the profits they took from the world with both hands in their younger days now stowed away at safer percentages, have bought into the island colony so they may spend what is left of their lives nursing their livers and improving their golf among their kind. They admit to the island only as many storekeepers, working-people, and similar riffraff as are needed to keep them comfortably served." Hammett had a social conscience which Carroll John Daly never dreamed of.

The knightly role aspect of the hard-boiled or *Black Mask* tradition was developed in "The Scorched Face," a story otherwise notable for its brutality and smashing tempo—both in content and style. The Op and Pat Reddy, a good young cop, moved in to clean up one of the California "mystical" cults which victimized naive, wealthy women. The cult operated by first taking compromising photographs of its victims and then controlling the susceptible women through threat of blackmail. Murder was done before the Op and Pat Reddy cleaned out the cesspool. As a policeman Reddy was obligated to turn over the murderer and all evidence, according to law; as an independent detective the Op took a more liberal view, according to his conscience. Because of his obviously higher law, the Op was able to persuade Reddy to cover the whole thing up, to destroy the evidence and let the murderer off—this prevented more suicides and protected womankind.

That Hammett was continuing to explore among literary techniques during the middle twenties can be inferred from "Ruffian's Wife," in which he worked with third person narration—the viewpoint used in *The Maltese Falcon*—and in which he introduced Leonidas Doucas, a fat man who suggested Casper Gutman of *The Maltese Falcon*. Created also in "Ruffian's Wife" was an unusual version of the tough guy. Guy Tharp was "hard-boiled, hard-nerved, to whom violence was no more than addition to a bookkeeper." But under the fat man's pressure, Tharp's image dissolved into weakness; for his wife, the "red wolf of a husband" became only an illusion, and all she had left was his "callous brutality."

The individualistic attitude toward law was made specific in "Corkscrew," wherein the Op, by going from San Francisco to the Arizona desert town of Corkscrew, found himself in the nineteenth-century West. Upon arrival, the Op was warned by the "better element"—which included Miss Janey, the false-toothed, sour-faced school teacher—against the violent element which included both the good and bad guys. The Op, who was not much of a rider, was tested by being given an unrideable horse. Preferring, obviously, the violent element to the better element, the Op attempted to prove himself worthy of his chosen group by continuing to mount the horse as long as his battered body could draw itself into the saddle. Having become accepted by his courageous display of guts, the Op was ready to enlist admirers. One of the most individualistic of these was Milk River, who was willing to work with the Op if he did not have to become a deputy; Milk River would not put himself in a position where, as he said, "I'll have to enforce no laws I don't like." In this "hard neighborhood" where the inhabitants were "hell-bent on proving to everybody that they're just as tough as the next one," the Op found himself a worthy antagonist and explained to the reader the joy of physical contact as he "smacked both hands into his body, and felt happy when the flesh folded softly around them." Not to be outdone, Milk River was "grinning" while he shot another contestant out of the saddle.

This was a different kind of philosophic attitude toward violent death from the one Stephen Crane had expressed a generation before in "The Blue Hotel." In Crane's story the Easterner explained to the cowboy how in every murder there are from a dozen to forty women involved, but in the death of the Swede only five men collaborated, including the poor gambler who wasn't even a noun, only an adverb. The cowboy cried out blindly and rebelliously against this "mysterious theory." There is no mysterious event to account for the violence in "Corkscrew"; Slim merely refused to pay for his meal at the Toad's eatery. Milk River summed it all up with his own brand of amoral humor: "Think of all them folks that were killed and maimed and jailed—all over a dollar and ten cents. It's a good thing Slim didn't eat five dollars' worth of grub. He'd of depopulated the State of Arizona complete!" It was but a short jump from the wild West back across the street to the violence of the big city, and Dashiell Hammett's Continental Op was now finely trained for the biggest criminal affair the country had to offer.

In February and May of 1927 the *Black Mask* carried two of Hammett's long stories—"The Big Knock-Over" and "$106,000 Blood Money"—which were subsequently published together as his first novel. One hundred and fifty of the country's finest crooks gathered together in San Francisco where they simultaneously knocked over The Seaman's National and The Golden Gate Trust. During the noisy affair sixteen cops were killed and three times that many wounded; twelve bystanders and bank clerks were killed; and the bandits lost seven dead and had thirty-one of their number taken as bleeding prisoners. In a case of this size it was decided that the Op could use some help in recovering the money, but two or three additional operatives from the agency sufficed. One was Dick Foley whose rule it was never to waste words. Another was Jack Counihan, "full of the don't-give-a-damn-gaiety that belonged to his youthfulness." And then there was the Continental Op at his cold-blooded best, deciding that the most effective way to get to the source and recover the money was to arrange for the hoods to eliminate each other. So within a few hours one house contained fourteen dead, the next six dead, and so on until the St. Valentine's Day Massacre which happened two years later back in Chicago began to look like a teenage tiff. The Op's part in the decimation of the hoods could be thought ethical only in his own eyes; the readers could accept his chicanery and double-cross only after accepting the role of the Op. Among other tricky moves, the Op befriended one of the hoods so he could later shoot him in the back, and at another point he arranged for one of his own operators to be shot. True, the operator had defected, but it was the Op who meted out the justice, with an additional motive of keeping clean the good name of the Continental Agency. Not since the days when eliminating inhuman Indians was a hero's duty had an individual's judgment caused the demise of so many.

If there is such a thing as a poetry of violence, Hammett achieved it, technically at least, in this novel. At the height of a scene of smashing, slashing, and sudden death, the Op was having the time of his life. As he saw a mouthful of teeth smashed in, a blackjack crunch an arm, a side of a face blown away, the Op got with the rhythmical spirit of the occasion: "It was a swell bag of nails. Swing right, swing left, kick, swing right, swing left, kick. Don't hesitate, don't look for targets. God will see that there's always a mug there for your gun or blackjack to sock, a belly for your foot." Without any perspective shots, the author kept the reader on the scene, and by using diction appropriate to the characters, the narrator was not allowed, except physically, to achieve the superiority which would destroy the unity of effect. From this vantage point the Op delivered one of his most poetic lines: "I swayed and broke a nose where I should have smashed a skull."

Short stories of this period, late twenties, continued to show the Op's various roles as the traditional hero. In "The Main Death" he was a knightly hero who got the murderer and collected his fee for it, but he refused to divulge to his client the knowledge of an affair which would implicate his client's wife. In "Fly Paper" the Op was exclusively the hard-boiled hero, with Hammett working his prose for all the violent effects he could squeeze from it. He could use it tight: "Babe liked Sue. Vassos liked Sue. Sue liked Babe. Vassos didn't like that. Jealousy spoiled the Greek's judgment. He kept the speakeasy door locked one night when Babe wanted to come in. Babe came in, bringing pieces of the door with him. Vassos got his gun out . . . Babe hit him with the part of the door that had the brass knob on it. Babe and Sue went away from Vassos's together." Or Hammett could resort to the smashing paragraphs.

> "I shot his right knee.
> He lurched toward me.

I shot his left knee.
He tumbled down."

During the thirty-two months from November 1927 to
June 1930, Hammett's four important novels were
published serially in *Black Mask: Red Harvest, The Dain
Curse, The Maltese Falcon,* and *The Glass Key.* They are
critically regarded as his best work, but they were successful only because he had previously worked out everything
in them in his short stories. The first two continued the
Op as the first person narrator, although he changed character somewhat in the second; the third developed the
swaggering Samuel Spade, told in third person; and the
fourth created a variation on the character in Ned Beaumont, also with the third person viewpoint.

Red Harvest, originally a group of separate stories referred to under the general title *The Cleansing of Poisonville,* revolved around the Op still at his hard-boiled best,
although he was much more concerned with the problems
of a collective society than he had been in his first novel.
The Op, completely hardened, played everyone off against
the middle, and by his own count totaled up one and a
half dozen murders. He admitted he could "swing the play
legally," but he decided that "it's easier to have them
killed off, easier and surer." Allowing himself no sexual
diversion, the Op went in only for heavy drinking, the
latter presumably because even he occasionally reacted to
piled-up violence: "I've got a hard skin all over what's left
of my soul, and after twenty years of messing around with
crime I can look at any sort of a murder without seeing
anything in it but my bread and butter, the day's work.
But this getting a rear out of planning deaths is not
natural to me."

The slight crack in the Op's armor, barely discernible in
Red Harvest, broadened to measurable proportions in *The
Dain Curse.* He was still the efficient operator, but he had
become humanized. The double-crossing and double-
dealing were gone. Murder was still present, of course, but
it was not the Op's doing; rather it was engineered or
performed by Owen Fitzstephan, a man with streaks of

insanity. The heavy drinking was cut down to just drinking, and although other people had realistic sexual experiences the Op still abstained. In his most humanitarian role so far, the Op began a benevolent and knightly campaign to save the misused and brutally treated Gabrielle who believed she was suffering from the Dain curse. She doubted her sanity, so the Op soothed her by saying that everyone except the very crazy and the stupid suspect themselves at times. She did not realize that it was her fears, her psychological maladjustment, and her dope habit that rendered her sexually ineffective. The Op consoled her by explaining that there were "a thousand women in San Francisco making the same complaint." As she gradually became convinced that her "differences" were held by other women, and that they could be cured or corrected, Gabrielle still doubted her ability to give up dope. But the Op also scoffed at that thought, saying, "You've been reading the Hearst papers." Well, Gabrielle was rehabilitated, but at what a price. Dashiell Hammett virtually traded a hard-boiled hero for a part-time sentimentalist, a character who could recognize in himself such emotions as might occasionally be acceptable in the traditional hard-boiled hero, but for Hammett it could mean only that his hero had grown old and soft. Long live the Op. He was ready for discard.

With his hero gone soft beyond redemption in *The Dain Curse*, Hammett created a new or at least variant version in *The Maltese Falcon*. Using the third person instead of the first, for a different viewpoint, the author presented Samuel Spade—several years younger than the Op, six inches taller, and looking "rather pleasantly like a blond Satan." Although definitely in the tradition, Spade was a cool hero who was a devil with the women but never called a spade a heart. As the character changed, in part, so did the style. Instead of allowing his hero to act, the author explained the action: "Spade flung his words out with a brutal sort of carelessness that gave them more weight than they could have got from dramatic emphasis or from loudness." This was not Hammett's style at its best, the writing was less objective and the situations too obviously simulated. Spade's role, however, was less impossible and therefore more believable; he was more as the average man romantically imagines himself—brave, heroic, exciting, and irresistible.

Ned Beaumont in *The Glass Key* was another variation of the hero, not a detective but a right-hand man to a big-time racketeer and politician. Perhaps more than any of the Hammett protagonists, Beaumont came the closest to being an amoral character of the kind which was developing in the tradition. Other than for certain loyalties, his motions were mechanical and his emotions were not there. He had a smooth manner and some refinement, but what he did or how seemed not to matter. "I don't believe in anything," Ned Beaumont said, "but I'm too much of a gambler not to be affected by a lot of things." Yet it is difficult for the reader to discover what things affected him. He was smashed to a pulpy mess, won a large amount of money, and became violently ill from too much drinking, without the author giving the reader a clue as to whether any of these acts pleased or displeased the hero. The words Beaumont did not use might have been supplied by Angel Grace who was pulled out of the bay in Hammett's first novel: "Why didn't they let me alone? It's a rotten thing, living."

Some time during the years from 1927 through 1930 Hammett reached his peak—I personally think with *The Dain Curse*—both as a stylist and as a contributor to the tradition of the American literary hard-boiled hero. His stories of the early thirties, published in *Black Mask, The American Magazine, Liberty,* and *Collier's* were quite ordinary. Many of them continued the exploits of Spade, while others were experimental. "Woman in the Dark" presented an unHammett-like hero who although he had chivalry, loyalty, and physical courage was without any of the hard-boiled qualities. Stylistically, a gauzy mellowness was substituted for the clipped prose: "The wind blowing downhill from the south, whipping trees beside the road, made a whisper of exclamation and snatched her scarf away."

There remains little to be said about Hammett's last major effort, *The Thin Man*, which was obviously written under Hollywood influence. The original version of the novel had been planned and begun in 1930, in the style of that period, but only sixty-five pages were completed. The setting was San Francisco and its environs, the viewpoint the third person, and the detective a kind of modified Op. The most interesting aspect of the fragment was the unreal quality that Hammett insisted on attaching to the hero who was referred to as untouchable, as not even a corpse but a ghost, as one with whom it was impossible to come into contact—like trying to hold a handful of smoke. It was three years, one of which was spent in Hollywood, before Hammett returned to his fragment. Unable or unwilling to continue with it he wrote a different novel.

For some, Dashiell Hammett wrote beyond the tradition by specifically expressing the giddy twenties and gloomy thirties. For those readers and critics his private eye spoke for men who had lost faith in the values of their society—during war, gangsterism, and depression. This view, perhaps, can be thought of as analogous to the attitude held by Eric Ambler's protagonist at the end of the thirties; looking at the body of Dimitrios Makropoulos, Latimer "saw him not as a corpse in a mortuary but as a man, not as an isolate, a phenomenon, but as a unit in a disintegrating social system."

After Captain Joseph Shaw, early in his career as editor of *Black Mask*, had decided on Dashiell Hammett as the leader of the writers who had a new kind of compulsion and authenticity, he set about to find a group good enough to follow the leader. He found them by the dozen, the best of whom he thought would "revolutionize" American literature. Among Hammett's colleagues were several good writers who first published their short stories in *Black Mask*, turned to writing novels, and ended up in Hollywood: Frederick Nebel, Raoul Whitfield, Norbert Davis, W. T. Ballard, George Harmon Coxe, Thomas Walsh, and Lester Dent, among others.

Frederick Nebel had a sound working definition of realism which was not at all hindered by his lack of feeling for humanity. As a writer he thought he should not allow himself any indiscriminate sentiment in viewing human derelicts, but rather he should use the ineffectual man, the "stranded flotsam," as a lesson in "understanding contrasts." He was pleased with one of his heroes who was "*born* hard-boiled," but he was almost equally interested in one of his hoods who was a "man of iron." In *Sleepers East* Nebel wrote a novel of murder and intrigue in politics in which the action is governed by the toughness and weakness in men. The theme, not infrequently appropriated by hard-boiled writers, concerns man's inability to control the incidents of life; man cannot really make the grade, but if he gives it a good try he may get some of what is coming to him if only for the wrong reasons. To live as much and as violently as one can—even for a single night—may be the only way.

The Hollywood setting provided color for much of the work of Raoul Whitfield. He had one big, rough, fearless, frontier-type of hero who rushed to meet danger wherever he sensed it, and he had a private eye who was "cold as hell." Whitfield had a habit of trying to make his hero tough instead of allowing him to be tough, but this was often the result of the hero's compelling drive as a reformer. There was a strong feeling for the joy of violence in the stories of Norbert Davis. Relying on his own sense of justice, the hero—"a gunman, gambler, and soldier-of-fortune"—smashed, shot, and killed all over town; but he was doing it for "good," and those who were maimed or killed were on the side of wrong. The principal character in the work of W. T. Ballard was a good deal like his counterparts in the stories of Whitfield and Davis. A liaison man for the General-Consolidated Studio in Hollywood, Ballard's hero used violence willingly, but only to combat violence; he was indifferent to human life generally, but he sometimes cared about "little people."

The "number one camera for the *Globe*" stood in lieu of the private eye in the *Black Mask* stories of George Harmon Coxe. Coxe's hero had already become what he told a girl she would be if she insisted on working for a newspaper. To the girl, newspaper work was like having a season ticket for the drama of life, but according to the cameraman she would soon become a "hard-boiled, vindictive, loud-mouthed dame with a cigarette throat; without an illusion or ideal—without an honest emotion left in her system." Thomas Walsh wrote tight, fast-moving, energetic fiction in which he used as hero a "strong, silent, and extremely fortunate man from Chicago," or he did equally well with a plain-clothes-man on homicide. In two of his stories Lester Dent presented a private dick who was as tough and violent as any hero who smashed and ice-picked his way through the pages of *Black Mask*. In his longer fiction, however, he depended on a financially successful man of violence, a man whose violence became sticky at times because of the sentiment behind it: "A door mat, Molloy believed, is good only to be stepped on. It gets nothing out of life but wear and tear. Therefore, Molloy had always fought viciously for what he considered to be his privileges as a human and an American-born."

There was at least one among the *Black Mask* boys whose writing contained something different. The wrappers of the first issue of a novel published in New York in 1933 carried the following statement: "now comes the hardest, toughest, swiftest novel of them all FAST ONE two hours of sheer terror written with a clipped violence, hypnotic in its power." If there ever has been an accurate blurb, this was probably it. *Fast One*, published in part in *Black Mask* in 1932, enjoyed, according to its author Paul Cain (Peter Ruric), a "spectacular critical reception but was not so hot at the box office." When it came out in England, however, it sold like "sixty or seventy."

Among the writers of the hard-boiled genre, there had been an ever-growing awareness of the attitude of negation toward life, a feeling of indifference about humanity which appears to have reached a kind of peak in the early depression years. Humanity was still in evidence around the country, but so were rocks. Again it must be remembered that the awareness of negation was not peculiar to the hard-boiled writers; it had appeared in various forms of literature in America, in the plays of Eugene O'Neill, for example. Nor was it new on the other side of the Atlantic, although a culmination of negation was clearly set forth in *Journey to the End of the Night* by Louis-Ferdinand Céline, published in France the same year that *Fast One* ran in *Black Mask*.

Gerard A. Kells, the protagonist of Cain's novel had the characteristics commonly found in the hard-boiled hero—the brutal, gutty, fearless man. Yet there was something more in Kells, a factor which gave him his violently "hypnotic" appeal. To account for this, one is tempted to turn to the existentialism of Jean-Paul Sartre. Man cannot, according to Sartre, be exclusively individualistic, for whatever man does for himself he does for all men. The one thing man has is freedom, but having it he must constantly make choices. Having no legislator but himself, man must do all the deciding for himself. Whatever choice he makes is acceptable, for he obviously could not or did not make the other. Because the overruling aim in each choice is freedom, man can choose either of two opposite moralities—in matters of choice they are equivalent. Gerry Kells, who appeared unaware of the existence of anyone but himself, was without doubt his own legislator. He also made choices, although to the reader they generally appear as unconscious acts. It did not, incidentally, occur to Kells that he was choosing between "two opposite moralities," for he was amoral. Yet this was not the amorality of Theodore Dreiser, who felt that because man was the victim of his environment and physical makeup he had no moral choice. Kells was aware of his options and alternatives, but being cognizant only of his own existence, he was indifferent even to choices.

Having acquired in the East two thousand dollars and a reputation for knowing how to play "rough," Gerry Kells arrived in Southern California. His reputation made it possible for him to begin taking over the Los Angeles rackets, which he proceeded to do by playing off one racketeer against another and by eliminating a few himself. Double-crossing, smashing, shooting, and ice-picking were all in the act; it mattered not at all to Kells how things went. He accumulated several thousand dollars and lost all of it but seventy cents, and he did not react to that. Like all memorable hard-boiled heroes, he had, however, points of vulnerability—his pride, some small feeling of revenge, and a tiny touch of loyalty brought about his end. He went as he had come, alone, "Then, after a little while, life went away from him."

About an hour before noon on a mid-October day in the 1930's, Philip Marlowe drove through downtown Los Angeles. The sun was not shining, and there was a "look of hard wet rain in the clearness of the foothills." The shabbiness of Bunker Hill made him think of its days of respectability. Soon he headed west on Wilshire Boulevard, through Westlake Park, across La Brea Avenue; turning to the north at La Cienega, he crossed Santa Monica and Sunset Boulevards and found his way into the hills of West Hollywood, to the home of General Guy Sternwood. As Marlowe entered the Sternwood mansion, he looked up to see, on a stained-glass panel, a knight in dark armor rescuing a lady who was tied to a tree. The lady was without clothes, but she was wearing long and convenient hair.

In this fashion, in *The Big Sleep* in 1939, Raymond Chandler introduced his hero, the hard-boiled detective who was to become the epitome of them all. In seven novels during the following two decades, Marlowe drove through the streets of Los Angeles, and the surrounding towns, looking for ladies to rescue, for the little fellow who needed help, for the big man who deserved a shot of old-fashioned justice. "Down these mean streets a man must go," wrote Chandler, and his story was "man's adventure in search of a hidden truth." From the skilled hands of this writer, one of the best literary portrayals of the *Black Mask* hero evolved.

Although Philip Marlowe was not introduced, by that name, until 1939, he had been developing in Chandler's short stories for a half dozen years. Chandler's original private eye, using the name Mallory, appeared in *Black*

Mask in December 1933. From that date through 1939, he performed in twenty short stories, usually as the private eye (fourteen times), but occasionally as a detective lieutenant, narcotic squad under-cover man, or hotel dick. He used ten different names and was twice nameless, but always he was a part of the man Marlowe was to become. In experimenting with viewpoint, Chandler used the first person twelve times and the third person eight. Once created, Marlowe was always a first person narrator; this technique kept him on the scene, involved in the lives of others.

Beginning with his first story, "Blackmailers Don't Shoot," Raymond Chandler established his hero as one good enough to compete in the violence found in abundance in the far western city of Los Angeles. The man was tall, with gray eyes and thin nose, and he had a "jaw of stone." He was tough, honest, loyal; women found him attractive and hoods played him carefully. He was a "business man" who got "paid [very little] for his work," part of which was dealing death to those on the side of wrong.

Raymond Chandler's style, at the outset, showed qualities which were to make him one of the best of the *Black Mask* detective writers. The restrained statements, the colorful similes and evocative images, the city of oil wells and jacaranda trees in bloom, the reliable lonely hero—it was all there at the beginning. The third story, "Finger Man," can serve as an example of the Chandler touch. Using an uncomplicated plot, Chandler developed his theme around the idea that when crooked politicians and crime choke a city's moral life, it takes the private eye to make the corrections. The police were willing and helpful, but because they were so necessarily a part of city politics their hands were tied. Only the free, uninhibited, and tough individual was able to move far enough and strongly enough in the right direction. At this early stage in Chandler's writing career, the hero was adequately noble and hard-boiled, but he was not yet the smooth nobleman that Marlowe was to be. In matters of style, however, one can see the similes and images beginning to take their places. Comments like "As a bluff, mine was thinner than the gold on a week-end wedding ring" were to become a Chandler trademark. But images like "I stopped beside a forgotten drugstore that slept behind two giant pepper trees and a dusty cluttered window" contributed to his reputation as a literary stylist. Yet one cannot overlook the fact that in weaker moments he sometimes used a cliché of the trade: "I saw that Canales had fired at least once, because Frank Dorr had no right eye." In the eyes of the knight, the moll was a lady, so she was allowed to escape. And the hero, who was more and more appropriating the role of the humanitarian, said, "It's a shame how little account some folks take of human life."

"Killer in the Rain," a short story Chandler later incorporated into *The Big Sleep*, continued the hero's efforts to help those in trouble. The nameless narrator didn't care about the "trash," but basically good people like Dravec, who had a neurotic daughter, deserved to be saved from a "little heartache," even when it meant ignoring legal requirements. The hero, who saw mankind in a melancholy plight, was provided by the author with a subtle mood through which he observed: "I stared at the window, watched the rain hit it, flatten out, and slide down in a thick wave, like melted gelatine. It was too early in the fall for that kind of rain."

Occasionally a Chandler story had a touch of the old West. The hero of "Nevada Gas" was a good-guy gambler helped by a hotel dick who carried a Buntline Special and said "I'm a tough guy. I used to be a Wells Fargo Dick." The cop in "Spanish Blood," covered for a friend, protected the girl (to whom he said, "Life seems to do nasty things to people"), and lost his badge. One infers that he got his badge back because he was honest and human. He could not help thinking, however, that had it been his grandfather—one of the best sheriffs the county ever had—the case would have been handled "with fewer words and more powder smoke."

Throughout the 1930's Chandler continued to dress his man in the clothes of the traditional hero. Mallory, Carmady, Dalmas, whatever his name, grew harder toward the wrong guys and softer toward the little people. Invariably it was the troubled poor who hired him, so he worked for beans he frequently didn't get. His all-American virility increased with a growing, impatient distaste for effeminate men like Lindley Paul—he had a dimple on his chin in which you could have "lost a marble," and he spoke softly "in the manner of a sultan suggesting a silk noose for a harem lady whose tricks had gone stale." He went to those places where a "hard-boiled redhead sang a hard-boiled song in a voice that could have been used to split firewood," and where a torch singer "sang of something very far away and unhappy, in a voice like old ivory." As he went he drank the "racket" beer which was as "tasteless as a roadhouse blonde."

Drawing from several years' writing experience and specifically from four short stories (three of which were in *Black Mask*), Chandler fashioned his first novel, *The Big Sleep*. The hero, theme, and style came together in a highly successful fruition. "To hell with the rich," Philip Marlowe said, "they make me sick." Yet for a small amount of money, most of which was used on the case, he risked his life many times in trying to help the wealthy Sternwood family. Most of Marlowe's sympathy was spent on old General Sternwood, once virile, now sick and helpless: only "a few locks of dry white hair clung to his scalp, like wild flowers fighting for life on a bare rock." The General's two problems were his two daughters, neither of whom had "any more moral sense than a cat." And Carmen, the younger, was hopelessly psychotic. In his knightly role, Marlowe rescued the ladies, who although beautiful were not very fair. In throwing the naked Carmen out of his bed, the hero brooded over his integrity and moral standards: "This was the room I had to live in. It was all I had in the way of a home. In it was everything that was mine, that had any association with me, any past, anything that took the place of a family." He said, as he moved a piece on his chessboard, "Knights had no meaning in this game. It wasn't a game for knights." Yet he played it as a knight throughout, meeting violence with violence, bringing a little peace of mind to a sick old man, and allowing the murderess to go free. The villains included a dealer in pornography, whose house "had a stealthy nastiness, like a fag party," a blackmailer, and a ruthless killer. They, with several others of their ilk, met justifiable deaths. For Marlowe the "world was a wet emptiness," full of violence and inhumanity, yet he moved through it with dignity and integrity, always, however, alone; in the febrile society in which he operated, the hero never deviated from his code. Occasionally, however, the rain stopped, allowing him to look at "the hard pale wild lilac of the California hills."

During the war years Raymond Chandler published three more novels of high quality in which the hero sought to bring some degree of justice and sympathy to those living in the world of violence. In 1949 *The Little Sister* included a sharp denunciation of Hollywood, and *The Long Goodbye* (1953) insisted on the value of loyalty in society, especially in a superficial society. When Chandler was nearing seventy he published *Playback*, a novel which clearly indicated a lessening of his talents. Feeling sorry for his lonely hero, the author, at the end of the novel, held out the prospect of marriage, although marriage, according to a younger Chandler, was impossible for his detective hero. With Chandler's death, Marlowe escaped a role for which he had never been fitted.

In the pages of *Black Mask* the detective hero contributed to the American myth of the hard-boiled hero. One component of the myth which *Black Mask* School utilized was a special attitude toward violence which provided both an ethical and an aesthetic justification for its employment.

In England, where an appraisal of popular American literature is often very discerning, Ernest Borneman held the opinion that the old *Black Mask* "was the training ground of such writers as Dashiell Hammett and Raymond Chandler; it established a new tradition of realism in the detective story; and it contributed to the development of what Mencken called 'the American language'—a prose style which, by transcending the limits of the crime story, has become part and parcel of the serious American novel."

The Poetics of the Private-Eye
The Novels of Dashiell Hammett

ROBERT I. EDENBAUM

> [The daemonic agent] will act as if possessed. . . . He will act part way between the human and divine spheres, touching on both, which suggests that he can be used for the model romantic hero, since romance allows its heroes both human interest and divine power. His essentially energic character will delight the reader with an appearance of unadulterated power. Like a machiavellian prince, the allegorical hero can act free of the usual moral restraints, even when he is acting morally, since he is moral only in the interests of his power over other men. This sort of action has a crude fascination for us all; it impels us to read the detective story, the western, the saga of space exploration and interplanetary travel.
> —Angus Fletcher, *Allegory*

RAYMOND CHANDLER, Dashiell Hammett's major successor in the tradition of the tough detective novel, Howard Haycraft, a historian of the form, and David T. Bazelon, a far from sympathetic critic, all agree that Hammett shaped the archetype and stereotype of the private-eye. Hammett's third novel, *The Maltese Falcon*, heads any list of tough guy novels of the thirties. The pre-eminence and popularity of that novel is not only due to its date of publication at the very start of the new decade, nor to the fact that eleven years later John Huston turned it into "the best private-eye melodrama ever made," according to James Agee (*Agee on Film*). And it is not only the vagaries of camp taste that have made Humphrey Bogart's Sam Spade a folk-hero a third of a century later. Sam Spade of *The Maltese Falcon* (1930), together with the nameless Continental Op of the earlier novels, *Red Har-*

vest and *The Dain Curse* (both 1929), and to a lesser extent Ned Beaumont of *The Glass Key* (1931) and Nick Charles of *The Thin Man* (1934) constitute a poetics of the tough guy hero of novel, film, and television script from 1929 to the present.

The characteristics of Hammett's "daemonic" tough guy, with significant variations in the last two novels, can be schematized as follows: he is free of sentiment, of the fear of death, of the temptations of money and sex. He is what Albert Camus calls "a man without memory," free of the burden of the past. He is capable of any action, without regard to conventional morality, and thus is apparently as amoral—or immoral—as his antagonists. His refusal to submit to the trammels which limit ordinary mortals results in a godlike immunity and independence, beyond the power of his enemies. He himself has under his control the pure power that is needed to reach goals, to answer questions and solve mysteries, to reconstruct the (possible) motivations of the guilty and innocent alike. Hammett's novels—particularly the first three, with which this essay will be primarily concerned—present a "critique" of the tough guy's freedom as well: the price he pays for his power is to be cut off behind his own self-imposed masks, in an isolation that no criminal, in a community of crime, has to face.

The Maltese Falcon is the most important of the novels in the development of the poetics of the private-eye because in it Hammett is less concerned with the intricacies of the detective story plot than with the combat between a villain(ess) who is a woman of sentiment, and who thrives on the sentiment of others, and a hero who has none and survives because he has none. As a result of that combat itself, the novel is concerned with the definition of the private-eye's "daemonic" virtue—with his invulnerability and his power—*and* with a critique of that definition.

The word "combat" has to be qualified immediately, for there can be only unequal combat when one antagonist holds all the cards and the other is always victim; when the one manipulates and the other is deceived; when the actions of the one are unpredictable and the responses of the other stock. These terms would seem to describe the villain and his victim in Gothic fiction from *The Mysteries of Udolpho* to *The Lime Twig*. But Hammett, in *The Maltese Falcon*, reverses the roles. Brigid O'Shaughnessy, the murderer of Sam Spade's partner Miles Archer, is the manipulated, the deceived, the predictable, finally, in a very real sense, the victim. Customarily in the detective story, the solution to the mystery—for example, the identity of the murderer—is known only to the murderer himself; terror makes everyone victim but the murderer, for only the murderer, the unpredictable element, can know what will happen next. In the first few pages of *The Maltese Falcon* Miles Archer is murdered, apparently by Floyd Thursby. Thursby is killed; that is apparently a mystery (though it takes no great imagination to settle on the young hood Wilmer as the likely culprit). The ostensible mystery, then, is why Thursby killed Archer, and why he in turn was killed. In the last pages of the novel, however, the reader (and Brigid O'Shaughnessy) discovers that he (and she) has been duped all along, for Spade has known from the moment he saw Archer's body that Brigid is the murderer. Spade himself, then, is the one person who holds the central piece of information; he is the one person who knows everything, for Brigid does not know that he knows. And though Spade is no murderer, Brigid O'Shaughnessy is his victim.

Once the reader knows, finally, that Spade has known all along that Miles Archer, with his pistol tucked inaccessibly under his arm, would not have gone up a dark alley with anyone but a girl as beautiful as Brigid, and therefore must have gone with *her*, he can make sense out of an apparently irrelevant anecdote that Spade tells Brigid early in the novel. The story, about a case Spade once worked on, concerns a man named Charles Flitcraft who had disappeared without apparent motive. The likely possibilities—as nearly always in Gothic fiction, sex and money—are eliminated beyond doubt. The mystery is cleared up when Spade finds the missing man. Flitcraft's life before his disappearance had been "a clean orderly sane responsible affair," Flitcraft himself "a man who was most comfortable in step with his surroundings." The day of his disappearance, on his way down a street, a beam had fallen from a building under construction and missed killing him by an inch. At that moment Flitcraft "felt like somebody had taken the lid off life and let him look at the works." He left his old life on the spot, for "he knew then that men died at haphazard like that, and lived only while blind chance spared them." Flitcraft spends several years living under that Dreiserian philosophy, working at a variety of jobs, until he meets another woman identical to his first wife except in face, marries her, has children identical to those by his first wife, leads a life identical to the one he had led before his black epiphany. Spade had returned to the first Mrs. Flitcraft to tell her what he had learned. Mrs. Flitcraft had not understood; Spade had no trouble understanding. Brigid O'Shaughnessy, despite her fascination with Spade's story against her will (she is trying to find out what he intends to do in her case) understands no more than Mrs. Flitcraft did.

Flitcraft moves from a life—and a commensurate philosophy—in which beams do not fall, to one in which beams do, back to one in which they don't. There can be no doubt which of the two Spade subscribes to: "Flitcraft *knew* then that men died at haphazard" (my emphasis). That commonplace enough naturalistic conception of the randomness of the universe is Spade's vision throughout. The contrast is of Spade's life (that of the private-eye) in which beams are expected to fall, and do fall, and that of the suburban businessman, in which they do not—or, at least, do not until they do. Since they did stop in the years between, Flitcraft merely adjusted himself back to a world where they did not. In Spade's world, of course, they never stop falling. If Brigid were acute enough—or less trammelled by conventional sentiment—she would see in the long, apparently pointless story that her appeals to Spade's sense of honor, his nobility, his integrity, and finally, his love, will not and cannot work. That essentially is what Spade is telling her through his parable. Brigid—totally unscrupulous, a murderess—should understand rather better than Mrs. Flitcraft, the bourgeois housewife. But she doesn't. She falls back on a set of conventions that she has discarded in her own life, but which she naively assumes still hold for others'. At the end of the novel, Brigid is not merely acting her shock at Spade's refusal to shield her; that shock is as genuine as Effie Perine's at Spade for that same refusal—and as sentimental. Paradoxically, in *The Maltese Falcon* the good guy is a "blonde satan" and the villain is as innocent as she pretends to be. For that matter Gutman, Cairo, even Wilmer, are appalled by Spade, and in their inability to cope with him are as innocent as Brigid.

This reading of the Flitcraft story accounts for Spade's over-riding tone of mockery with Brigid whenever she appeals to his gallantry and loyalty based on her trust and confidence in him. His response to her talk of trust is, "You don't have to trust me . . . as long as you can persuade me to trust you." But, as we have seen, that is impossible from the very start, and Spade's saying so is a cruel joke on an unsuspecting murderer. To Brigid, Spade is "the wildest person I've ever known," "altogether unpredictable." Had she understood the Flitcraft story, she would have known that he is not unpredictable at all, but simply living by Flitcraft's vision of meaninglessness and the hard knowingness that follows from that vision. Spade is in step with his surroundings as much as Flitcraft is in step with his. Except for a brief (but important) moment at the end when he is nonplussed by Effie, Spade is never surprised by anyone's actions as Brigid is continually surprised by his. Spade several times picks up mockingly on Brigid's words "wild and unpredictable." She asks at another point what he would do if she were to tell him nothing about the history of the falcon and the quest for it; he answers that he would have no trouble knowing "what to do next." Sam Spade (cf. Humphrey Bogart) never has to hesitate about what to do next. Brigid, of course, has no idea what he will do. When a thousand dollar bill disappears from the envelope holding Gutman's "payment" to Spade, the detective takes Brigid into the bathroom and forces her to undress so that he can make sure she does not have it hidden on her person. Brigid, incredulous, responds with the appropriate clichés: "You'll be killing something." "You shouldn't have done that to me, Sam . . ." But Spade will not be stopped by "maidenly modesty," for he knows that Gutman is testing him to see what he will do. The fat man finds out; Brigid still does not, and learns only when it is too late.

The rejection of the fear of death, perhaps the most obvious characteristic of the tough guy in general, is but another aspect of the rejection of sentiment. Spade fully expects those falling beams, and thus detective work is as much a metaphor for existence as war is in *The Red Badge of Courage* or *A Farewell to Arms*. In an exchange with the driver of a rented car on its way to one unknown destination in the unending series that is the fictional detective's life, the driver comments on Miles Archer's death and on the detective business.

> "She's a tough racket. You can have it for mine."
> "Well [Spade answers], hack-drivers don't live forever."
> "Maybe that's right . . . but just the same, it'll always be a surprise to me if I don't."

The driver is a working-class Flitcraft; Spade, on the other hand, is heading towards another potential falling beam—though, in fact, the trip turns out to be a wild-goose chase planned by Gutman. And the final sentence of the dialogue—"Spade stared ahead at nothing . . ."—bears a double force.

Hammett's reversal of the trap of naturalism gives his heroes a kind of absolute power over their own destiny, a daemonic power, in Angus Fletcher's useful phrase. To stare into nothing and know it; to be as dispassionate about death as about using others—Wilmer, Cairo, *or* Brigid—as fall-guy: all this means that Spade can rob a Gutman of his ultimate weapon, the threat of death.

When Gutman threatens Spade, the detective can argue that the fat man needs him alive; Gutman returns that there are other ways to get information; Spade, in his turn, insists that there is no terror without the threat of death, that he can play Gutman so that the fat man will not kill him, but that if need be he can *force* Gutman to kill him. Who but the tough guy can *make* the beam fall? In that lies the tough guy's power to set his own terms in life and death, a power that is the basis of his popularity in detective and other fiction.

To a generation of readers suckled on the violence of Mickey Spillane and Ian Fleming, it will hardly come as a shock to learn that detectives are as unscrupulous and amoral as "the enemy," as Spade calls them. In this book, though, Hammett seems to be consciously defining the nature of that unscrupulousness through Spade's relationship with Brigid, a relationship which itself becomes the major subject of *The Maltese Falcon* and itself exemplifies the terms of the detective's existence in the novel and in the fiction that ultimately derives from it. The dialogue between Sam Spade and Brigid does much of the work of developing that definition. For example, at one point Brigid says that she is afraid of two men: Joel Cairo and Spade himself. Spade answers, with his total awareness of what she means and what she is, "I can understand your being afraid of Cairo . . . He's out of your reach" (that is, because he is homosexual). And she: "And you aren't?" And he: "Not that way." Under the terms I am suggesting, this exchange must be read as follows: she says she is afraid of him; he says that that's not true because he's not out of her reach; he's right, she's not afraid of him; she should be because he *is* out of her reach. If she thinks him unscrupulous it is because she thinks he is after her and / or her money. She "seduces" him, thinking it will make a difference, but it doesn't. As soon as he climbs out of bed in the morning he steals her key to ransack her apartment, to find further evidence of her lies, though once again the reader doesn't know what he finds until the very end. The fact that Spade does not "cash many checks for strangers," as his lawyer puts it, is the key to his survival, and it leaves him outside the pale of tenderness.

One further key to Hammett's demolition of sentiment is the all but passionless figure of Sam Spade and one further indication of the price immunity exacts is Effie Perine, the archetypal tough guy's archetypal secretary. Spade pays Effie the highest compliment of all in the classic line, "You're a damned good man, sister," but unlike many of her later peers Effie is not tough. In the course of the novel Spade baits Effie again and again by asking what her "woman's intuition" tells her about Brigid O'Shaughnessy; Effie is "for her"; "that girl is all right." The point is not simply that Effie is wrong. Even at the end, knowing that she has been wrong all along, that Brigid has murdered one of her bosses, she responds as a woman, with a woman's (from Hammett's point of view?) sentimental notions, with appalled distaste for *Spade*. The last word in the novel is Effie's. She has learned of Brigid's arrest through the newspapers; Spade returns to his office.

> Spade raised his head, grinned, and said mockingly: "So much for your woman's intuition."
>
> Her voice was queer as the expression on her face. "You did that, Sam, to her?"
>
> He nodded. "Your Sam's a detective." He looked sharply at her. He put his arm around her waist, his hand on her hip. "She did kill Miles, angel," he said gently, "offhand, like that." He snapped the fingers of his other hand.
>
> She escaped from his arm, as if it had hurt her. "Don't, please, don't touch me," she said brokenly. "I know—I know you're right. You're right. But don't touch me now—not now."

Effie's response amounts to a definition of sentiment: the impulse that tells you to pretend that what you know to be true is not true, to wish that what you know has to be, did not have to be. In the vein of the romanticism of action that becomes doing what everything sensible tells you you cannot do. You're right, you're right, but couldn't you better have been wrong? As Hammett has made sufficiently clear in the course of the book, and particularly in the final confrontation with Brigid, exactly the point about Spade—and about the tough guy in general—is that he could not have.

The confrontation of Spade and Brigid rather than the doings of Gutman, Cairo, and Wilmer, who are disposed of perfunctorily offstage, is the climax of the novel. Spade makes Brigid confess to him what, as we have seen, he has known all along—that she is Miles Archer's murderer; then he tells her, to her horror, that he is going to "send her over." His theme throughout this sequence is, "I won't play the sap for you." Though he says, "You'll never understand me" (anymore than Mrs. Flitcraft understood her husband), he goes on, in an astonishing catalogue, to tote up the balance sheet on the alternatives available to him. He ticks off the items on one side: "when a man's partner is killed he's supposed to do something about it"; "when one of your organization gets killed it's bad business to let the killer get away with it"; a detective cannot let a criminal go any more than a dog can let a rabbit go; if he lets her go, he goes to the gallows with Gutman, Cairo, and Wilmer; she would have something on him and would eventually use it; he would have something on her and eventually she couldn't stand it; she might be playing him for a sucker; he could go on "but that's enough." On the other side of the ledger is merely "the fact that maybe you love me and maybe I love you."

The tabulation of pros and cons suggests that Spade is a bookkeeper calculating the odds for getting away with breaking the law. But that is inaccurate, for his final statement demolishes his own statistics and suggests that something else is at stake: " 'If that [all he has been saying] doesn't mean anything to you forget it and we'll make it this: I won't because all of me wants to—wants to say to hell with the consequences and do it—and because—God damn you—you've counted on that with me the same as you counted on that with the others.' " The rejection of sentiment as motivating force, i.e., of senti-

mentality, is at the heart of the characterization of Sam
Spade and of the tough guy in general. It is not that Spade
is incapable of human emotions—love, for example—but
that apparently those emotions require the denial of what
Spade knows to be true about women and about life. The
sentiment Spade rejects is embodied in all three women in
The Maltese Falcon—Brigid, Iva Archer, and Effie: murderer, bitch, and nice girl, respectively. It is in this theme
itself, paradoxically, that *The Maltese Falcon* has been
weakened by the passage of time. As one reads the novel
now, Spade himself still retains his force; he is still a
believable, even an attractive (if frightening) character.
Brigid, on the contrary, is not. (Just so, Hemingway's
assertion of Jake Barnes' stoical mask in *The Sun Also
Rises* still works, but the attack on Robert Cohn's romanticism seems to be beating a dead horse.) And yet it is the
pitting of Brigid's sentimental platitudes against Spade's
mocking wisecracks that may make this book the classic it
is. This theme, too, signals a reversal in the naturalistic
novel, for the tough guy in the tradition of Sam Spade can
no longer be the victim of sentiment (cf., for example,
Dreiser's Hurstwood or Clyde Griffith, or a Hemingway
character defeated by the death of the woman he loves).
On the contrary, he hedges himself so thoroughly against
betrayal that he lives in total isolation and loneliness.
Spade is last seen shivering (temporarily) in revulsion as
Effie Perine sends the moral slug Iva in to him. The
attractions of Brigid given up to the law, the possibilities
of Effie lost, Spade is left with only Iva—or an unending
string of Iva's successors.

The Hammett detective most pure, most daemonic, is
the Continental Op of the first two novels, his purity
indicated even in his namelessness. The Op, perhaps more
than Spade, is free of sentiment, of the fear of death, of a
past, of the temptations of sex and money. Like Spade he
is capable of anything that his opponents are in the pursuit of his goals; in *Red Harvest* he goes further than
Spade ever does in his responsibility for setting criminals
against one another murderously. The Op in *Red Harvest*

is much like Mark Twain's mysterious stranger that corrupts Hadleyburg: the stranger drops the bag of "gold" in the laps of the townsmen and watches them scramble; and so the Op in Personville (pronounced Poisonville). Both manipulate matters with absolute assurance and absolute impunity (cf. Spade as well). In *Red Harvest* twenty-five people are killed, not counting an additional unspecified number of slaughtered hoodlums, yet the only mishaps to befall the Op are to have a hand creased by a bullet and an arm stunned by the blow of a chair-leg. His powers come to seem almost supernatural, his knowledge of the forces that move men (sex and money) clairvoyance. His single-minded mission is to clean up the corruption no matter what the cost in other men's lives. The Op's own explanation of his motives—like those voiced to Gutman by Spade, a kind of personal grudge against those who have tried to get him—is not particularly convincing. It is tempting to say that the Op's apparently personal response to being picked on is the equivalent of the response of Hemingway's characters when they are picked off, but Hemingway's characters do have identifiable human emotions, whether disgust, or relief from disgust, or love; Hammett's, because of the purely external mechanistic method, do not. The superhuman is so by virtue of being all but nonhuman.

Red Harvest offers a perfect role for the Hammett private-eye. Elihu Willsson, aristocratic banker-boss of Poisonville, gives the Continental Detective Agency in the person of the Op ten thousand dollars to clean up the town because Willsson thinks the local gangsters responsible for the murder of his son. After the Op discovers that the crime was one of passion (if passion bought and sold) unrelated to the bootlegging-gambling-political corruption of the town, Willsson tries to dismiss the Op, who refuses to be dismissed, " 'Your fat chief of police tried to assassinate me last night. I don't like that. I'm just mean enough to want to ruin him for it. Now I'm going to have my fun. I've got ten thousand dollars of your money to play with. I'm going to use it opening Poisonville up from Adam's apple to ankles.'" Ten thousand dollars of *your* money to play with—there is the role of invulnerable power with the most possibilities open. The Op almost seems to forget he has the money; aside from his day-to-day expenses, all he uses of it is $200.10 that he reluctantly pays Dinah Brand for information. Hammett seems to want to establish the financial freedom of his character: with ten thousand dollars in hand how can the Op be suborned? Once that immunity is established it does not matter how (or whether) the money is spent.

The Op's immunity from temptation indicates something of the allegorical nature of these novels. Rather than being amoral, they establish moral oppositions of the simplest kind: if the proletarian novel is a version of pastoral, in William Empson's witty formulation, the tough detective novel is a version of morality, with allegorical combat between the forces of good and evil, and the most obvious of object lessons. Don't be a sucker for sex (read "love"): better Spade with Iva than Spade with Brigid. Don't be a sucker for money: it leaves you wide open for the crooks *and* the cops. Myrtle Jennison (a minor character in *Red Harvest*) was once as beautiful as Dinah Brand: now she's bloated with Bright's Disease (and Dinah herself dies of an ice-pick wound). Twenty-five men, slaughtered, were once alive (*Red Harvest*). And so on.

The morality of Hammett's detectives is basically defensive, as it must be in the Gothic world posited. As I indicated earlier, in the traditional Gothic novel (and as well in the naturalistic novel in this century) corruption and evil stem from two sources of power, two kinds of end—money and sex. Innocence (virginity in the older Gothic) is eternally threatened, usually for money; sex is used to gain money, and is in turn corrupted by money. Sexual and financial power are at most equatable, at least inextricable, for it is money which makes sex purchasable and sex which makes money attainable. The Op functions as a monkish ascetic who in order to survive must stay clear of money and sex, the only real temptations. Presumably he could walk off with Elihu Willsson's ten thousand, but of course he is no more tempted to abscond than he is to seduce Dinah Brand (he is just about the only male in the novel who doesn't). He unfixes a prize-fight, lets Dinah win a pile of money, but does not himself bet. When Dinah, puzzled, questions him, he claims he was not sure his plan would work; but there is no evidence that that is anything but bluff. Dinah no more under-stands the Op's immunity to cash than Brigid understands Spade's to love. For Dinah, trying to get money out of the Op in exchange for the information she has on the inner workings of Poisonville, "It's not so much the money. It's the principle of the thing." The Op, refusing, parodies her with her own words: "It's not the money . . . It's the principle of the thing." Everything about Dinah, particu-larly her body, can be bought; nothing about the Op can be, by money or sex or sentiment. In self-defense he must be untouchable; otherwise his invulnerability would be seriously compromised.

Like Spade, the Op in his immunity from temptation becomes god-like, perhaps inseparable from a devil, his concern not a divine plan but a satanic disorder. "Plans are all right sometimes . . . And sometimes just stirring things up is all right—if you're tough enough to survive, and keep your eyes open so you'll see what you want when it comes to the top." The Op's way of unravelling the mess in Poisonville is to "experiment," in his word, to see if he can pit one set of crooks against another, when he unfixes the prizefight, for example. The result, in that case and always, is more murder and further chaos impending. Dinah Brand's irony—"So that's the way you scientific detectives work"—is Hammett's as well. The Op's meta-phor makes him the same kind of godlike manipulator the naturalist novelist himself becomes in *his* experiments with the forces that move human beings to destruction. The stranger in "The Man That Corrupted Hadleyburg" may drop the bag of money in the town, but it is Mark Twain who drops the stranger there; and Hammett the Op in Poisonville. The bitter enjoyment may be Ham-mett's and Mark Twain's as well as their characters'.

Ultimately the Op does discover that he is paying the price for his power—his fear that he is going "blood simple like the natives." "Play with murder enough and it gets you one of two ways. It makes you sick or you get to like it," he says as he tabulates the sixteen murders to that moment. The blood gets to the Op in both ways. He finds that he cannot keep his imagination from running along murderous lines on the most common of objects; he carries an ice-pick into Dinah's living room, and Dinah asks why.

> "To show you how my mind's running. A couple of days ago, if I thought about it at all, it was as a good tool to pry off chunks of ice." I ran a finger down its half-foot of round steel blade to the needle point. "Not a bad thing to pin a man to his clothes with. That's the way I'm betting, on the level. I can't even see a mechanical cigar lighter without thinking of filling one with nitroglycerine for somebody you don't like. There's a piece of copper wire lying in the gutter in front of your house—thin, soft, and just enough to go around a neck with two ends to hold on. I had one hell of a time to keep from picking it up and stuffing it in my pocket, just in case—"
>
> "You're crazy," [Dinah says].
>
> "I know it. That's what I've been telling you. I'm going blood-simple."

Out of his head on the gin and laudanum which he takes to relieve his own morbidity, the Op wakes the next morning to find his hand around the ice-pick, buried in Dinah's breast. It is not surprising that not only the authorities but one of the other operatives sent down from San Francisco and the Op himself think he may be Dinah's murderer. If the Op, like all men, is capable of all things, then he is capable of unmotivated murder. If the calculatedly nonhuman yields to human emotion and human weakness, defenses are down; loss of control and near-destruction follow. The point would seem to be, don't let your defenses down. No one, including the detective, is exempt from the possibility of crime. Thus, in *The Dain Curse* and *The Thin Man* the murderer turns out to be an old friend of the detective; in *The Maltese Falcon* it is the girl the detective loves (or may love); in *The Glass Key* a father (and U. S. Senator) murders his own son; and in *Red Harvest* there is no one who might not be a killer—and most of them are, given those twenty-five some odd murders.

In *The Rebel* (Vintage Books) Albert Camus offers a brilliant analysis of the implications of the fear of emotion in the tough guy novel. The concomitants of the rejection of sentiment is the rejection of psychology itself and of everything that comprises the inner life in favor of the hedges themselves.

> The American novel [the tough novel of the thirties and forties, Camus explains in a note] claims to find its unity in reducing man either to elementals or to his external re-actions and to his behavior. It does not choose feelings or passions to give a detailed description of . . . It rejects analysis and the search for a fundamental psychological motive that could explain and recapitulate the behavior of a character . . . Its technique consists in describing men by their outside appearances, in their most casual actions, of reproducing, without comment, everything they say down to their repetitions, and finally by acting as if men were entirely defined by their daily automatisms. On this mechanical level men, in fact, seem exactly alike, which explains this peculiar universe in which all the characters appear interchangeable, even down to their physical peculi-arities. This technique is called realistic only owing to a mis-apprehension . . . it is perfectly obvious that this fictitious world is not attempting a reproduction, pure and simple, of reality, but the most arbitrary form of stylization. It is born of a mutilation, and of a voluntary mutilation, per-formed on reality. The unity thus obtained is a degraded unity, a leveling off of human beings and of the world. It would seem that for these writers it is the inner life that deprives human actions of unity and that tears people away from one another. This is a partially legitimate suspicion . . . [but] the life of the body, reduced to its essentials, paradoxically produces an abstract and gratuitous universe, continuously denied, in its turn, by reality. This type of novel, purged of interior life, in which men seem to be

observed behind a pane of glass, logically ends, with its emphasis on the pathological, by giving itself as its unique subject the supposedly average man. In this way it is possible to explain the extraordinary number of "innocents" who appear in this universe. The simpleton is the ideal subject for such an enterprise since he can only be defined —and completely defined—by his behavior. He is the symbol of the despairing world in which wretched automatons live in a machine-ridden universe, which American novelists have presented as a heart-rending but sterile protest (pp. 265–66).

Camus' analysis isolates both the success and the sadness of the tough novel. The success is that of the serious novel in general in that the correlation between the "voluntary mutilation" performed on reality by the author and that of the characters is complete; technique is subject matter in Hammett as much as in Joyce (though the analogy ends there). The excision of mind and emotion in tough dialogue, the understatement, the wise-guy joke-cracking cynicism—all the characteristics of Hammett's particular stylization—are matter as much as method. The sadness lies in the thinness of the world that remains and in the terror that is the common denominator of all men, who must fear all other men *and* themselves, and whose primary occupation would seem to be the development and maintenance of a reflexive self-defense. Finally, the detective's motives are as hidden as the murderer's and as indeterminable. The inner world is so thoroughly left to shift for itself (if it exists at all) that there is some question as to whether Hammett's characters *are* more than Camus' "wretched automatons"—with credits to Hollywood for the terrorless charms of Bogart, Greenstreet, *et al.*

The Dain Curse is one of the more interesting of Hammett's novels, in part because it is concerned with the implications and consequences of the mechanistic method and the mechanical world, with the difficulty of discovering, not only the motives of the actors, but the actual events that took place. As a result *The Dain Curse* is by far the most complicated of the novels. It consists of three separate plots concerning the events surrounding the drug-addict Gabrielle Leggett, events which eventually include the deaths of her father, mother, step-mother, husband, doctor, and religious "counselor," among others. In the first sequence, an apparently trivial theft of a batch of inexpensive diamonds leads to several murders and to incredible disclosures about the history of Edgar Leggett and his two wives, the Dain sisters Alice and Lily, a history that includes, for example, Alice's training of the three-year-old Gabrielle to kill Lily. In the second sequence, her father and aunt / step-mother dead, Gabrielle, a virtual prisoner in the quack Temple of the Holy Grail, is involved in another round of deaths, and the Op does battle with a man who thinks he is God and with a spirit that has weight but no solidity. In the third, after still more murders and maimings—a total of nine, plus three before the time of the novel—the Op discovers that there was, as he had suspected, a single mind behind the many criminal hands at work in all three apparently unrelated sequences of events. The man the Op has known for several years as Owen Fitzstephan is actually a Dain, a mastermind whose prime motive is—love for Gabrielle.

After the second part, the Op gives the still-unsuspected Fitzstephan his reconstruction of the events at the Temple of the Holy Grail, then adds,

> "I hope you're not trying to keep this nonsense straight in your mind. You know damned well all this didn't happen."
>
> "Then what did happen?" [Fitzstephan asks]
>
> "I don't know. I don't think anybody knows. I'm telling what I saw plus the part of what Aaronia Haldorn [the woman who runs the Temple, and, it is later disclosed, Fitzstephan's mistress and tool] told me which fits in with what I saw. To fit in with what I saw, most of it must have happened very nearly as I've told you. If you want to believe that it did, all right. I don't. I'd rather believe I saw things that weren't there."

And again the Op asks, "You actually believe what I've told you so far?" Fitzstephan says that he does, and the Op answers, "What a childish mind you've got," and starts to tell the story of Little Red Riding-Hood. In these novels there is no question of the complexity of, say, the relativity of guilt, for there is no ambiguity in human actions. As I have suggested, the allegory is fairly simple. The complexity is in the mystery of motive which results in the thorough-going ignorance that even the detective must admit to. What, finally, does move any human being—here, a criminal—to act? Put together a gaggle of the criminal and semi-criminal, the tempted and the merely self-interested, and it may be nearly as difficult to find out what happened as why. Similarly in *The Thin Man* Nora Charles is thoroughly dissatisfied with Nick's "theories" and "probablys" and "maybes" in his reconstruction of the events surrounding the death of Clyde Wynant. To the Op "details don't make much difference," details, that is, such as whether Joseph Haldorn really came to think himself God or merely thought he could fool everyone into thinking he was God. All that matters is that Joseph "saw no limit to his power." The same impossibility of determining truth recurs at the end of the novel: is Fitzstephan a sane man pretending to be a lunatic or a lunatic pretending to be sane? It's not clear whether the Op himself thinks Fitzstephan sane. That again is a detail that doesn't make much difference, especially since people are capable of anything. Fitzstephan, like Haldorn, saw no limit to his power. The exact terms of the curse are irrelevant; he is lost in any case.

In *The Dain Curse* Hammett once again explores the detective's mask by means of a woman's probing, but the Op's motives are no more susceptible to analysis than the criminals'. Gabrielle wants to know why the Op goes to the trouble of convincing her that she is not degenerate or insane, cursed by the blood of the Dains in her veins. She asks the questions the reader might ask: "Do I believe in you because you're sincere? Or because you've learned how—as a trick of your business—to make people believe in you?" The Op's response—"She might have been crazy, but she wasn't so stupid. I gave her the answer that seemed best at the time . . ."—doesn't answer the question for the reader any more than it does for the girl. *Is* it only a trick of his business or does he have a heart of gold beneath his tough exterior? Gabrielle is asking unanswerable questions, finally, because the removal of one mask only reveals another beneath. That may amount to saying that the toughness is not a mask at all, but the reality.

In their next encounter Gabrielle asks specifically why the Op went through the ugliness of supervising her withdrawal from drugs. He answers, with exaggerated tough guy surliness, "I'm twice your age, sister; an old man. I'm damned if I'll make a chump of myself by telling you why I did it, why it was neither revolting nor disgusting, why I'd do it again and be glad of the chance." By refusing to expose himself he is suggesting that he is exposing himself. Certainly his words suggest love for the girl, but he's hardly to be believed. He pretends to be hiding his sentiments under his tough manner, but it is more likely that he is pretending to pretend. Gabrielle has been the object of the "love" of a whole series of men: of the insane passion of Owen Fitzstephan and the only less insane of Joseph Haldorn, the High Priest and God of the Cult of the Holy Grail; of the petty lechery of her lawyer, Madison Andrews; and of the fumbling, well-meant love of Eric Collinson, who gets himself (and nearly Gabrielle) killed as a result. This view of love as destructive force, as we have seen, is an essential part of the occasion for the tough role. The Op, like Spade, has to think himself well out of it, though the reader does not have to agree.

In the last of this series of interviews in which Gabrielle, acting as the reader's friend, tries to comprehend the Op's tough guy role, the girl accuses the detective of pretending to be in love with her during their previous talk.

"I honestly believed in you all afternoon—and it *did* help me. I believed you until you came in just now, and then I saw—" She stopped.

"Saw what?"

"A monster. A nice one, an especially nice one to have around when you're in trouble, but a monster just the same, without any human foolishness like love in him, and— What's the matter? Have I said something I shouldn't?"

"I don't think you should have," I said. "I'm not sure I wouldn't trade places with Fitzstephan now—if that big-eyed woman with the voice [Aaronia Haldorn] was part of the bargain."

"Oh, dear!" she said.

It's tempting to take the Op at his word here, at least, and believe that he has been hurt by Gabrielle's unwittingly cruel words. But the pattern I have been developing makes it difficult to accept the Op's sensitivity about his toughness. It is more reasonable to assume that he is telling her, once again, what she wants to hear, suggesting that she is in some way unique in his life. If no sentiment whatever is involved in his actions, he *is* the monster she calls him. And, in fact, that is the case with the Op as with Sam Spade. Seen as figures in stylized romance, both men may be seen as daemons; as characters in realistic fiction they are monsters both.

The Glass Key is Hammett's least satisfactory novel, perhaps precisely because it is not allegorical Gothic romance, lacking as it does a godlike Spade or Op. It may be the case, as David T. Bazelon writing in *Commentary*, suggests, that Hammett was trying to write a book closer to a conventional novel, one in which characters are moved to action for human reasons such as loyalty and love. But Hammett's mechanistic method is unchanged and, as a result, it is still impossible to tell what is under Ned Beaumont's mask. Does Ned take the punishment he does out of loyalty to the political boss Paul Madvig, because Madvig picked him out of the gutter fifteen months earlier? Perhaps the reader's sense of propriety or decency fills in that answer, but there is no evidence that it is accurate. It can be argued, on the contrary, that Ned takes the vicious beatings, not out of loyalty but out of indifference to death (to falling beams, if you will). He "can stand anything [he's] got to stand," a gangster's sadism no more and no less than his (apparent) tuberculosis or a purely fortuitous traffic accident in a New York taxi. But "standing" punishment stoically (or suicidally) is not loyalty, not a basis for positive action; and without some clarification of motive, the sense of Ned's activities is merely muddy.

In a sequence that goes on for four brutal pages Ned tries repeatedly to escape his enemies despite being beaten after each attempt. But nothing stops him; as soon as he regains consciousness, he goes to work on the door again. It is tempting, once again, to take this behavior (which includes setting fire to the room) as motivated by loyalty, by Ned's overwhelming desire to warn Paul. But nothing of the sort is possible, for Hammett's descriptions of Ned's actions make it clear that most of his behavior—both his attempts to escape and to kill himself—are instinctual. He remembers nothing beyond his first beating, we are told. Action is determined mechanistically—or animalistically.

Ned's motives are essential to make sense of the climax of the novel when Ned allows Janet Henry, Paul's ostensible fiancée, to go off with him. His response to her "Take me with you" is hardly romantic: "Do you really want to go or are you just being hysterical? . . . It doesn't make any difference. I'll take you if you want to go." Yet there are indications earlier that Hammett wants to suggest the development of some kind of love between the two, growing out of their original mutual dislike, a love about which Paul Madvig has no doubt. The men have a falling out when Paul accuses Ned of lying to him because of Ned's own interest in Janet; at the end of the novel, Paul is confronted with the couple going off together. The question remains whether Paul was right in the first place, whether Ned acted out of desire for the girl rather than loyalty to Paul, or for neither reason. But there is no basis for judgment, by Janet *or* the reader. Motives are once again indeterminable, but in this book it is necessary that they be determined. The result is not the richness of fruitful ambiguity but the fuzziness of inner contradiction.

The title of this novel, from a dream recounted to Ned Beaumont by Janet Henry, suggests once again the fear of unhedged emotion and thus of all human relationships despite the matching of Ned and Janet with which it ends. In the dream Janet and Ned are starving and come upon a locked house within which they can see food—and a tangle of snakes. To open the door there is a glass key; to get access to the food is to release the snakes. The fragile key breaks as the door opens, and the snakes attack: apparently to get at the heart's need is to open a Pandora's box. Given the tawdriness of the "love" relations in *The Glass Key*—Taylor Henry's unscrupulous use of Opal Madvig's love, Janet Henry's of Paul's—there is not much chance that Ned and Janet will escape the snakes ("I'll take you if you want to go"). Once again in these novels it would seem that the only safety is in not letting down your guard in the first place: do without the food and you escape the snakes.

It is perhaps significant that Ned Beaumont is not actually a detective, though he functions as one in trying to clear up the mystery of the murder of Taylor Henry. However, there is a professional detective in the novel, Jack Rumsen, who is interesting for his unHammett-like behavior; it is not Sam Spade or the Op who would say to a man trying to solve a crime, " 'Fred and I are building up a nice little private-detective business here . . . A couple of years more and we'll be sitting pretty. I like you, Beaumont, but not enough to monkey with the man who runs the city.' " That modification of the private-eye character in the direction of the cynicism and timidity of self-interest prepares the way for Hammett's last novel, *The Thin Man*, published three years later. Nick Charles is the least daemonic of Hammett's heroes, but then he's only an ex-detective. However indifferent he may have been to death in the past, now he wants to be left out of danger, to be able to enjoy his wife, her wealth, and his whiskey. Nick Charles and his boozing is what happens to the Op/Spade when he gives up his role as ascetic demi-god to become husband, man of leisure, investor in futures on the stock market.

The Thin Man is perhaps less concerned with murder and the private-eye than with the people around the murder—with a wide range of social types spiritually sibling to the Alfred G. Packer of the long entry Gilbert Wynant reads in *Celebrated Criminal Cases of America*. The man-eaters Mimi, Dorothy, and Gilbert Wynant; Christian Jorgensen, Herbert Macauley, the Quinns, the Edges; as well as underworld characters like Shep Morelli and Julia Wolfe are little less cannibalistic than Packer. Nick Charles has no interest in their problems; it is his wife who drags him into the search for the missing Wynant against his will. The martini-for-breakfast cracking wise of William Powell and Myrna Loy more than anything else accounts for the popularity of *The Thin Man*. Despite Nick Charles' tough manner, Hammett's tough guy had been retired for good before this book appeared.

In Hemingway's story "In Another Country" the Italian major whose wife has just died fortuitously of a cold says, "[A man] must not marry. He cannot marry . . . If he is to lose everything, he should not place himself in a position to lose that. He should not place himself in a position to lose. He should find things he cannot lose." Knowing that, and despite that knowledge, Hemingway's characters of course always put themselves in a position to lose. They continually fall in love, knowing just how vulnerable that makes them, and they continually lose. Their hard exterior is merely a mask for the fine sensibility on a perpetual quest for good emotion. Hammett, in his best novels, literalizes the Hemingway mask and produces "monsters" who take the major's advice. The Hemingway mask is lifted every time the character is alone; he admits his own misery to himself—and to the reader—and exposes his inner life. The Hammett mask is never lifted; the Hammett character never lets you inside. Instead of the potential despair of Hemingway, Hammett gives you unimpaired control and machinelike efficiency: the tough guy refuses "to place himself in a position to lose." For all (or most) intents and purposes the inner world does not exist: the mask is the self. It is that "voluntary mutilation" of life that is the subject matter of these novels as much as Hemingway's stoical mask is of his. Hammett uses the relationships of Sam Spade with Brigid O'Shaughnessy, of the Continental Op with Dinah Brand and then with Gabrielle Leggett as proving grounds to indicate just how invulnerable his tough guys are. In each case the woman tries to find out what the man is; in each case the toughness is tested—and found not wanting. In the fantasy of detective novel readers and movie-goers who are themselves victims of a machine-ridden universe, loneliness is not too high a price to pay for invulnerability.

Focus on *The Maltese Falcon*
The Metaphysical Falcon

IRVING MALIN

DASHIELL HAMMETT is usually praised for his "effective clipped dialogue," "brutal characters," and "violent action"—I am quoting from the publisher's blurb in the Vintage *Maltese Falcon*—but he is more than a simpleminded, tough novelist. He refuses to give us easy documentaries of crime; he presents, instead, unsettling and inverted ceremonies. He is "metaphysical," not merely "physical."

In the first chapter of *The Maltese Falcon* many physical details—Spade's face, Miss Wonderly's clothing, cigarette ashes which dot the desk—are described at length. We assume that they are superficial, that they can be quickly observed and understood. But Hammett disturbs us. He makes them mysterious (or sees their mystery). He tells us, for example, that Spade's face makes him look "rather pleasantly like a blond Satan"; he insists that Miss Wonderly's eyes are "both shy and probing"; he notes the "twisting" and "crawling" ashes as the wind blows them. The solid details become deceptive, fluid, nonsubstantial.

The mystery is intensified throughout the novel. Not only does Spade have to explore the significance of the objects—statuettes, guns, newspapers—he must come to terms with underlying *motives*. Miss Wonderly changes her identity, becoming Miss Leblanc and Miss O'Shaughnessy. (The latter is her real name, but it reveals little about her personality.) Joel Cairo acts so "queerly" that he cannot be trusted to sit still. Iva Archer calls at unpredictable times. The police try to frustrate Spade when he least expects it. In the middle of his quest, Spade relates an anecdote (or it is a parable?) of Flitcraft, the man who suddenly left his family and then turned up years later with another family. What caused his transformation? It seems that he ran away because a falling beam almost killed him. "He knew then that men died at haphazard like that, and lived only while blind chance spared them. . . . What disturbed him was the discovery that in sensibly ordering his affairs he had got out of step, and not into step, with life." He decided to end his unnatural life; *he became someone else.* Spade is obviously fascinated by this parable; it incarnates the lives he and all "detectives" live every day.

Ironies multiply. Spade plays the cosmic game, as Flitcraft did, by trying to outwit it. He lies, cheats, and masquerades. He becomes others; he wears them (as they wear him). He agrees, for example, with Dundy that he "really" did kill Archer. He informs Gutman that he will deliver the falcon. He goes along with Miss O'Shaughnessy. He masters life (or yields to its playful, haphazard rhythm?) by tricking it—at least for a while.

Thus Spade is our "hero." He understands that he is alone (his partner is killed in the second chapter) and that he can never depend on anyone. His secretary, who seems helpful and knowing, is fooled by Miss O'Shaughnessy. She admits this gullibility finally by saying, "I know—I know you're right. You're right. But don't touch me now—not now." Spade cannot even trust himself, especially with women who are always "beyond" him. Although he apparently has a definite, strong identity (it resembles the physical details I have mentioned), we and he know that he is shadowy, wavering, and changeable. Perhaps he can be himself only when he participates in the various ceremonies he invents.

Spade is always ceremonial. After he learns about Archer's murder—the phone rings in darkness; a man's voice speaks from "nowhere"—he makes a cigarette.

> Spade's thick fingers made a cigarette with deliberate care, sifting a measured quantity of tan flakes down into curved paper, spreading the flakes so that they lay equal at the

ends with a slight depression in the middle, thumbs rolling
the paper's inner edge down and up under the outer edge
as forefingers pressed it over, thumbs and fingers sliding to
the paper cylinder's ends to hold it even while tongue licked
the flap, left forefinger and thumb pinching their end while
right forefinger and thumb smoothed the damp seam, right
forefinger and thumb twisting their end and lifting the other
to Spade's mouth.

This elaborate ceremony reminds us of Nick Adams' in
"Big Two-Hearted River." But Spade does not avoid "the
swamp"; on the contrary, he dives into it. He continually
lives by his low "religion." Miss O'Shaughnessy may
tempt him to convert—she sees no need to go to jail as a
murderess, especially because she loves the detective. But
Spade holds fast. He methodically offers six or seven reasons for turning her over to the police, hoping thereby to
keep himself intact. He is miraculously complete (or
empty?) when he functions, not when he thinks.

Spade eludes us—as he eludes his other selves. He shares
the archetypal qualities of such mythic heroes as Odysseus, Samuel, and Jesus in a peculiarly contemporary way.
He is as resourceful as Odysseus, but he believes in playful
chance as *the deity, not as one divine attribute.* San Francisco is his kingdom—one he must win or lose daily. His
first name, Samuel, suggests his biblical namesake who can
identify the first Hebrew ruler. Perhaps he is also prophetic in his uncanny ability to see through the details to
the mysteries within. Spade as Jesus? Yet he is ready to
sacrifice himself for the truths (or are they lies?) he em-
braces ironically. He is the man between thieves and
police, unsure of his mission, but foolish or wise enough to
die for it. Hammett is able to undercut traditional values
of heroism, quest, and romance by disguising idealism as
cynicism, prophecy as sham, serious play as "sport." He
resembles Spade: Hammett too eludes us as we try to
determine the underlying motives for his curious, new
mythology.

The falcon is the deity of the mysterious world I have
suggested. Joel Cairo is the first to describe it as a "statuette," the "black figure of a bird." But it is as paradoxical

as Spade's face or Miss Wonderly's eyes. The more we learn about it, the more "metaphysical" it becomes. This is the secret—the falcon changes. It is at times great wealth for Gutman, Cairo and all the thieves who want to possess it; it is also haphazard justice (the oxymoron is at the heart of the novel) for Sam Spade. Although it has a long history (it was "worshipped" in the Middle Ages), it has somehow transcended time. It is *a changing symbol of change itself*. It can never really be grasped; it vanishes triumphantly.

In the chapter of revelation all the "detectives" discover that they have been deceived. The statuette which Gutman as black priest finally uncovers is a *fake*.

> Gutman turned the bird upside-down and scraped an edge of its base with his knife. Black enamel came off in tiny curls, exposing blackened metal beneath. Gutman's knife-blade bit into the metal, turning back a thin curved shaving. The inside of the shaving, and the narrow plane its removal had left, had the soft grey sheen of lead.
>
> Gutman's breath hissed between his teeth. His face became turgid with hot blood. He twisted the bird around and hacked at its head. There too the edge of his knife bared lead. He let knife and bird hang down on the table while he wheeled to confront Spade. "It's a fake," he said hoarsely.

Because the falcon *is* fake, it divinely judges their own deception. How fitting that they "die" for untruth! Gutman and Cairo may think that they can get the original statuette back from the Russian who tricked them with this hoax, but we are made to believe that the original, if it can be found, is also fake.

I have stressed the metaphysical currents of *The Maltese Falcon* because they are often slighted. Most critics tend to discuss technique—if only in clichés about toughness and Americanism—without realizing that it is symbolic. Hammett tries to be flat and impersonal when he describes the "surface," but he suggests that it contains deep truth. Consider this lengthy, representative example. After Spade learns of Archer's death, he walks to the scene.

Spade crossed the sidewalk between iron-railed hatchways that opened above bare ugly stairs, went to the parapet, and, resting his hands on the damp coping, looked down into Stockton Street.

An automobile popped out of the tunnel beneath him with a roaring swish, as if it had been blown out, and ran away. Not far from the tunnel's mouth a man was hunkered on his heels before a billboard that held advertisements of a moving picture and a gasoline across the front of a gap between two store-buildings. The hunkered man's head was bent almost to the sidewalk so that he could look under the billboard. A hand flat on the paving, a hand clenched on the billboard's green frame, held him in this grotesque position. Two other men stood awkwardly together at one end of the billboard, peeping through the few inches of space between it and the building at the end. The building at the other end had a black grey sidewall that looked down on the lot behind the billboard. Lights flickered on the sidewall, and the shadows of men moving among lights.

Spade turned from the parapet and walked up Bush Street to the alley where men were grouped. A uniformed policeman chewing gum under an enameled sign that said *Burritt St.* in white against dark blue put out an arm and asked: "What do you want here?"

"I'm Sam Spade. Tom Polhaus phoned me."

"Sure you are." The policeman's arm went down. "I didn't know you at first."

The first impression is that Hammett is simply giving us "what happened." Here are many details—the noise of the car, the "blank grey" wall of the building, the gum of the policeman—which suggest that Spade is committed to physical reality. Notice, however, that he is the "private eye" somewhat removed from the scene. He must identify himself to the policeman. (Throughout the novel identity is questioned, as in Miss Wonderly's changing names, Flitcraft's disappearance, the bird itself.) He must master the movement and the fog which distort safe, static evaluations. The movement itself—the lights flickering, the car roaring, the arm extending—mirrors the violent processes Spade confronts. He is, continually, the running man who must keep up with or "outrun" events. He cannot sit still, waiting for things to happen. The foggy darkness is a symbolic condition—the latter is especially noticeable in the drug-induced sleep of Spade and Gutman's daughter. This lengthy passage, therefore, effectively demonstrates Hammett's descriptive power. Because he can fuse "blank" reality and teasing symbol, he is philosophically agile.

Although there are many other strong descriptions—Gutman cutting the bird is probably the most violent, beautiful passage—the novel consists largely of devious "interviews" in which the dialogue is as flat and complex as the descriptions. There are quick movements again; sentences begin and end abruptly as the characters hide or disclose their motives. Communication is difficult. In the first chapter Miss Wonderly speaks "indistinctly"—the adverb can modify all the interviews, because words and motives are separate. I don't want to imply that Hammett employs the "absurd" dialogue of Beckett or Pinter, but he does stress the *nonbelief of conversation*. Even his characters do. Miss Wonderly says, "He wouldn't tell me anything, except that she was well and happy. But how can I believe that? This is what he would tell me anyhow, isn't it." Spade agrees, "Sure . . . but it might be true." Unanswered questions and curious hints abound. Cairo screams for help, at one point, while the police are visiting Spade, but he and the detective claim it is all a joke. Gutman deliberately avoids "crude" statements. No wonder that Spade often flees from the elliptical, suggestive, and social uses of language into the ceremonies I have discussed. These ceremonies are silent, comforting, and true—until they are interrupted by other unrelenting interviews.

Hammett's "clipped dialogue," "violent action," and "brutal characters" are not employed for mere sensationalism and toughness but, rather, for metaphysical subtleties. In its many symbolic, odd descriptions and conversations *The Maltese Falcon* transcends the hard-boiled school of detective writing. It is a special "case"—one that we "detectives" will not easily solve.

Man Under Sentence of Death
The Novels of James M. Cain

JOYCE CAROL OATES

A WORLD IMMENSE with freedom, women hellish and infantile by turns, money, power, the tantalizing promise of
adventure—these are the common elements of James M.
Cain's novels. His reputation is by this time a vague one,
grown generalized and perhaps sentimentally overrated
(along with the reputations of Dashiell Hammett and
Raymond Chandler) since he is no longer "read." We
have Camus, we have the films of Jean-Luc Godard, we
have any number of cryptic realists who can give us Cain's
pace and excitement without Cain's flaws—*and* in the
form of art. Though he deals constantly with the Artistic,
Cain, it will be said, never manages to become an artist;
there is always something sleazy, something eerily vulgar
and disappointing in his work. Let us abandon all claims
for Cain's "place in American literature" if it is literature
only that is significant, and let us concentrate instead on
the relationship between Cain's work and his hypothetical
audience, America of the thirties and forties, and the
archetypal rhythms of his works whether the works themselves ultimately satisfy as art.

The freedom of women and money and power, and the
promise of adventure—all this is dangled before us in
Cain. These are his tricks, his gimmicks, but how cynically
he exploits them as "gimmicks" that lead his heroes to
their deaths! The trickery, while dramatically heightened,
seems somehow to grow out of Cain's dream-like landscapes; one must not criticize him as unrealistic in his

plots, out of a misconception of his being realistic in his settings. Consider how casual everything appears to be in Cain's world, accidental and contingent and apropos of nothing. *The Postman Always Rings Twice* opens: "They threw me off the hay truck about noon. I had swung on the night before, down at the border. . . . They saw a foot sticking out and threw me off. I tried some comical stuff, but all I got was a dead pan, so that gag was out. They gave me a cigarette, though, and I hiked down the road to find something to eat. That was when I hit this Twin Oaks Tavern." *Double Indemnity* opens: "I drove out to Glendale to put three new truck drivers on a brewery company bond, and then I remembered this renewal over in Hollywoodland. I decided to run over there. That was how I came to this House of Death, that you've been reading about in the papers." *Serenade* opens: "I was in the Tupinamba, having a *bizcocho* and coffee, when this girl came in." But beneath this apparently contingent surface is an iron-hard pattern of necessity. Everything is "past," finished, when the narrator begins; the stories themselves are no more than recountings of events, not intended to represent events themselves.

Cain's world is by no means "realistic": coming to him from the great psychological realists, Joyce and Mann, one understands how barren, how stripped and bizarre this Western landscape has become. It is as if the world extends no farther than the radius of one's desire. Within this small circle (necessarily small because his heroes are usually ignorant), accidental encounters have the force of destiny behind them. It is as if no other accidental encounters are imaginable: when Frank sees Cora in the restaurant their fates are determined; when John Howard Sharp sees his Mexican Indian girl their fates are determined; even the improbable machinations of fate in *The Butterfly* operate with a relentlessness out of all proportion to the people involved. This casualness is in operation even when Cain apparently doesn't know what he is doing, as in the beginning of *Mildred Pierce*: "In the spring of 1931, on a lawn in Glendale, California, a man was bracing trees. It was a tedious job. . . . Yet, though it was a hot afternoon, he took his time about it, and was conscientiously thorough, and whistled. He was a smallish man, in his middle thirties." But this time the beginning is indeed apropos of nothing, for the novel has little to do with Herbert Pierce and everything to do with his wife Mildred. Cain's method is to single out an ordinary human being, center in upon him with every acknowledgement of his being still ordinary, and bring him into an encounter with his "fate." *Mildred Pierce* (1941), overlong and shapeless, must surely owe its flaws to the third-person omniscient narration, which takes us too far from the victim and allows us more freedom than we want. To be successful, such narrowly-conceived art must blot out what landscape it cannot cover; hence the blurred surrealistic backgrounds of the successful Cain novels, *The Postman Always Rings Twice* (1934) and *Serenade* (1937).

The fable of the man under sentence of death, writing to us from his prison cell or from the cell of his isolated self, is in one of the great literary traditions. Stendhal's Julien Sorel does not write a journal, but he speaks most passionately and eloquently of the education that his imprisonment makes clear. Far superior to any of Cain's heroes, Julien makes extravagant leaps from level to level, person to person, exploiting all resources (especially himself) to gain some kind of transcendence, or a place at least for his talents—only to wind up, of course, in a prison cell, from which he contemplates a world governed by the middle class that will execute him and sees it as both beneath and beyond comprehension, absurdly simple and complex at once: man is an ant accidentally crushed beneath a hunter's boot. *The Red and the Black* stands at the beginning of so much of modern literature that its influence can no longer be isolated. The essential loneliness of the hero, his deracination from society and from individuals, his tragic split of self between egoism and love mark him off from the picaresque hero, and by now these elements are commonplace and inevitable; we have passed beyond them. Julien's late cousin, Meursault, will make the same trip to prison cell and nonrepentance, a negative of Julien, almost a parody of his egoism, though able finally to state with Camus' peculiar eloquence the basis upon which life must be lived: the consciousness of its being absurd.

Cain's heroes have an aura of doom about them, suggested to us by the flatness of their narration, their evident hurry to get it said. They follow the same archetypal route, obeying without consciousness the urges that lead them (and their tragic ancestors) to disaster. But the European works are concerned obsessively with the "why" behind such accidents; in the sub-literary world of American popular writing, it is the "how" that is important—"what happens next," "what happens finally." And what happens finally is always repentance, for the Cain hero is no more metaphysically inclined than he is morally substantial. Though we deny Cain's landscapes the technical realism others credit to him, let us admit that between Frank Chambers and Meursault one believes ultimately in Frank: he is as probable as the roadside sandwich joint we have all seen. Aggressor but really victim, a man's man but susceptible to tears, Cora's passionate lover but her nervous betrayer—all that is painful, embarrassing, and much more credible than the transformation of the clerk Meursault into a man of prodigious imagination. But *The Stranger* is "art" and *Postman* is "entertainment."

It is the fact that such pessimistic works are entertainment that fascinates. No happy endings, no promise of religious salvation, not even the supposition that society has been purged of evil—society is always worse than Cain's victims! Nothing is handed out to the reader; no obvious wish is fulfilled. A course of action is begun with terrifying abruptness, once begun it cannot be stopped, and it comes to its inevitable conclusion with the same efficiency criminals are usually brought to "justice," with their photographs appearing at once in the tabloid press. Edmund Wilson, in his famous essay "The Boys in the Back Room," talks of Cain as a poet "of the tabloid murder." He uses the word "poet" loosely enough, so loosely indeed that it has no meaning, and one would not want to call Cain an "observer" either, or a "philosopher"; in the end one can call him simply an "entertainer." But he is an entertainer with an uncanny knowledge of the perversities of his audience, the great range of their vulgarity and their demand for social "justice," the eradication of the impulsive heroes whose exploits have been enjoyed vicariously. Yes, they are bold and masculine, but after all, the memoir comes to us from a prison cell; and it is irrelevant to question this technique. The sense of confinement and doom is what makes Cain's work palatable to a popular audience, just as a more literate, conservative audience of readers can delight in the crudities of Dostoevsky's violence, and the yet more incredible crudities of his resurrections of the spirit.

Cain's heroes fight a losing battle with the forces of the unconscious (which they may describe in a number of ways). But, since they go beyond the point of self-control, a vigorous and all-powerful social unit awaits them and will protect us from them. The social instruments by which justice is granted may be no more moral than the victims who are punished, but if so, this is one more element of the tabloid poetry that pleases a popular audience: the sadism of Cain's heroes will always be turned against them, and the phenomenon of an audience both identifying with and rejecting a victim is not surprising. It is the very ordinariness of Cain's heroes that make them fit victims for "justice." If they were wiser, more clever, more audacious or evil they might escape, but then they would be monsters and valueless to a reading public, which demands characters with whom one can identify. But the fact that they are non-heroic heroes, animalistic or even mechanical in their responses, even (in the case of John Howard Sharp) masculine only by effort and luck, and somehow losers in the economic struggle of America, will necessitate their total failure.

That Cain as entertainer is entertaining his audience in a highly masterful and intelligent way is indicated by his remarks on his own writing. So far as he can sense the "pattern of his mind," Cain says in his preface to *The Butterfly*, he writes of "the wish that comes true, for some reason a terrifying concept, at least to my imagination." At the very basis of neurosis is the terrifying fact of the wish that threatens to come true; Freud recognizes the dynamic struggle of the mind's levels with what is wished for and what must be tolerated, the kernel of tragedy being the fulfillment of the monstrous wish in one form or another, enacted by the hero or by someone else who works as his agent. Cain's narratives are not imagined on a particularly subtle or even surprising level. The Freudian insight Cain acknowledges is best suited for a work in which the central consciousness is deep, deeper than the consciousness which the reader brings to the book. In Cain, however, one can always see beyond the central characters, who are involved so passionately with one another that they are, in a sense, blind. The overt wish, then, is an ego-wish and whatever the basis for its power in the id, it remains largely on the conscious, calculating level. Therefore, victims are generally irrelevant to the hero's relationship with his woman. Frank kills the Greek, Cora's husband, but not because the man disgusts him; the killing is pragmatic; they need money, they can't run away and be bums. The insurance salesman of *Double Indemnity* agrees to murder a man he hardly knows, again for pragmatic reasons. The murder of a victim beyond the killer's emotional radius characterizes Cain's works as crime or suspense novels, but it would be a mistake to look no further into them. In *Serenade* the "forbidden wishes" are dealt with in typically dream-like and unconvincing fashion: to bring the action to the fantastic point at which a man might sing five lines of "Cielito Lindo" and with that kill a woman! This is the wish as pure action, so outlandish as to dissociate itself entirely from ordinary considerations of verisimilitude. If the conscious wish of *Serenade* is to be a man, free from homosexual weakness, then surely the unconscious wish is to destroy whatever threatens this weakness—obviously, the female who pre-

vents the comfortable illicit relationship with the male
lover, artist, musician, man of taste, of wealth, etc. Is it
possible that Cain did not understand what he was doing
in *Serenade*?

And *Mildred Pierce* has at its center a forbidden wish
made articulate: that a mother may possess her daughter
completely as if the daughter were a lover, that she may
control not only this daughter but all people, all men
within her orbit, and even achieve a kind of apocalyptic
economic success out of the ruins of the Depression—
exactly the formula for a popular audience, though all
these wishes are ultimately thwarted. *Mildred Pierce* is the
most convincing of Cain's central works in its plodding,
repetitious, unimaginative progress, its depiction of a
strong / weak heroine whose profound ignorance is
matched perfectly by the characters who surround her.
The lure of the unconscious is suggested crudely by means
of the daughter, Veda, who is not only extraordinarily
beautiful but also a singer, thereby having access to the
mystical reservoir Cain associates with music.

The Butterfly (1947) is an incredible Caldwellesque
extravaganza concerning a weak victim whose apparent
daughter is in love with him. The "forbidden" wish is the
father's incestuous desire for the girl, who does in fact
turn out to be someone else's daughter (Cain is daring but
not depraved!), and the realization of this wish leads to
his own doom. But the characterizations and motivations
of this novel are so strangely inconsistent that critical
analysis is probably out of place. Again we have a mysteri-
ously-gifted singer, whose hypnotic effect is not enough to
prevent his being brutally murdered by the hero. It is the
pretentious interweavings of fates that make *The Butterfly*
fail, for in it Cain is attempting to create a truly predes-
tined disaster, a kind of sub-tragedy whose hero / victim is
doomed by his false interpretation of the butterfly birth-
mark which links father and grandson. With his plot so
rigidly determined, Cain's casual style is thwarted and the
result is awkward melodrama.

In general, however, Cain's craftsmanship has been admired even by critics who disapprove of him. In *The Novel of Violence in America*, W. M. Frohock declares that nothing of Cain's is "outside the category of trash," and goes on to discuss *Postman* in the past tense, as if it no longer existed as a novel to be read. Yet Frohock will say, in his discussion of James T. Farrell in the same book, that Cain, though less deserving of attention than Farrell, can "give him cards and spades" when it comes to writing dialogue—using, even, imagery he must have garnered from Cain's writing!

David Madden argues in "James Cain and the 'Pure' Novel" (*University Review*, Winter, 1963) that Cain's main interest is *technique*—and certainly the deliberately sordid stories are triumphs of a kind of technique, faltering only when a more traditional narrative is attempted (as in *Mildred Pierce* and *Love's Lovely Counterfeit*). *Double Indemnity* is a continuous assault upon the reader's imagination, for Cain is determined to end every short chapter with a twist or a new development. It is only when we are asked to believe in the hero's sudden integrity that the craftsmanship fails—it can perform dazzling tricks but it cannot quite make us believe in them. However, Cain's novels are paced so fast that one usually does not have time to question the authenticity of the deepening or waning passions, and this is deliberate. Madden quotes Simenon, that extraordinary popular writer, in relationship to the kind of pure novel Cain attempts: "And the beginning will always be the same; it is almost a geometrical question: I have such a man, such a woman, in such surroundings. What can happen to them to oblige them to go to their limits? That's the question. It will be sometimes a very simple incident, anything which will change their lives" (in *Writers at Work*, 1959).

Simenon sometimes deals with the relationship between members of a family—the literal working-out of unconscious feelings of guilt and hostility, as in *The Brothers Rico*. And it must be admitted that his psychology and his writing are superior to Cain's. Cain is determinedly and flat-footedly American, while Simenon probes into his victims with so morbid a curiosity as to make the reader recoil with frustration, as if forced to participate in a sadistic act. Simenon's people are doomed but their doom is more obviously self-willed; Cain, catering to and certainly a part of the American desire for simplicity, will allow certain initial choices that lead (indirectly) to doom, but will occasionally force his characters to suicide only when there is no other alternative, as in *Double Indemnity*. Murder is one thing, but suicide is clearly another—it involves an entirely different kind of temperament, an introverted one in which the fatal wish is never quite brought up into consciousness and never exorcized. That is why Simenon, perhaps, has never caught on in America and is probably regarded as a little depraved; murder for money and a woman is a fairly healthy act, but suicide is somehow . . . unlawful beyond murder, since society cannot deal with it.

Let us consider *Postman* as an example of Cain's craftsmanship at its finest. In this novel everything is slick and professional; even the unintentional comedy ("I kissed her. . . . It was like being in church.") is somehow just right, perfect. This is precisely what Frank Chambers would think and he would express it in just that way, knowing none of the uses of rhetoric or the ways by which conceits of passionate and spiritual love are devised. Chambers comes out of nowhere, is thrown off a hay truck and wanders to the roadside sandwich joint that is "like a million others in California." The novel's beginning is far superior to the beginning contrived for the famous movie made from it, since it says nearly nothing, promises little, and emphasizes the accidental nature of everything in Frank Chambers' world. The movie contrives to make the hero a recognizable citizen, definitely not a bum, well-dressed and actually in search of work—while Cain's Chambers responds not at all to the offer of work, though he needs money, but only to Cora. That he is a bum, "no good," worthless, is insisted upon and accepted by Chambers himself.

The colloquial, compressed style, the common man's

halfway cynical objectivity, make the reader feel that this is a man whose opinion can be trusted. He is no pretentious intellectual; he doesn't waste time describing nature or even people. He doesn't bother with a psychological background. Food is important to such a person, so we get a catalogue of the seven items Frank will have for breakfast. The woman appears as a mirage, less detailed than the breakfast, a blurred picture of Woman: "Then I saw her. . . . Except for the shape, she really wasn't any raving beauty, but she had a sulky look to her, and her lips stuck out in a way that made me want to mash them in for her." Later on, uncharacteristically talkative, Frank assures Cora that she doesn't look "Mex": "You're small, and got nice white skin, and your hair is soft and curly, even if it is black." Cain structures the scene around Frank's obvious interest in Cora and Cora's defensive attitude about being married to a Greek, which is the crack in her sulky demeanor that lets Frank and the reader know that she will be vulnerable. At dinner Frank can "smell her" and her presence excites him so that he vomits up everything he has eaten: about the most concise way of letting the reader know that this is serious business, since food itself is serious enough. This running-together of sexual desire and nausea is factually preposterous, but as a sensational device it works so well that few readers would ever pause to criticize it. (Nor would they criticize the love-making at the scene of the murder, which is just as unlikely for two normal people.) There is nothing tentative about Frank's assessment of the initial situation, and Cain manipulates his audience into accepting whatever Frank says as the truth.

The undercurrent of gratuitous violence in this novel has more to do with the sex-obsession than with the actual murder. And, as I remarked earlier, there seems to be no necessary relationship between this violence and the pragmatic, calculated violence that ends in the Greek's death. One does not lead into the other, as it would in a superior work—*Light in August*, for instance. Cain's lovers respond to each other at once in the most animalistic of ways: "I took her in my arms and mashed my mouth up against hers. . . . 'Bite me! Bite me!' I bit her. I sunk my teeth into her lips so deep I could feel the blood spurt into my mouth." A few days later he sees Cora by herself and "swung my fist up against her leg so hard it nearly knocked her over." This is without provocation indeed; nothing comes before it or after it; it is a kind of act of love in itself. Cora, understanding perfectly, snarls "like a cougar. I liked her like that." But the infantile quality of their relationship can have its tender side as well, equally simple-minded: " 'You like blueberry pie?' 'I don't know. Yeah. I guess so.' 'I'll make you some.' " Women are associated with food, whether they bake pies like Cora and Mildred Pierce or offer their own bodies, like Juana, to whom Sharp says, "I know now, my whole life comes from there."

Frank and Cora are representative of a competitive society that has bypassed them, but they are not informed of its spiritual values. There is no question of their being "immoral" since, within the confines of their world, no morality exists. When they are dragged out of their particular world and confronted with superior, intelligent people—their lawyer, for instance—they recognize without surprise the same lust for power and indifference toward human life. (Their lawyer even makes a present of the $10,000 insurance money to the murderers, and never flinches or shows the slightest sign of disapproval toward what they have done.) All this is in line with popular sentiment: the sense of universal corruption, the sly, knowing low-brow familiarity with the evil in all men, which is the precise corollary (and, indeed, sustained by the same audience) of the idea that everyone is really good. Brutality and sentimentality are closely related; the vulgar degrade all notable qualities, especially that of subtlety. What is not exaggerated will be passed by.

Amoral though the lovers are, they do develop a sense of responsibility for their crime and for each other which arouses in them unexpected feelings of guilt. "That's all it takes," Huff says in *Double Indemnity*, "one drop of fear, to curdle love into hate." Genuine moral responsibilities are developed in Cain, particularly in *Serenade* and *The Butterfly*. But the moral commitments are always temporary, varying with the emotions of the characters, and by no means can they be depended upon. (Kady of *The Butterfly* is warm and loving on one page, depraved on another, sympathetic on another, and finally murderous.) Only within a certain emotional radius do relationships exist; Cain's people have one set of values for each individual occasion, each person with whom they are involved. Out of the murder plot of *Double Indemnity* arises a legitimate, selfless love in Huff that is unusual in Cain. More often, as in *Postman*, an initial love-relationship is intensified and expressed in violence of one kind or another.

Cain's fast-moving narrative is sometimes so economical, so oblique and knowing, that one feels the reader must participate as a kind of writer himself. He must, at least, be reading between the lines; because there is such barrenness everywhere, he is forced into the position of imagining what is not given. For instance, the beginning of chapter 6 deals with Frank's attempt at poolhall hustling: "I made shots that Hoppe couldn't make. . . . He never made a shot that Blind Tom . . . couldn't have made. He miscued, he got himself all tangled up on position . . . he never even called a bank shot. And when I walked out of there, he had my $250 and a $3 watch. . . . Oh, I was good all right. The only trouble was I wasn't quite good enough." Here, Cain is relying upon his audience to anticipate the outcome of the hustling, so that the narration itself is only a kind of summary, almost an allusion.

Edmund Wilson and others have remarked upon the contrived quality of the murder scene, where the dead man's high note (the Greek has been singing) is echoed back from the mountains after his death. But the line between Hollywood gimmick and surrealistic touch is fairly thin—note the skillful use of the cat motif in the novel, a cinematic technique as well, but one that seems to work. Cora is described as a "cougar" and defines herself, a little hesitantly, as a "hellcat" (that is, a woman prepared to murder for love); the first murder attempt is endangered by the presence of a policeman who notices a cat climbing up the ladder to the window of the bathroom, and it is this cat's stepping on a fuse box that thwarts the murder attempt and saves the murderers, this time. Frank and the policeman later find the cat "laying on its back with all four feet in the air"—a Hollywood cat, surely, perhaps even a cartoon cat.

After the murder is successfully committed, the lovers fall into the inevitable period of accusations and misery. Just as they were attracted to each other through a kind of sexual tropism, so at the first sign of trouble they are willing to betray each other, and the memory of their traitorous behavior haunts them. There is no tenderness in their love, but only a kind of preposterous violence: Cora is imaged as the "great grandmother of every whore in the world," an incredibly foolish metaphor until one remembers who has said it. Gradually, Cora emerges as the stronger figure. It is she, like Mildred Pierce of the later novel, who wants to do something substantial, to go into business by adding a beer garden to the restaurant. Cain's men usually want a kind of infantile freedom, but the women seem to gravitate toward permanent and conventional patterns of behavior. The cat motif comes in again in the peculiar episode in which Frank goes with a girl puma-trainer down to Mexico. There is a brief cryptic conversation about big cats.

"What's an outlaw?"
"He'd kill you."
"Wouldn't they all?"
"They might, but an outlaw does anyway. If it was people, he would be a crazy person. It comes from being bred in captivity. These cats you see, they look like cats, but they're really cat lunatics."

If the cat lunatics are symbols for the lunatic people, it is not really Cora who is cat-like so much as it is Frank, whose recklessness finally results in her death. The colloquial style keeps leading one to think that Frank is a kind of American innocent, an older Huckleberry Finn whose very stupidity prevents him from being evil. When he thinks, at the Greek's funeral, "I got to blubbering while they were letting him down. Singing those hymns will do it every time, and specially when it's about a guy you like as well as I liked the Greek," it is possible that Cain is being ironic, but that's doubtful; Frank is so simple that he becomes ambiguous! Cain intends a kind of ritualistic cleansing when Frank and Cora, now married, go swimming. Frank says, "and with my ears ringing and that weight on my back and chest, it seemed to me that all the devilment, and meanness, and shiftlessness, and no-account stuff in my life had been pressed out and washed off, and I was all ready to start out with her again clean, and do like she said, have a new life." But his good intentions are thwarted when he passes a truck and has an accident which is fatal to Cora—but apparently doesn't injure Frank.

The plot is a reversal of *The Stranger*, in which a man is found guilty of a crime because of his prior unnatural behavior toward his mother. In *Postman* Frank is found guilty and declared a mad dog not for the original murder, which he did commit, but for the alleged murder of Cora, which was an accident. For some bizarre reason the puma kitten given to Cora by Frank's temporary girl friend is brought into court, and Frank comments, "It was an awful looking thing, and it didn't do me any good, believe me." Thus the hellcat motif is sounded a final time, in connection with Frank now, not Cora.

At the end of the novel, Frank says, "There's a guy in No. 7 that murdered his brother, and says he didn't really do it, his subconscious did it. I asked him what that meant, and he says you got two selves, one that you know about and the other that you don't know about, because it's subconscious. It shook me up. Did I really do it, and not know it?" It is evident that the inner rhythm of the story deals with the unleashing of unconscious, violent urges, turned not toward the usual targets of the impoverished or marginal—the police, the rich—but toward the person who enters into an emotional unit with the hero. It is the arousal of lust which precipitates violence, and indeed the two are precisely the same thing; the infantile ego always lashes out against any force that threatens an end to selfishness. The promise of maturity, of marriage and fatherhood, necessitates Frank's final act of violence, whether it is conscious or not. Significantly, Frank ends his confession with a wistful vision of heaven in which he and Cora are together, and he asks the reader to pray for them. Only in literature do men under sentence of death transcend their situations and understand themselves and society—in real life nothing of the sort happens, as Cain tells us so convincingly. We fall deeper and deeper into our old delusions, which we believe fervently, and at the end of life our commitment is still atomistic. In Cain, life is a bungling process and in no way educational. There is one lesson: love turns into hate if fear is introduced. But, significantly, "fear" comes from without, from the threat of a legal system, and not from an internal code or conscience. There is no education, then, in moral terms at all. *Mildred Pierce* points out the all-too-human predicament in the series of confrontations and exposures of the daughter Veda's hatefulness and the constant failure of Mildred Pierce to understand. Tedious, intolerable, yes, but totally believable. Frank, begging the reader to pray for him and Cora, is the very voice of mass man. There is no doubt but that brutality brutalizes, and sentimentality is but one form of brutality.

Cain's most interesting novel is *Serenade*, a dream-like blend of many elements: the exoticism of the primitive; the "terror" of the archetypal female, the Artist disguised in rags and anonymity; the amazingly simple conquest of the world (via singing); the alter-ego who threatens to obscure one's identity. Juana is the archetypal female, best seen as an Indian who lives in a timeless time, who functions as a kind of Jungian anima for the hero. John Howard Sharp is the Artist, in disguise when we first meet him, having lost all connections with the world of music;

in further disguise, we learn gradually, not only from the world but from himself, and his little lady of terror sees directly into his soul: "When I closed my eyes I'd see her looking at me, seeing something in me, I didn't know what, and then I'd open them again and look at the fog. After a while it came to me that I was afraid of what she saw in me. There would be something horrible mixed up in it, and I didn't want to know what it was." When Juana confronts Sharp with this vision, later, he collapses and admits the truth: that he is victimized by a homosexual attraction he cannot control. Juana is that which must be faced and acknowledged; her terror is her primitive relentlessness, which Cain feels possesses the truth. She is always in control of herself, while Sharp, a typical man, is often not in control of himself. Fleeing Mexico, Sharp looks out over the water and sees a shark's fin, and the music-loving Captain (a kind of Prospero who saves the couple twice) remarks, " 'The water, the surf, the colors on the shore. You think they make the beauty of the tropical sea, aye, lad? They do not. 'Tis the knowledge of what lurks below the surface of it, that awful-looking thing, as you call it, that carries death with every move it makes. So it is, so it is with all beauty. So it is with Mexico. I hope you never forget it.' "

While Juana is the primitive, the ageless, the "real," Winston represents the decadence of civilization. He is intelligent, wealthy, generous, powerful, and depraved. It is only through a compromise and an alliance with this "civilization" that the Artist can express himself—but the paradox is that, in so doing, in demanding a public expression of his art, he falls from the real and is threatened with a loss of self. Sharp's manhood determines his singing voice. In Cain's imagination the voice of the singer is an expression of his sexual normality, perhaps psychologically determined. Sharp's failure as a singer is the result of his unnatural attraction for Winston, who was once so important to him that Sharp "depended on him like a hophead depends on dope." Through an accidental meeting with Juana, the power of the alter-ego is lessened and nearly

conquered. Juana explains the mystique of music and sex:
"I know when you sing. . . . these men who love other
man, they can do much, very clever. But no can sing.
Have no *toro* in high voice. . . . Sound like old woman,
like cow, like priest." When Sharp admits she has spoken
the truth, he collapses and has a vision of the shark's
fin—a phallic symbol that seems somehow connected with
death.

The bullfighting scene in which Juana kills Winston
may be criticized as sensational, but in the context of the
novel's exoticism and the particular exoticism of the party
of perverts in Winston's apartment, it seems perfect. Here
Juana takes on the role that should by nature have been
Sharp's: he should have killed the homosexual in himself.
But Juana, with her primeval strength, kills her rival and
wins Sharp. The irony is that their fleeing from civilization results in a period of aimlessness and disorder similar
to the post-murder sequence in *Postman*. Sharp gets fat,
has to wear glasses; Juana "looked like an old woman. . . .
If she had had a donkey beside her, it would have been
any hag from Mexicali to Tapachula." Their love disinte-
grates without any public outlet for the Artist's talent, and
it is ultimately Sharp's public exposure of his identity (by
way of singing) that leads to Juana's death.

As a parable of the Artist and his relationship to both
society and his inspiration, nature, *Serenade* is an ambiguous work. It seems doubtful that Cain was conscious of
his intention in killing off Juana; he must have had in
mind the creation of a kind of tragedy in which the Artist
must choose, though either choice will result in disaster.
But Sharp's attraction to Winston is an attraction to a
fuller, more powerful version of himself. Like Chambers
and other Cain heroes, Sharp is most himself when he is
kicking free of demands of tenderness, or when he is
pushing people around and browbeating stereotypes of
people in power. He learns from Juana what it is like to
depend upon a woman, but this education is but a temporary one. Significantly, it is not the Artist who is destroyed
(in the typical parable it would have been) but the inspi-

ration for his art, the archetypal female—destroyed by the very masculinity of the force she has created. If the shark's fin suggests Winston, the ugly and primitive iguana suggests Juana; as she is being lowered into her grave, an iguana appears, bringing to mind the iguana she and Sharp ate in the country church prior to their love-making. The iguana is the "terror," but the shark's fin is also the terror—between the two of them the hero is doomed.

Finally, it is not Cain's writing so much as the success of that writing which is interesting. His works may be discussed as mirrors of the society that gave birth to them and rewarded their creator handsomely for them, but the ambiguities and paradoxes of the works bear analysis. Money is important, but it is important secondarily. Of first importance is the doomed straining toward a permanent relationship—an emotional unit which the male both desires and fears. Whether love or sex, it is certainly dominated by unconscious motives, a complex of impulses which shuttle between violence and tenderness. Thus the innocent victim of *The Butterfly* becomes a moonshiner and, rather abruptly, a brutal murderer because of his confused feelings toward his "daughter"; and once his power is relinquished to her, his doom is certain. To love and therefore to relinquish one's power are tantamount to being destroyed. One must remain solitary and invulnerable, yet one cannot—and so the death sentence is earned. Mildred Pierce, masculine in her determination for economic success and possession of her daughter, survives only because in her novel, Cain attempts to write a realistic story, without the structural contrivance of murder and retribution. Mildred is "destroyed" in a thematic sense, but in the suspense-novel genre she would have been killed.

Cain's parable, which is perhaps America's parable, may be something like this: the passion that rises in us is both an inescapable part of our lives and an enemy to our lives, to our egoistic control of ourselves. Once unleashed it cannot be quieted. Giving onself to anyone, even temporarily, will result in entrapment and death; the violence lovers do to one another is no more than a reflection of the proposed violence society holds back to keep the individual passions in check. Freud speaks in many of his works of the strange relationship between the impulse of love and the impulse of destruction, how the sadistic impulse (see *Civilization and its Discontents*) may be an expression of Eros—but an Eros concerned with the self and its survival. The self cannot fulfill its destiny without the alter-ego or anima, but, in relinquishing its power to external agents, it becomes vulnerable to destruction from without. The highest expression of Eros, which is spiritual, is of course beyond Cain's infantile characters. Just as the soap operas and the American movies not only of the thirties and forties but of the present have played back again and again certain infantile obsessions to the great American public, so Cain's novels serve up, in the guise of moral tracts, the lesson of the child who dares too much and must be punished. And there is satisfaction in knowing he will be punished—if not for one crime, then for another; if not by the law, then by himself or by an accomplice. In any case the "postman," whatever symbol of fate or death or order in the form of a uniformed and familiar person, will "ring twice"; there is no escape.

There is perhaps no writer more faithful to the mythologies of America than Cain, for he writes of its ideals and hatreds without obscuring them in the difficulties of art.

Focus on *Appointment in Samarra*
The Importance of Knowing
What You Are Talking About

MATTHEW J. BRUCCOLI

> I feel I have a duty to get down as much of what I know
> as I can.—John O'Hara [1]

JOHN O'HARA is what he called Hemingway in 1950, "the most important author living today." [2] Although he did not specifically analyze the importance of Hemingway in the review of *Across the River and into the Trees*, he particularly praised Hemingway for "pre-paper discipline"—which "means, first of all, point of view" or "the expression of an attitude." O'Hara's work has a controlled, uninvolved point of view—which is one of the reasons he is regarded as hard-boiled—as well as the competence and clarity he admired in Hemingway; but his real importance comes from a commitment Hemingway also had: the duty to tell how it was. "The United States in this century is what I know, and it is my business to write about it to the best of my ability, with the sometimes special knowledge I have. The Twenties, the Thirties, and the Forties are already history, but I cannot be content to leave their story in the hands of the historians and the editors of picture books. I want to record the way people talked and thought and felt, and to do it with complete honesty and variety" (*Sermons and Soda-Water,* 1960).

There are more elegant stylists, more profound thinkers, more sensitive spirits. There is no working writer who matches O'Hara's importance as a social historian. When the next century wants to know how Americans lived between 1920 and 1940, it will find what it wants to know in O'Hara. It will find the names of things—the right names—but it will also find accurate analyses of the social structure and characters who are both real and representative. The stories and people may not always fall within the individual reader's experience, but it is difficult to doubt that O'Hara's wide knowledge and deep commitment to the truth would permit him to falsify his material.

There are subjects—such as the labor movement and national politics—O'Hara has never tried to study in depth. Despite the gaps in his coverage, he has a much broader scope than his competitors—think of James T. Farrell, Louis Auchincloss, John P. Marquand. His closest competitor is James Gould Cozzens, whose commitment to history is modified by his philosophical-ethical concerns. Social history has not been widely admired in American literature, and the second-rate practitioners, such as Henry James and Edith Wharton, have been overrated because they were not reliable observers. Indeed, most influential critics seem to feel that social history belongs to a lower order of endeavor called reportage. Note the of-course and to-be-sure way these chaps admit that John O'Hara does have a sharp ear before they move on to his crudeness. Critics like authors who make them look good. Since O'Hara writes fiction that does not require—or permit—brilliant explication, the critics picket him.

John O'Hara's first novel, *Appointment in Samarra* (1934), employs techniques of tone and point-of-view, materials, and language found in the *Black Mask* school; but it is more ambitious and varied. Historically, it is considered tough or hard-boiled today partly because it was so labelled by its reviewers. Jamesian R. P. Blackmur put O'Hara in the school of Hemingway, James M. Cain, and Benjamin Appel—the school of pointless toughness—and charged that *Appointment in Samarra* was actually distorted and unrealistic (*The Nation*, August 22, 1934, 220–21). Genteel Henry Seidel Canby was so upset by the dirty language and "water closets" that he was inspired to write one of his triumphantly opaque reviews in which he cited "incident recorded only because it happens" and characters without any meaning "except a sociological importance." This review is worth reading. It concludes: "It makes one long for the good old days of the Restoration when in a literature equally thin, equally without values, equally unrepresentative of what was happening in a society at large, and far more wittily erotic, one encountered sometimes a *Millimaunt* and felt the saving presence of a beauty that certainly never waved its wings over Gibbsville" (*The Saturday Review of Literature*, August 18, 1934, 53, 55).

Appointment in Samarra has certain resemblances to two other novels published in 1934, Dashiell Hammett's *The Thin Man* and Cain's *The Postman Always Rings Twice*—uninvolved viewpoint, economical style, accurate speech, dirty words, frank sex. But it is much closer to F. Scott Fitzgerald's *Tender Is the Night* in its interest in character deterioration and in money. *Appointment in Samarra* is a long way from both James T. Farrell's *The Young Manhood of Studs Lonigan* and Henry Roth's *Call it Sleep*. It is not a Depression novel, although the action takes place in 1930 and some of Julian English's troubles are financial. O'Hara has cited Sinclair Lewis and Fitzgerald as the chief literary influences on this novel— and he has discounted the influence of Hemingway (*Appointment in Samarra*, Modern Library, 1953). Hammett, Raoul Whitfield, and Paul Cain—all of whom had published their best work by 1934—are not on the list of secondary influences, which includes Galsworthy, Tarkington, Owen Johnson, Hemingway, Lardner, and Dorothy Parker. Raymond Chandler, the best social observer to come out of *Black Mask*, did not publish his first detective story until 1933.

If there is a connection between O'Hara and the *Black Mask* school, it comes from a shared obligation to the first generation of American naturalists. Although O'Hara does not seem to have been directly influenced by Crane, Norris, or Dreiser, his work reflects their interest in documentary verisimilitude, social stratification, sexual force, and the unpretty aspects of American life—and Crane's perspective on the fate of his characters. O'Hara is a determinist, but he is happily free from the cosmic theorizing and nature-questing of the pioneer naturalists. His characters' lives are controlled by forces they cannot themselves control: by social position—which is not just environmental—and appetite. Their possessions—the things they spend their money and mortality on—are the symbols of their bondage to deterministic forces. O'Hara's genius for meaningful cataloguing of the objects and systems of environment is striking, but he also exhibits a certain commitment to simple hereditary determinism. In *Appointment in Samarra* there is the obvious possibility that Julian's suicide may not be unrelated to his grandfather's. The metaphor of the title obviously says that Julian's fate was determined, though it is left to the reader to assess the influence of the several forces which operate on Julian. As I have indicated, heredity in *Appointment in Samarra* must include such things as the social position and family traditions one inherits at birth. Being born on a certain street to certain parents with certain memberships and being early impressed with the knowledge that one will be expected to attend certain schools where one will join—or be able to join—certain organizations, after which one will honor certain family obligations and marry into a certain social level: these are as deterministic in O'Hara as a family taint of idiocy is in Zola. Always in O'Hara there is the money; and inherited money is better than new money.

The neat theory that O'Hara's work stems from his poor boy's pain at being excluded from Pottsville, Pennsylvania, society has been widely—gleefully—accepted along with the joke about "let's all take up a collection and send John O'Hara to Yale." These wound-and-bow analyses are supposed somehow to discredit his work, although the childhood wounds—preferably sexual—of other writers are deemed respectable. However, the story of O'Hara's socially deprived youth, at least as commonly interpreted, is not true. For the record, he has written, "In 1918, in a store on Chestnut Street in Philadelphia, my old man bought me a pair of riding boots for $55.00 and the first pair of wing-tip brogues I had ever seen, for $26.50. He paid cash, and we didn't have to thumb it home. That didn't last but don't say it never happened." [3] The anti-O'Hara school would of course claim that this statement—especially the last sentence—exposes his overconcern with the thing he is denying. It is possible, even probable, that as a Catholic, O'Hara experienced prejudice and exclusion, which is not the same as making him the little match boy. Religious bias is covered in his work—notably in *Appointment in Samarra*—but it is hardly a preoccupation. To say that O'Hara writes as an outsider is too simple because so much of his work depends on inside information.

Edmund Wilson has stated that the cruel side of social snobbery is O'Hara's main theme (*The Boys in the Back Room*, 1941). It is one of his themes, but not his chief one. However, snobbery—interpreted as all the machinery of social conduct and social stratification—is his main subject. The main theme within this subject is not the cruelty of exclusion, but the futility and tragedy of the waste of life within the social system. In *Ten North Frederick*, a minor character sums up what he has learned about the system: "The safest way to live is first, inherit money. Second, marry a woman that will cooperate with you in your sexual peculiarities. Third, have a legitimate job that keeps you busy. Fourth, be born without a taste for liquor. Fifth, join some big church. Sixth, don't live too long." There is authorial irony here, of course, for these are rules for a safe, happy, and futile life. But they really are good rules for a safe life in society. It is worth noting that of the six rules, four concern things we normally do not control and which have social consequences: inherited wealth, sexual peculiarities, alcoholism, and life-span; and the other two involve social relationships. The job is not for income or satisfaction, and the church is not for religion.

O'Hara has been tagged a hard-boiled writer partly because of his realistic treatment of the rougher aspects of life, and mostly because of his detachment from his characters—or what has been described as his sardonic attitude toward them. It is said that he is indifferent to their fates and refuses to judge them. It is even said that he hates his rich people, in which case he can not be detached at all. True, he is interested in the underworld and its show-business fringes—for example, Al Grecco and Ed Charney in *Appointment in Samarra*. But he is much more interested in the middle and upper classes—the Flieglers and the Englishes—because they are more complicated. The rich are different; and the richer they are, the more different they are. Like Fitzgerald, O'Hara is impressed by the charm and grace the rich can achieve; and like Fitzgerald, O'Hara is disappointed by what these privileged people actually do with their lives. It is also true that O'Hara shares an interest in the varieties of sexual conduct with the hard-boiled writers—and is more explicit about it. But his scope is wider, his ambition greater. When he describes people in bed, he is trying to show that most people do and say the same things, or that some people do not.

O'Hara's work is free from the deliberate shock element found in hard-boiled detective fiction—the detailed beatings and the descriptions of bullet-holes in foreheads; the exaggerated indifference of the protagonists to pain, even their own; the matter-of-fact inventories of alcoholic consumption; the refusal to display emotion. Where O'Hara does cover the same ground—Julian's or Luther's drinking, for example—he makes it part of the bigger job of showing how the character lived, how the drinking was part of social rituals. Critics have complained that O'Hara supplies needlessly elaborate case histories for minor characters in *Appointment in Samarra*—that there is too much about Al Grecco for his importance in the novel—but these biographical sketches are clear indications that the novel was intended as a sociological study as well as a character study. O'Hara is interested in the man who had the appointment and in Samarra; in fact the social organization of Samarra determines the nature of the appointment.

What has been assumed to be O'Hara's indifference to his characters—his hard-boiled attitude—has been confused with his disciplined authorial point of view. He is not an intrusive author, and he does not get emotionally involved with his characters. This is not to say that he does not approve and disapprove of them. He thinks Dr. William Dilworth English is a choice son-of-a-bitch, and the reader knows that he does. O'Hara's procedure is to tell as much as he can about his characters' histories and then to let them reveal themselves through their behavior and speech while he avoids open judgment on them. That O'Hara offers no open judgment does not mean that there is no judgment. The very acts of selecting material, of inventing characters, of having them act, of creating speech—all involve judgment. He does not instruct us in how he wants us to feel about Julian, but it is clear that O'Hara is not without feelings about him. The novel shows us that Julian is weak and self-indulgent, but not wholly contemptible and certainly not vicious. He is doomed by forces of character and circumstance he cannot cope with; and because he does not merit his doom, he deserves pity. But only a little pity because there is nothing in particular to admire about him. There have been complaints that he is a surface characterization, that O'Hara fails to make the reader understand Julian, that we never really know why he commits suicide. That is what O'Hara intended. The novel is not superficial: Julian is a superficial human being. He is not a tragic character and was not intended as one. *Appointment in Samarra* is a sociological novel, not a psychological novel.

When O'Hara does openly comment, it is clear that his controlled handling of his material conceals the fact that he is a sentimental man who can be very sentimental about sex, love, and marriage. It may be that O'Hara's uninvolved point-of-view is his tactic for disciplining his sentimentality, a sentimentality that has become more apparent in his recent work—"Imagine Kissing Pete," for example. In *Appointment in Samarra*, when Julian and Caroline have intercourse after he has failed to apologize to Harry Reilly, O'Hara does comment: "It was the greatest single act of their married life. He knew it, and she knew it. It was the time she did not fail him." If Julian's reaction to Caroline's refusal to keep their love-making date at the country club seems extreme, the point is that this time she fails him again when he desperately needs reassurance. Julian fails Caroline, of course, but he needs her more than she needs him. The English marriage is contrasted with the Fliegler marriage, which opens and closes the novel. Luther and Irma do not fail each other. If Julian can be considered the victim of one particular thing, he is the victim of Caroline's bitchiness. In her grieving for Julian, she recognizes that she would have failed Julian again, that it is better for both of them that he killed himself. "But this time she knew she would not have come back this afternoon, and he had known it, and God help us all but he was right. There was nothing for him to do today. . . . There, that was settled. Now let the whole thing begin again."

O'Hara's plain style adds to the impression that he is a hard-boiled writer. His prose moves; it is clear and exceptionally readable—which in some quarters counts against him—but it lacks the grace of Fitzgerald's prose. To be sure, O'Hara has a good ear, and his dialogue includes words that used to upset people. His writing is uncomplicated and notably bare of simile and metaphor. Allegory he eschews along with ambiguity and ambivalence. He creates no white whales; but he has an unsurpassed skill with his kind of symbols, which are the names of things. That Julian is a Cadillac dealer is appropriate and meaningful. The characters may not always understand what their possessions reveal about them, but O'Hara does. He knows what he is talking about.

You may not like what he writes about, but "don't say it never happened."

Horace McCoy's Objective Lyricism

THOMAS STURAK

MEASURED BY the standard that William Faulkner once applied in his assessment of Thomas Wolfe's preeminence among his contemporaries, Horace McCoy (1897–1955) —considered simply as a hard-boiled or tough guy novelist—would have to stand at the head of his class. If, like all writers, the so-called "poets of the tabloid murder" ultimately failed, then McCoy made the best failure because he tried hardest to say the most. But it should be evident that his five novels do not submit to such limited categorization, either by subject matter or approach.

In terms of his career as a novelist, McCoy's own experiences in the down-and-out world of the Hollywood extra during the early thirties were crucial and determinative. Besides providing him with raw materials for two books, the initial shock of failure and the struggle for success set the emotional bent of his creative imagination in all of his subsequent serious fiction. "I think that if a man has the urge to be an artist," Georges Simenon once said, "it is because he needs to find himself. Every writer tries to find himself through his characters, through all his writings" (*Writers at Work*). From his beginnings as a writer (even in his pulp stories), McCoy showed signs of an inward-turning artistic sensibility whose thematic preoccupations and stylistic aims reflected the major impulse of twentieth-century literature. The real subjects of his fiction are the existential conflicts arising out of an acute self-awareness and the inevitable consequences of self-division. Like that of many another modern novelist, McCoy's work comprises an emotional autobiography; his fictional world becomes a symbol of his creative imagination.

Following the publication of his first novel, *They Shoot Horses, Don't They?* (1935) —upon which this essay will focus—McCoy landed his first major film-writing assignments. In his twenty-year career as a Hollywood writer, he contributed to approximately one hundred filmed screenplays. His second novel, *No Pockets in a Shroud* (1937), was written in fits and starts between 1935 and 1936, and "touched up" in the same manner over another year in an unsuccessful quest for an American publisher. Accepted by Arthur Barker of London, it was further revised and emasculated to meet the demands of England's "invisible censorship." Barker was optimistic about the book's prospects "of making a real hit" in England —"assuming," he wrote to McCoy, "we don't go to gaol on it and in spite of having had to cut a certain amount out." How extensive was this cutting we can't know; but it may have further weakened a plot already notorious for its lack of depth and failure to correlate adequately external acts and motives. In the years prior to World War II, this fast-paced but unevenly inspired story of a crusading journalist's fatal battle against crime, corruption, and a Klan-like organization of native fascists became McCoy's most translated and best known work abroad.

In its original form, it has never been published in this country. The so-called "First U. S. Edition" brought out by the New American Library in 1948 was extensively rewritten by McCoy. Also, at the last minute an NAL editor, worried that critics might give it a Marxian interpretation, made several major alterations, e.g., he changed the heroine from a Communist into a sexual pervert! In its anti-Fascism, anti-Hearst passages, *No Pockets in a Shroud* bears a seeming resemblance to certain "proletarian novels" of the thirties. For McCoy, as for the majority of American artists and intellectuals, the Communist movement of the 1930's was an inescapable influence. But this is not a "leftist" novel, because its hero, Michael Dolan, is neither sinister nor subversive politically. He is simply a very angry young man. Created during an era of social consciousness, he is nonetheless drawn in the image of the disillusioned individualist of the twenties, and ultimately postures like "the young reformer" of pre-World War i muckraking novels—who, as Malcolm Cowley has described him, "single-handedly fought the corrupt politicians, besides courting the daughter of the biggest boss of all" (*The Literary Situation*). Though the book's nominal heroine, Myra Barnovsky, is a Communist, she functions as little more than a vaguely symbolic Doppelgänger; her fatal influence upon Dolan seems more occult than ideological. That so much space is given to his affairs with two wealthy debutantes suggests that the individual acts of rebellion arising from what he calls his "social phobia" are as operative in his destiny as any crusading idealism or love for downtrodden humanity.

Privately, McCoy called *No Pockets in a Shroud* the closest thing to an autobiography that he ever wrote. (It is his only novel written in the third-person.) To an extent, it is a *roman á clef* based upon his own activities as an editor in Dallas during the late twenties. Published when he had already turned forty, it reads very much like an immature and early book by a talented writer, akin to those commonplace "so-called autobiographical novels" of the 1920's which Frederick J. Hoffman has described as "too often excuses for conduct rather than explanations of it" (*The Twenties*).

McCoy's next novel, *I Should Have Stayed Home* (Knopf, 1938) was also hurriedly written and expediently revised under pressure from its editors. Closely patterned after *They Shoot Horses, Don't They?* (e.g., in the submitted manuscript, the hero committed suicide), this brutally realistic story concerns the hapless lot of two young movie extras, Mona Matthews and Ralph Carston. The latter's monolithic simple-mindedness—he is surely one of the most "soft-boiled" heroes in American fiction—

undercuts the book's effectiveness as propaganda about what he calls "the most terrifying town in the world." If McCoy were pointing the moral, "keep away from Hollywood," he was not only warning gulls like his incredibly naive hero, but also empathizing with "sellouts" like the minor (but most vibrant) character, Johnny Hill, an idealistic writer turned cynic, who evidently served as his *persona*. As the *Saturday Review* recognized, "Horace McCoy hates Hollywood, not enough to stay away from it but enough to get all the bile out of his system in a short, bitter, name-calling novel."

McCoy himself struck no tragic figure as a Hollywood writer; his public image was hardly that of an *artiste manqué*. Privately, however, he felt himself intrinsically a failure. But during the years following the publication of *I Should Have Stayed Home*, when he was submerged in (as he put it in a letter to Victor Weybright) "the bottomless muck" of Hollywood, his work in translation won a following abroad. During World War II, his first two novels enjoyed an underground—literally—fame on the continent, particularly in France. In 1946, the open publication by Gallimard of *On achève bien les chevaux* (*They Shoot Horses, Don't They?*) sent his reputation skyrocketing, especially among the existentialists (inevitably he was called "the first American existentialist"). The following year a new translation of *No Pockets in a Shroud* (*Un linceul n'a pas de poches*) was issued as the fourth volume—and the first by an American—in the extremely popular *Série Noire*. Word began to drift back to the United States that in Paris "everyone in the knowledgeable world talks about American writers, about a curious trinity: Hemingway, Faulkner, and McCoy." [1] Another report described McCoy as "the most discussed American writer in France." [2]

Flattered and frightened by this sudden "spectacle of a dead man rising" (and free of movie work for the first time in fifteen years) McCoy made his fourth novel, *Kiss Tomorrow Goodbye* (Random House, 1948), the acid test of his creative genius and artistic talents—to prove, as it were, both to himself and to the world that his first novel had not been a fluke and that his revival abroad was not merely a Frenchman's fancy. As its publishers advertised, this book is "a kind of success story"—at its simplest, an example of the popular drama of the rise and fall of a gangster. But it is also, to use a phrase of Malcolm Cowley's, "an inquisition into the unknown depths" of McCoy's own mind; subliminally, it is his most damning novel about himself in Hollywood.

In 1947 McCoy told his literary agent, Harold Matson, that he had been thinking about *Kiss Tomorrow Goodbye* "for a long, long time." The shadowy prototype for its Phi Beta Kappa killer briefly appears in his last *Black Mask* story, published in 1934. Five years later, when he was working on a series of "supporting features" (i.e., B movies) based on FBI cases against notorious criminals of the thirties, he seems to have begun his "psychological story of a pathological killer." [3] In its final form, *Kiss Tomorrow Goodbye* became McCoy's most intriguing and ambitious novel. In its thematic preoccupations with states of awareness, failure and success, death and rebirth, and the quest for self-identity, it reflected a period of crisis in his own life which was dominated by a mood of disintegration and complicated by a promising turn of fortune so sudden and unexpected that it was, he wrote to Matson, "something like a miracle, to be revived after all these years with such a fanfare." Time and again in his personal letters, he spoke of his new book's importance to him "as a symbol" of his regeneration as a writer. In itself this novel stands as both the climax of his career and a paradigm of his creative imagination.

Kiss Tomorrow Goodbye's unique first-person protagonist, who goes under the dual alias of Ralph Cotter and Paul Murphy, has been understandably called "one of the most brutal of the hard boiled characters in American fiction." [4] At the same time, he narrates his violent story with a peculiar brand of lyricism that in the book's climactic stream-of-consciousness passage and poetic and haunting final paragraphs exceeds, strictly speaking, the limits of objectivity. Before *Kiss Tomorrow Goodbye* went to press, McCoy appealed to Random House, as he had with each of his previous publishers, that they take a strong stand to disassociate his work from "the 'James Cain' school." In reassuring McCoy, Editor Allan Ullman remarked in 1948, "you have given me the best kind of clue when you talk about the 'lyricism' of your own brand of brutality." Unfortunately, McCoy's letter to Ullman is lost; but we know that this peculiar stylistic concept had engaged his creative imagination since at least the time of *They Shoot Horses, Don't They?* In 1937, he wrote "there were decadence and evil in the old walkathons—and violence. The evil, of course, as evil always has and always will, fascinated the customer and the violence possessed a peculiar lyricism that elevated the thing into the realm of high art" (quoted in an unidentified Dallas newspaper clipping). Shortly after the publication of his first novel, he explained his "literary aims," in an informal lecture, "dwelling on the lyrical quality that lies in any dramatic action and the transfer of that lyrical quality to the pages of a book by means of graphic and telling words" ("Writer Is Heard / In Informal / Address / Horace McCoy Talks / to Shakespeare / Club Juniors," *Pasadena Star-News*).

In 1945 Raymond Chandler had written that "the possibilities of objective writing are very great and they have scarcely been explored." [5] Three years later, only a few readers of *Kiss Tomorrow Goodbye* sensed that in attempting a lyrical, first-person, psychoanalytical novel about a "master-mind" criminal, McCoy had tried those possibilities to the limits. In 1949, however, Philip Durham asserted that in *Kiss Tomorrow Goodbye* McCoy had carried "the objective technique" (America's "most original contribution to the art of fiction") "to its furthest development." In doing so, he had enhanced the coherence and complexity of both a traditional American fictional manner and a modern American popular drama.

McCoy had hoped that *Kiss Tomorrow Goodbye* would buy his escape from what he called "this whoring" in

Hollywood. But in the end, his one-way ticket proved to be a "brass check." In 1949, a paperback abridgment (made with his permission by an editor) sold well; and the story was soon bought by the movies. Try as he would, he had never before been able to interest film makers in any of his novels. Of *Kiss Tomorrow Goodbye*, he had written to his agent: "I do not think there is a picture in the book." With this ironic success, McCoy, financially strapped (as always) and in poor health, once again resigned himself to his destiny as "a Hollywood hack." In his last novel, *Scalpel* (1952), he reversed his course as a creative writer in more ways than might be evident from a reading of this "popular" story of an incredibly successful surgeon who on the final page thinks to himself, "God was in His Heaven and all was right with the script writer." We can read *that* as a sardonic authorial commentary on the only novel McCoy ever "made" from one of his screen stories. Early in 1951, he had sold an original "treatment" of a "medical yarn" to Hal Wallis Productions for something between fifty and one hundred thousand dollars. This "book" was bought by Appleton-Century-Crofts, who commissioned McCoy to turn it into a novel. (The posthumously published *Corruption City* [Dell: N. Y., 1959] is an unaltered screen treatment which McCoy wrote for Columbia Pictures in 1950. Originally titled *This Is Dynamite*, it was screened as *The Turning Point*. Though it is not a novel, and McCoy himself never considered it as such, since his death it has also been published in Italian [twice] and Portuguese. During his lifetime it appeared only in a French translation in the *Série Noire*. In 1950, McCoy's agent had submitted the manuscript to the New American Library, but the paperback house would have nothing to do with it unless McCoy agreed to do a complete revision. Apparently, he wasn't interested.)

McCoy's longest book and only "best-seller" in hard covers, *Scalpel* epitomizes Albert Van Nostrand's phrase, "the denatured novel." [6] Despite the uncharacteristic leisurely manner and over elaborate and too neatly worked out plot, it nonetheless displays all of the familiar signs of the characteristic McCoy fable. In fact, a collection of selected passages—amounting to perhaps 1500 of its 150,000 words—would comprise a virtual compendium of his major themes, character types, and dramatic conflicts. For example, from time to time the narrative is interrupted for explicit glosses on ambition, success, self-doubt, self-division. Similarly, the conflict is merely—but repeatedly—asserted. In a word, everything has been stylized—and "stylization exaggerates gestures and attitudes" (Van Nostrand). In padding out his original screen story, McCoy imitated and borrowed from his previous work, most of all from *Kiss Tomorrow Goodbye*. We need only scratch the surface to discover, for example, that "genius" surgeon Doctor Thomas Owen and "genius" criminal Cotter-Murphy are blood brothers under the skin. In substance, *Scalpel* is *Kiss Tomorrow Goodbye* turned upside-down. Whereas the latter is a bitterly black parody of the Horatio Alger myth, the former is a cynically rosy revival.

McCoy's divided character fashioned his destiny as a novelist. At times, the most disparate elements coexisted in his imagination seemingly without any awareness on his part. During the final doldrums of his literary career, a Hollywood reporter claimed that he had once heard McCoy "admit, on television, that he is the best writing man in America today." About the same time, in a letter he asked his agent to keep after his foreign publishers for copies of translations which, he wrote, "would be as welcome as the money, even more so." Basically sensitive and honest, he was torn all his life between the crude material values of fame and fortune, and a dream of enduring greatness. It was his inner, fatal weakness. "In the domains of creation, which are also the domains of pride," Valéry wrote, "the need to distinguish oneself cannot be separated from existence itself." Throughout his life, McCoy struggled with a compulsion to fulfill a heightened conception of himself as an artist. The clash of this romantic illusion and the inexorable realities of time and existence resulted in deep feelings of guilt, self-doubt, and self-division. Transmuted by his imagination, these reactions inform all of his fictional dramas as failure, success, corruption, and unrequited ambition.

In 1962 a commentator on the literary scene of the thirties paired Horace McCoy and Nathanael West as novelists of that decade "whose work was important and is still read today," and has "had surprising influence on later writers. Witness, for example, . . . *They Shoot Horses, Don't They?* (1935) with its setting a marathon-dance contest—in France the existentialists call it 'great.' " But at the same time another critic could only recall with dismay that thirty years ago many Americans did not discriminate "between naturalistic writings having social significance" and such works as *They Shoot Horses, Don't They?* "which had no social significance of any kind." These two assessments together epitomize the critical divergence and confusion in this country regarding the nature and value of McCoy's remarkable first novel.

Published during a grim period for the American book trade, *They Shoot Horses, Don't They?* was an unquestionable *succès d'estime,* but hardly a best seller. Despite some impressive reviews, it soon slipped into the limbo of neglected books, beyond the grace of established criticism. In 1940 Edmund Wilson, rising from "a long submergence in the politics and literature of the nineteenth century," took a quick look into what "people were reading." The results were some uneven and often inaccurate "notes" on "the California writers"—the infamous "boys in the back room"—in which a few general remarks were devoted to McCoy's two novels about "the miserable situation of movie-struck young men and women who starve and degrade themselves in Hollywood." Wilson found *They Shoot Horses, Don't They?* "worth reading for its description of one of those dance marathons that were among the more grisly symptoms of the early years of the Depression" ("The Boys in the Back Room"). This faint praise—the sum and total of serious American criticism of the book—has been piously re-echoed down to the moment. Writing in 1966, Robert M. Coates could only elevate it, so to speak, from Low to High Camp: "The book is in the highest, and in many ways the best, meaning of the term, a period piece."

Wilson also laid the mark of James M. Cain and the onus of "writer for the studios" on McCoy's fiction. Both of these insinuations were undiscerning and unenlightening. *They Shoot Horses, Don't They?* (Simon and Schuster, 1935) was not one of those books "which apparently derived" from Cain's sensational first novel, *The Postman Always Rings Twice* (1934). By November of 1933 McCoy had completed a first draft, which was essentially an amplification of an unpublished short story of the same title that he had written no later than August 1932. McCoy himself always inveighed, justifiably, against the specious, "almost obligatory" comparison to Cain's *Postman*. In 1948 he wrote to his paperback publishers (who also reprinted Cain's books), "I do not care for Cain's work, although there may be much he can teach me. I know this though—continued labeling of me as of 'the Cain school' (whatever the hell that is) and I shall slit either his throat or mine."

If it can be said that McCoy ever belonged to any school of fiction, it would have to be as a wayward member of Joseph T. Shaw's boys in the *Black Mask* during the late twenties and early thirties (when Cain was still an essayist and closet dramatist for Mencken's *American Mercury*). Editor Shaw himself in 1932 named McCoy among "the older writers who helped establish the *Black Mask* standard." But despite the implied parity with the work of such so-called "hard-boiled" classicists as Carroll John Daly, Raoul Whitfield, and Dashiell Hammett, McCoy's contributions—when measured against Shaw's own avowed aims—are most interesting for their violations of the *Black Mask* "formula" that demanded character in constant action. Moreover, he often indulged in symbolistic and lyrical techniques that Shaw once told him were "almost too fine writing." Unlike almost every other *Black Mask* regular who "graduated" to hard-cover publication, McCoy did so extracurricularly. Writing under the patient and encouraging tutelage of Joe Shaw taught McCoy much about the craft of fiction, and sharpened his techniques of objective writing; but he never directly used or adapted any of his pulp materials in his subsequent short stories and novels. Significantly, he persuaded Simon and Schuster not to use either the word or the idea "hard-boiled" in the promotion and advertising copy for his first novel.

In writing *They Shoot Horses, Don't They?* (and also his third novel, *I Should Have Stayed Home*) McCoy drew upon his own early experiences and observations in Hollywood. He had come to California from Dallas — leaving behind him a ten-year career as a newspaperman and a national reputation as a little theatre actor — early in 1931, full of self-confidence and the highest ambitions. But until well into 1933, while striving to break into motion pictures as an actor and writer, he shared the hardships, disappointments, and anxieties common to the 20,000 extras reportedly out of work during these cruelest years of the Great Depression. The story that he actually worked as a bouncer in a marathon dance contest is apocryphal, though there is evidence that he may have *acted* the role in a film. He definitely witnessed such contests, which were regular attractions in dance halls on the ocean piers in nearby Venice and Santa Monica. According to his widow, he was always deeply disturbed by the bestiality of these spectacles. All of which is not enough, of course, to explain the evolution of his marathon-dance story into a novel of considerable artistry. As Sartre has said: "The writer makes books out of words, not out of his sorrows."

Marathon dancing, which had originated in the twenties as another zany fad, became in the thirties a vicious racket. Whether or not it was part of McCoy's conscious intention to write a "sociological novel" — as some of his admirers still view *They Shoot Horses, Don't They?* — condemning by implication the social and economic system responsible for such brutalization of human beings, the work certainly rises above mere calculated sensationalism. McCoy's latent reformist tendencies—revealed in a brief fling as the editor of a crusading magazine in Dallas—were suited to the "mood of social evangelism" so strong "among writers and critics and the intellectual elite generally" during the thirties (Frederick Lewis Allen, *Since Yesterday*). But by any meaningful definition (i.e., ideological commitment), he was never a proletarian writer. The doctrinaire left-wing reviewers of the day ignored *They Shoot Horses, Don't They?* although one English critic thought that the book ("emphatically not just another example of that fake American, romantic tough writing") implied "a condemnation of American civilization severe enough to satisfy the standard of the Third International." From a perspective of thirty years, however, it is clear that the enduring radicalism of the novel resides in no political program or ethical system; its implied message is perhaps best summed up in Clifford Odets' plea, "Life should have some dignity."

In great part, the continuing interest in *They Shoot Horses, Don't They?* is a result of McCoy's lack of commitment to a priori literary or political theories. In writing the novel he consciously minimized topical allusions to the Depression, consistently cutting explicit references, for example, to "bread lines" and the plight of "people who work in factories," which had appeared in the original short story. Always, in this compact narrative, the descriptive details and motifs contribute to the creation of a dominant effect and the elucidation of the human drama.

Technically, *They Shoot Horses, Don't They?* is a brilliant tour de force—but not one without serious purpose and significant implications. In the unpublished original short story (c. 1931–32), the central narrative of the marathon dance was set within the frame of a courtroom trial at the climactic moment of sentencing. In drafting the novel McCoy retained this structure, but carefully reworded the judge's pronouncement which runs through the text in cadenced fragments preceding each of the thirteen chapters, with the last page of the book bearing the final phrase "MAY GOD HAVE MERCY ON

YOUR SOUL." The book's designer, Philip Van Doren Stern, thought this idea such a good one that he attempted to make (he wrote to McCoy) "the typographical treatment an integral part of the story" by setting these fragments in black capitals which progressively increase in each section one degree in point. His notion that the final phrase "in huge type" would hit "the reader with a terrific bang—as it must have hit the prisoner at the dock" is questionable on both counts; but the effect is startling, and in a way these scareheads seem to fit the tabloid sordidness of the subject matter and the rising intensity of the story's action. Certainly, the device heightens both the dramatic and ironic contrast between the clipped, colloquial urgency of the narrated events of over a month's duration and the measured, pompous rhetoric of the legal formula spoken in a matter of seconds. Nietzsche somewhere remarked that in the courtroom he would acquit everyone but the judge. By implication in McCoy's minor American tragedy, a condemning society shares in the guilt for the transgressions which precipitate the destruction of two human beings. On this level, the plot of the novel is in the conflict between the "criminal" facts of the narrator's case and another set of "facts" or extenuating circumstances.

The book's first words "THE PRISONER WILL STAND"—standing alone on a page—graphically preamble the narrator's *de trop* situation as he briefly recalls in vivid detail how he shot "*Gloria . . . in the side of the head . . . out there in that black night on the edge of the Pacific. . . . She did not die in agony. She was relaxed and comfortable and she was smiling. It was the first time I had ever seen her smile. . . . And she wasn't friendless. I was her very best friend. I was her only friend.*" No such exposition as this appeared in the short-story manuscript. It is a dramatic prologue—told within the condemned man's mind (indicated by italics)—portraying the protagonists at the catastrophe of their tragic relationship. Immediately in the next one-page chapter we learn that the boy—who remains nameless until the judge intones (before chapter 8), "YOU ROBERT SYVERTEN, BE DELIVERED"—has killed the girl as "a personal favor." The crime is against not only society but seemingly also against nature.

They Shoot Horses, Don't They? is obviously no murder mystery. Without a complete sacrifice of suspense, however, McCoy set himself the task of making this killing-out-of-friendship understandable and inevitable. He applied, as it were, Joseph Shaw's dicta to subject matter beyond the range of any popular magazine formula: as in the best *Black Mask* detective stories, the emphasis is on "character and the problem inherent in human behavior"—the "crime, or the threat" being "incidental." [7]

Gimmicky as the novel's design may appear, it serves in many ways, as suggested above, to integrate the various motifs and themes. For example, within Robert's recital of events there occur several critical passages (always italicized) which momentarily either thrust the narrative back into his childhood or tie it to his present position in the courtroom. These textual in-turnings are concomitant with the repetitive, circular movement permeating the story on all levels—e.g., the monotonous routine and incessant motion of the dancing and the "derby" races; the singsong introductions of celebrities; Robert's ludicrous pirouetting to follow the moving spot of sunlight each afternoon; his habit of psychological reversion, which in the end triggers his bemused but fatal decision to help Gloria off their futile "merry-go-round" existence.

These brief, italicized, reversed flashbacks within the narrative, together with the interpolated phrases between chapters, remind us that Robert is for a minute or two standing in court listening to a judge pronounce sentence. But only if we should choose to force our interest away from the developing drama and onto the set frame must we imagine that the related happenings of thirty-seven days are literally passing through his mind. In fact, *They Shoot Horses, Don't They?* reads easily and seems a simple story told simply. It speaks highly of McCoy's handling of point of view that the typographical and structural devices neither blur nor support the drama, but instead help to hold our attention and to heighten our sense of inevitability and of what Camus called the "secret complicity that joins the logical and the everyday to the tragic" (*The Myth of Sisyphus*).

With a boldness characteristic of all his writing, McCoy overrides certain difficulties inherent in employing a first-person narrator who is also a main actor, and succeeds in gaining immediacy and authenticity of expression without sacrificing plausibility. Unlike the vernacular hero of *The Postman Always Rings Twice*, for example, we are not in the end asked to believe that Robert Syverten is literally *writing* his own story. For that matter, most of the time we are less aware of him as a narrator *of* than as a participant *in* the action. In creating a first-person narrator who is at once both outside and inside the story, McCoy is able to command, direct and, in this case, literally frame the reader's attention. All we read of the experiences which constitute the novel's subject is filtered through Robert's rather limited sensibility. It follows almost of necessity that McCoy would use dramatic scenes as the principal device to objectify this indirect approach and give it self-limiting form. Jamesian as all of this may sound, it is also a refinement of the old *Black Mask* "formula." Certainly from Robert's point of view, the story is not so much about what happened as what he feels about what happened.

Through the *persona* of Robert, McCoy selects and organizes his realistic observations for effect rather than for proof. Patently lacking weight of naturalistic "documentation," the undeniable power of this short novel resides in its intensity of mood. Indeed, atmosphere is of the greatest importance—as the narrative progresses it creates the characters. The crime immediately laid bare, the only interest lies in the how and why of the circumstantial "threats"—the physical and psychological forces—which bear unrelentlessly upon the protagonists, in particular upon the central figure of Gloria Beatty.

Among American fictional females, Gloria is unique in

her unremitting, evil-tempered, nihilistic despair and total estrangement. Metaphorically, her existence is the point of the title's terrible question. It is *her* story Robert tells; the fact that as he unfolds it he is being condemned to death fuses the intricately patterned ironies of theme and drama.

> IS THERE ANY LEGAL CAUSE WHY SENTENCE
> SHOULD NOT NOW BE PRONOUNCED?
>
> What could I say? . . . All those people knew I had killed her; the only other person who could have helped me at all was dead too.

The "only other person" being old Mrs. Layden, the wealthy and eccentric "champion marathon dance fan of the world," who takes such an unusual interest in Robert and his future, and whose accidental killing by a stray bullet is the death blow to the marathon and a foreshadowing of Gloria's resolution to have herself shot.

Morbid and ineffectual as she is, Gloria is nonetheless the *anima* and from the outset the seeming arbiter of the world of the novel. As a minor character sarcastically says, she does Robert's "thinking for him." She also dictates his fate, as well as her own, and to an extent even that of the marathon dance. By the end of the book we accept her character and condition because McCoy has succeeded in creating a protagonist who is at once the dramatic matrix of the narrative and the embodiment of the novel's theme.

Since Gloria literally dominates Robert, what he tells us of the setting and action is largely determined by her reactions to their surroundings and activities, or otherwise serves to emphasize their predicament, and their physical and spiritual deterioration. By extension, her character sets the pervading mood of the novel. The Sisyphean routine of the marathon dance itself is clearly symbolic of her view of life in which the one value of existence supersedes all others. In an amoral world nothing is immoral; nothing is meaningful. Robert says he feels sorry for a contestant picked up by detectives for a murder. " 'Why,' said Gloria, 'what's the difference between us?' " There is literally no exit out of their absurd world—to open an outside door is to risk disqualification; no chance of getting anywhere, either inside or out. "This whole business is a merry-go-round," Gloria tells Robert. "When we get out of here we're right back where we started."

Gloria's predicament is, however, only in part of her own making, and even that part is shown to be the result of her having been born an orphan into a world she never made—the fact that constitutes her character. Estranged and ineffectual, she is engulfed in a universal amorality. "I wish God would strike me dead," she says. But any sign of God is literally shut out of this insulated dancehall world. When, after the marathon's closing, she and Robert finally walk out onto the pier, he looks back at the building and says, "Now I know how Jonah felt when he looked at the whale." In the end, under the moonless, starless sky, Gloria tells him to "pinch hit for God."

The climactic episode, in terms of Gloria's tragedy, occurs in the tenth chapter, when she confronts two dowager representatives of the Mothers' League for Good Morals and, in a scene that is the emotional high-point of the novel, routs them with the terrible force of all her pent-up frustration and bitterness. Her castigation of the women reformers—delivered in the most notorious four-letter terms—is grounded upon her own experience which has proven "morality" an empty word, always dependent upon circumstances, e.g., dancing in a marathon is better than starving. At the end of her tirade she slams the door behind the routed ladies, sits down, and for the first and only time in the story begins to cry: "She covered her face with her hands and tried to fight it off, but it was no use. She slowly leaned forward in the chair, bending double, shaking and twitching with emotion, as if she had completely lost control of the upper half of her body. For a full moment the only sounds in the room were her sobs and the rise and fall of the ocean which came through the half-raised window." At this moment in the narrative, McCoy brings together the sum total of the amoral environment—the dancehall, the social system, an indifferent nature—that envelopes Gloria, smothering her last hope, reducing her to whimpering despair. The Mothers' League instigates a public campaign against the contest that makes its demise inevitable. The sound of the ocean, a recurring image suggestive of death, foreshadows Gloria's final resolution. The next time we hear its rise and fall she is dead.

Much more could be said about this critical episode in which the cumulative forces of character and environment at last break Gloria's resistance to her fate. (Nothing even remotely like this incident occurred in the original short-story.) Shortly afterward, Gloria makes the explicit declaration: "This motion picture business is a lousy business. . . . I'm glad I'm through with it." The irony is, of course, pathetic. At this point in his narration, Robert, standing in the courtroom listening to the closing phrases of his death sentence, thinks, "*I never paid any attention to her remark then, but now I realize it was the most significant thing she had ever said.*" In the night, out on the pier, Gloria looks "down at the ocean toward Malibu," where, as Robert has pointed out a moment before, "all the movie stars live": "Oh, what's the use in me kidding myself—," she says. "I know where I stand."

"The embodiment of the outcast, unemployed and unemployable, miserable, cynical, foul-mouthed, without faith in anything or anybody, very nearly worthless"—as the *TLS* reviewer characterized Gloria—she is nonetheless "to some small extent redeemed by honesty and pitiless self-knowledge." And also by a lucidity denied to her bemused partner: Robert, looking at the same distant lights of Malibu, still can only think about Hollywood, "wondering if I'd ever been there or was I going to wake up in a minute back in Arkansas." Though near the end, he petulantly complains to Gloria that before meeting her he didn't see how he "could miss succeeding" and "never thought of failing," it is not simply by the sheer force of her passionate unhappiness that she is able to draw him into her fatal orbit. She is obviously no villain. A melodramatic or moralistic interpretation would have to ignore the details and nuances of the relationship between the protagonists, and consequently miss altogether the novel's telling psychological import. In this respect, the scant ten pages of chapter 3—the beginning of the narrative proper —are critical to an understanding of how Gloria is able to exercise such mastery over Robert, and how *They Shoot Horses, Don't They?* expresses a universal human dilemma.

Robert begins, "It was funny the way I met Gloria." The vernacular idiom not only pegs his social caste and suggests the limitations of his comprehension, but also strikes a note of mordant humor which counterpoints his essentially grim narrative throughout, down to its final line, "They shoot horses, don't they?" Gloria accidentally runs into his life in a sardonic burlesque of a *Saturday Evening Post* or *Collier's* story opening—on a streetcorner in Hollywood, yet—swearing at a missed bus and interrupting his childish daydreaming of riding in a Rolls Royce, "the greatest director in the world." The blending of stark realism and grotesque drollery produces an ironic tension which is almost Kafkaesque—as do other features of this nightmare story told by a confused man on trial for "trying to do somebody a favor." "How it all started . . . seems very strange" to Robert, and he can't "understand at all" as he stands and waits for the judge to sentence him to death. Good-natured and basically decent, he is also a fool (in the Jamesian sense) whose constant muddlement promotes a "comicality"—but, in this case, of a distinctly modern distemper.

The morning Robert meets Gloria he isn't "feeling very well" and is "still a little sick" from intestinal flu, which had made him "so weak" he had had "to crawl." Images of sickness and physical disorders quite naturally arise throughout the story and function on many levels, especially those tied to Robert. In more ways than one he is weak and susceptible to contagion. About Gloria there is, almost literally, a faint odor of corruption. In an early rough draft of chapter 3 McCoy had Gloria describe a "laughable" fact concerning her sexual history ("I've never been laid on a bed in my life, . . ."), and Robert "began to feel a little like heaving" while at the same time fascinated enough to think of her as being like "an unpleasant odor that was very interesting" (Typescript held by author). The degradation of her past life and circumstances have inoculated her irremediably with a moral taint as contagious as a disease. Significantly, she tells Robert how she had gotten "the idea of coming to Hollywood . . . from the movie magazines" while recuperating in a hospital from an attempt at suicide by poison. He doesn't say so directly, but we gather that his naive ambitions had been "poisoned" back on the farm in Arkansas from much the same source. Both of them are sick, so to speak, with the same disease and suffer the common hallucinatory hope of "discovery" in Hollywood.

The central scene of the third chapter takes place at night in a stage-like setting of a small, secluded park where Robert takes Gloria to sit and talk. In a few pages of dramatic exposition, mainly dialogue, the two unemployed extras confide in each other with that queer, precipitant intimacy which so often transpires between chance acquaintances who are lonely and share a common predicament. Compact in the extreme, the episode moves naturally, but at one and the same time directly and indirectly, to introduce the characters and to establish the pattern and tone of their relationship. Dramatically this is Robert's big scene—or, more significantly, it *should* be. Armed with money "made squirting soda in a drug store" for a friend who "had got a girl in a jam" and had to take her out of town "for the operation," Robert diffidently asks Gloria "if she'd rather go to a movie or sit in the park." Directly and decisively she takes command: "I got a bellyful of moving pictures. . . . If I'm not a better actress than most of those dames I'll eat your hat—Let's go sit and hate a bunch of people." She dominates the ensuing conversation, and we hear most about her background and what she thinks—about Hollywood in particular and life in general. Since Robert is the narrator, we discover his character by indirection and apposition; and since he is a hypersensitive and dreamy fellow, it is doubly appropriate that we learn most about him through his heightened and emotional internal responses to events, actions and, in particular, his surroundings.

Unaffected by Gloria's caustic outburst, Robert is only "glad she wanted to go to the park." This "very dark and very quiet" place "filled with dense shrubbery" and surrounded by tall palm trees gives him "the illusion of security." He imagines the palms are "sentries wearing grotesque helmets: my own private sentries, standing guard over my own private island." For him the park is a regenerative oasis in a desert of hard knocks and fading mirages, to which he retreats "three or four times a week" to fantasize: "Through the palms you could see many buildings, the thick, square silhouettes of apartment houses, with their red signs on the roofs, reddening the sky above and everything and everybody below. But if you wanted to get rid of these things you had only to sit and stare at them with a fixed gaze . . . and they would begin receding." Gloria, looking at the same "red, vaporish glow," recalls that West Texas, where she comes from, is "a hell of a place." Unable, like Robert, to stare reality out of countenance, she leads him out of his private square-block Eden into the hell of "an enormous old building that once had been a public dance hall . . . built out over the ocean."

Interestingly enough, the characterizations of both Robert and Gloria in the short-story version were more "round" (e.g., in the park, he speaks of failure; she smiles often and says the park is "lovely"); they seemed more like people in real life—inconsistent and often, perhaps paradoxically, less interesting. Given the objective manner and dramatic structure in which McCoy chose to write his novel, he inevitably was forced to delineate his characters in bold, theatrical strokes. Gloria, in particular, is "fore-shortened" (in Henry James's phraseology) "to within an inch of her life"; but few readers, I think, would deny that she is thoroughly alive and memorable. McCoy avoids caricaturizing either protagonist by maintaining an "exquisite chemical adjustment" of the psychological affinities which inexorably draw these two dispossessed people together into a tragic, almost sado-masochistic, trap. Though their personalities differ, we sense that fundamentally they have more in common than their social and geographical origins and bad luck in Hollywood. Given their individual limitations of intelligence and sensibility, Robert's self-centered enthusiasm and Gloria's inverted egotism effectively block any chance of mutual insight or understanding—until after it is too late. When next these two sit and talk together at night, looking at distant lights, external forces of degradation will have eroded away all vestiges of balance and control.

Years before, in one of his earliest published short stories, McCoy first crudely dramatized the familiar notion of the divided personality that was to inform so much of his subsequent fiction. In *They Shoot Horses, Don't They?* the characterizations of Robert and Gloria, taken together, reveal a dramatic particularization of the common dilemma of young and naive ambition up against a frustrating, hobbling, and even destructive world in which the truths of existence run contrary to all logic, morality, and dreams. As previously noted, despite the inescapable theatricalness and sensationalism of locale and setting— which are to the very point of the story—McCoy has not written a simplistic melodrama. Robert and Gloria— Couple No. 22 in the dance contest—are not antithetical types in a modern morality play. In the original short-story version, Robert liked Gloria "because she talked to me the way I would talk to a boy if I were a girl." His obsessive ambition and her obsessive despair are opposite sides of the same overvalued coin.

If, as Van Nostrand says, "fiction is the fashioning of an occasion appropriate to one's deepest need, which is to justify oneself," then *They Shoot Horses, Don't They?* can be read as McCoy's first serious attempt to resolve the inner tensions of his own actions and ambitions in Hollywood. (In this and the following paragraph I have found Van Nostrand's general critical terminology useful.) Any fiction is, of course, "a bizarre exaggeration of mere actuality"; but the uniqueness and force of this book are in part due to the fact that the actualities of Hollywood and of a marathon dance are to begin with bizarre. However, because McCoy exercised such controlled and dispassionate objectivity, we are satisfied that these things could not have happened otherwise (given what we learn about the characters); and we recognize that their implicit meanings transcend the narrative. The necessity of inevitability which rules this novel resides to a great extent in the natures of the characters in conflict—i.e., if we accept the underlying divided-personality motif, in the nature of the conflict within a limited individual driven by an internal compulsion abetted by external corruption. As in any serious novel, the essence of *They Shoot Horses, Don't They?* lies "in the way it repeats and amplifies its substance to appraise it"; and in the way it "represents by metaphor, by analogy to things known," in particular by the metaphor of conflict which is held to be the substance of all narrative fiction.

We should not, of course, hold to any rigorous set of criteria for "the novel" in evaluating such a unique work as *They Shoot Horses, Don't They?* Lacking largeness and breadth, it falls within the dominant tradition of "the best American writing," which is characterized, as Malcolm Cowley has noted, "by narrowness and intensity." Like so many short contemporary American novels, it is more akin to a long short story, from which it derived. More properly, perhaps, we should call it a novelette. But more to the point is the degree to which McCoy develops his subject matter, within his self-imposed limits of size and form, into an intricate system of analogues. Close attention to certain patterns of images and arrangement of incidents reveals a "developing of involvement," that makes "the most of the least material."

For example, there is much to do about intimate man-woman relationships throughout the novel (but not in the short story version), especially the institution of marriage. From Robert's viewpoint, marriage seemingly would be Gloria's only salvation short of "discovery" (but she is, he says, "too blonde and too small and looked too old" for the films) —though, he assures Mrs. Layden, *he* is not going to marry Gloria "or anything like that." But her childhood environment and adult experiences and observations have long since conditioned her to fear and reject this natural solution: "I've thought about it plenty," she tells Robert. "But I couldn't ever marry the kind of man I want. The only kind that would marry me would be the kind I wouldn't have. A thief or a pimp or something." When the dance promoters offer the two a chance to be married in a public wedding—"it don't have to be permanent . . . it's just showmanship"—Gloria adamantly refuses.

All the variations on the motif of marriage culminate in the travesty of the public wedding in the climactic penultimate chapter. This grotesque scene is a dramatic nexus in which the various themes of the novel are self-reflexively appraised: "The entire hall had been decorated with so many flags and so much red, white and blue bunting that you expected any moment to hear firecrackers go off and the band play the national anthem." To the howling, sellout crowd, the master of ceremonies announces: "Remember, the entertainment for the night is not over when the marriage is finished. That's only the beginnin' . . . After the wedding we have the derby——." Before the grand march of the contestants—who have been costumed in rented tuxedos and dresses—begins, the local merchants "who have made this feature possible" are introduced in the same tedious Academy Awards manner used in previous episodes for visiting Hollywood celebrities. The wedding-ceremony finale to this sordid, almost surrealistic parody of a Busby Berkeley musical-comedy film is performed by the Reverend Oscar Gilder.

> "——And I now pronounce you man and wife——"
> Dr. Gilder said. He bowed his head and began to pray:
> *The Lord is my shepherd . . .*

Set all in italics, the Twenty-third Psalm at this moment in the narrative reminds us that Robert, standing in court, has just heard the judge pronounce sentence of death. This funereal hymn would be blatantly inappropriate, of course, to any real wedding ceremony (except, perhaps, at a marathon dance near Hollywood), but in the context of the novel it is a brilliant stroke of indirect commentary, structural fusion, and ironic mood music. As the minister finishes the prayer, a gunfight breaks out in the dance-hall's beer garden ("the Palm Garden") and Mrs. Layden—the epitome of the perverted audience—is shot in the head by a stray bullet. Looking upon the dead body, Gloria says under her breath, "I wish it was me——." In an "afterword" to the most recent edition of *They Shoot Horses, Don't They?* (Avon, 1966), Robert M. Coates found himself concerned over "the tendency to equate" McCoy's first novel with Nathanael West's *Miss Lonely-hearts* (1933), "though the outlook of both was thoroughly pessimistic, West's approach was basically and deeply poetic, while McCoy's was stringently matter-of-fact throughout." I would agree that McCoy can not be superficially equated with West (though this has never been done "so often" as Coates suggested)—or, for that matter, with any other contemporary American novelist. But if by a poetic approach is implied an attempt by a writer to express his most imaginative and intense perceptions of his world, himself, and the interrelationships of the two, then McCoy possessed a profoundly lyrical creative imagination. The deep strain of "symbolism" in *They Shoot Horses, Don't They?*—and not the hard-boiled surface—is its dominant aesthetic characteristic.

Surely, in his first novel Horace McCoy stepped out in new directions. Chandler once wrote of "little lost books . . . which are not perfect, evasive of the problem often, side-stepping scenes which should have been written . . . but somehow passing along crystalized, complete, and as such things go nowadays eternal, a little pure art." [8] In the long run, the atmospheric intensity and inevitable fatality of *They Shoot Horses, Don't They?* speak more convincingly for McCoy's artistry than any amount of categorizing or close analysis. With bold originality and a high degree of literary skill, he imbued his story with the bitter and disquieted mood from which he wrote, creating one of the most original works of contemporary American fiction.

Beyond any conscious intention and artistic control—with the power of intuition that always distinguishes an original creative imagination—McCoy's handling of his story's unique setting and *in extremis* resolution projected it beyond the social and ethical preoccupations of its time and place. Much more than a documentary of a grisly symptom of the early years of this country's Great Depression, more than an objective correlative of the world of Hollywood's extras, McCoy's marathon *danse macabre* has become an universally applicable parable of modern man's existential predicament. Its grotesque and morbid fantasia has echoed with meaning through the literal and spiritual undergrounds of the past quarter-century—among the existentialists of occupied France, the disaffiliated of postwar America. "There is but one truly serious philosophical problem," Camus argued in *The Myth of Sisyphus* (1942), "and that is suicide." Its corollary, he pointed out elsewhere, is the problem of killing others. It should no longer be difficult for American critics to understand how *They Shoot Horses, Don't They?* has received the serious attention of writers and intellectuals abroad, for both its literary techniques and implicit meanings. As Sartre explained twenty years ago: "What we looked for above all else in the American novel was something quite different from its crudities and its violence."

Focus on *You Play the Black and the Red Comes Up:* "No Bet"

E. R. HAGEMANN

> "Leave it on the red," I said. There was thirty-two hundred dollars there. I didn't know what to do.
>
> "No bet," the man said. They didn't start the wheel.
> —*You Play the Black and the Red Comes Up*, Richard Hallas

NOT LONG AGO, I conducted a little field work. I spoke to a gambler about the Wheel, about roulette, that is. He was contemptuous. "It's a sucker's game. You know, you bet even money, say on the colors, the red or the black; only you are not up against even money odds. There's the oh and the double-oh. You don't get paid there, neither."

"The chap I have in mind, call him Dick Dempsey, was playing a wheel that had a diamond also."

He looked bewildered. I explained.

"He's nuts. It's bad enough, a game like that, the house holding the edge at $5\frac{5}{19}$ per cent. You know, it's pure luck. Now, you got to have luck, but there's skill, too, in 21, or the dice, even the horses. With a diamond . . . The percentage . . . I don't know. The guy was nuts."

"Only luck?"

"Luck only, mister. The wheel's going one way, the ball the other. You're going to tell me there's something besides luck?"

He lit a good cigar. It didn't go with his Robert Hall suit. Maybe, I thought, luck was something he had not always had.

"This chap, Dick, was trying to lose."

The gambler looked at the floor in a kind of fury.

"Yeah, you *can* do that. But why was *he*?"

I didn't tell him Dick Dempsey had won $3200 in his game. That would have been too much. Rather, I told him to read a novel, *You Play the Black and the Red Comes Up*, by a man named Richard Hallas. I pushed it across the desk—bright red covers. Published back in April 1938. Thirty years ago. Only his name wasn't really Hallas. It was Eric Knight. I pointed to a novella on my shelves—we were in my study—*The Flying Yorkshireman* by Sam Small. Same writer. Same locale. Same year, 1938. He'd been around Hollywood as a screen writer. Been in the War. In the 1930's, the War was World War I. In the 1940's, the War was World War II, and Knight was killed in January 1943 in the Southwest Pacific. He was 46. He was a major and he had written one of the "smash" novels of the War, *This Above All*. Tyrone Power had been in the movie.

"Yeah," the gambler said, "I understand they gambled out on the Coast in the Thirties. I wasn't there. Vegas wasn't Vagas then. I'm only 45 myself. At my age, I need to read a book about losing? You play the black—you play the wheel—and, mister, the red does come up. You know what I mean?"

His Robert Hall suit (right off the racks) bunched around the collar of a good shirt. I walked with him to his car. A 1963 Comet. "Not splashy, you know. It runs. It's mine."

He drove away. It wasn't a Bugatti—and Dick Dempsey—which isn't the hero's real name in *You Play the Black* (but he looked like the Champ)—once owned a Bugatti; maybe it was blue, maybe it was a Type 37A. Dick didn't say. After he had won on the wheel, he bought it for $500 cash. That was a lot of money, in the Depression, to spend on a car. But he loved *good* motor cars. And a Bugatti was the best there was. Only one problem: he never drove it.

In 1938, one of the cavils of the critics was that Hallas (Knight) was parodying the hard-boiled school and style. The reviewer for the *Springfield Republican* said that "the reader is likely to feel the work would have been better as burlesque." And J. Fenwick, in *The New York Herald-Tribune Books*, said, "this is a phony, but it is a pretty slick job. . . . James Thurber, himself, couldn't have done a better parody. . . . After it is all over you feel sort of disgusted with yourself for having strung along with him." This is demonstrably incorrect, for Hallas (Knight) was too good a writer, too much a talented observer, to waste his efforts on such as that. Parody can be awfully cute, awfully cheap. No, *You Play the Black and the Red Comes Up* is a carefully written novel; but more important, it is a carefully structured novel, too. And in structure there is meaning—for the careful reader.

The key to the novel's meaning and action is chapter 12, where Dick bucks the wheel with the diamond. As a matter of record, it is not exactly a wheel, but an arrangement of lights. He knows the odds and he spells them out very carefully, 7 to 6 against him, and he decides to play the colors. He must lose the money. His *modus operandi* is most important. He loses, almost idly, $200 in $5 chips. He takes another $100 (we'll begin here) and plays the red five times and the black comes up five times. He's lost $300. He buys another $100 in chips and plays black. He wins, and he wins the next four spins, ten in all for black. Dick has $1600. He switches to red on his eleventh bet. He wins. He has $3200. The house won't cover his twelfth bet. But he has almost $4000 when he gets home to his apartment.

There are twelve "bets" in the novel, i.e., chapter-groupings concerning an action (or actions) in which Dick bucks the odds, not, it is true, in the same win-lose chronology as his twelve bets in Mannie Gottstein's place on the beach, but nevertheless pertinent to the red-and-black, or seeming even money, motif. Essentially an honest and decent, not-too-bright young man, his desertion from the Marines notwithstanding, Dick Dempsey is in the tradition of the flawed rogue-hero often encountered in hard-boiled literature, a tradition, unbelievably enough, that can be traced back to as unlikely a character as Miles Coverdale in *The Blithedale Romance*.

These twelve bets, or actions, are framed neatly by the

first and last chapters (there are 50): Dick either entering or departing Los Angeles, riding the freight trains, and crossing the mountains. Quentin Genter (we will meet him later) once commented on those mountains: "You can bring men from other parts of the world who are sane. And you know what happens? At the very moment they cross those mountains . . . they go mad. Instantaneously and automatically, at the very moment they cross the mountains into California, they go insane." He has a point—he, himself, illustrates it.

Now, I have said that Dick loved good motor cars. Well, he loved a woman, too, in Oklahoma, and this started him off one night when he came home from work at the zinc smelter and found Lois and Dickie, their son, gone from the restaurant they ran on the side. He hopped the local freight. So much right now for the frame.

The first bet (chapters 2–3) is a pretty good one on the surface of things. After beating it into L.A., he can find the address where he expects Lois to be staying. Only thing is, she's now living on Las Olas (The Waves) in San Diego. It's still a good bet as Dick thumbs a ride south on U.S. 101, until a real three-dollar bill, Quentin Genter (not quite a gender), movie director, picks him up and thus becomes the o and o–o in the game. Dick finds Lois in Dago, but he raises so much hell trying to break into 137¾ Las Olas, she calls the cops. Dick barely evades them. Does he come up winner? It's a fact he doesn't have his son, Dickie; on the other hand, it's a fact the cops don't have Dick. Call him winner.

He beats it back through San Pedro and into a beach town (Redondo? Hermosa?) where the second bet is laid out (chapters 4–5). Maurice Gottstein plans a phony hold-up. He'll deal Dick in for $10.

> "I've got it all figured. You stop me, see, take the bag. Then you run. I'll give you lots of chance to get a good start. Then I'll yell."
> "And what do you get out of it if I get the money?"
> "I've got that figured out. I'll show you a garden where I want you to throw the money."

He seems to have it all worked out "to perfection." Dick takes the $10, eats on it, and goes through with the caper. It looks like even money, but the cops kill Gottstein and Dick flings the hold-up bag into an acacia tree. He doesn't lose here either, for there are two floozies, Mamie Block and Patsy Perisho, to drink beer with; and he escapes the cops again. They arrest Hernandez Felice for Dick's crime. Dick is a peculiar guy—he likes Mexes.

When you run into floozies as he does, both drawing $50 a week alimony, who love beer, and who're from Jersey, a guy on the lam is naturally going "to hang around." He lives with Mamie. With some instantaneous help from Genter, Patsy gets moving one of those outlandish Southern California political movements. The Ecanaanomic Party, Genter christens it. It looks like a good bet. As Patsy says: "All you do is give everyone five dollars the first week, on condition they've got to spend it within a week. Then the next week you give them six dollars each. And each week you give them a dollar more than last week." This is the day of EPIC (End Poverty in California), Upton Sinclair, I, Candidate for Governor, and Dr. Francis E. Townsend's plan of a $200-a-month pension for every person over 60. Nathanael West was in town, writing scripts for Republic studios, and contemplating the Day of the Locust. Genter sums it all up: "It's Armageddon." Dick recovers the hold-up money ($1380) and is about to send it to the cops when they release Felice. Dick cuts the bag into strips and flushes them down the toilet. Then, in chapter 12, he tries desperately to lose the money in Gottstein's beach joint. After all, it's better than even money he'll lose. It's his fourth bet (chapters 9–13); he cannot seem to lose.

On his next bet (chapters 14–17), it's money, money; there's $500 for the Bugatti, a grand to the Party, a white fur coat for Mamie. They live high, and they get "married" in the garden of Genter's Hollywood mansion. Suddenly the money's gone. He takes a job running a "shoot-the-chute" concession in the beachtown after his new friend, Al Smith, ex-gob, goes back home to Iowa. "It was something to do, and it got me away from hanging round the apartment and listening to Mamie."

Very neat. He is midway. He's made his sixth bet. Yet, he hasn't been betting seriously, except there at Gottstein's; he has been refining his *modus operandi*. Then one night Dick rescues out of the sea the mad and lethal Sheila Devon. She comes from nowhere; she lives nowhere, truly. She is really only camping out in Palos Verdes. He sees her again and she's in a Packard roadster, and that's a good motor car. She *is* a serious bet. Dick makes his play in the midst of some pretty funny business concerning the Ecanaanomic Party which is delightful in its evocation of the Great Unwashed loose in Southern California in the 1930's. Sheila's weird, she's strange, she's unearthly. Briefly: she bolsters Genter's "Armageddon" generalization. The chips are piling up. A question: Are they all Dick's?

They are for the nonce. Smitty's returned. There's a long flashback: Dick's sharecropper-bindlestiff background and his old man's death at the hands of the cattlemen who hold the water rights. Retrospection is momentary, Dick being unable to stop thinking about Sheila. Hallas handles this flashback quite well and thereby avoids the cynicism which V. S. Pritchett charges is necessary in hard-boiled novels (*New Statesman and Nation*, February 19, 1938). They play and play, in Malibu, or down in Palos Verdes, or by the mission in the San Fernando Valley which was so beautiful before it was spoiled. Then in a dirty tourist cabin, this side of Bakersfield, he has her for the night. She is a *woman*. He swears he will never see her again, and he tries honestly to tell her so, but she plays Debussy for him. Her name is derived from St. Cecilia; but it's only a derivation. She's named Sheila and you don't hedge a bet like her. Put it another way: Dick's *modus operandi* is now a *modus vivendi*.

She is a *woman* and she proves it soon enough: she's pregnant. Get rid of Mamie; the trouble is, she knows of the phony hold-up. A plumber found the strips. Her threat is not subtle. Get rid of Mamie, anyway. Genter helps: "You, A, love Sheila, B, but are barred from the goal by Mamie, C. How can you remove C from the [plot] structure?" Dick's not stupid. This is a real bet. And it's murder.

He plays the bet (chapters 36–42) desperately, comically. He tries drowning her off Avalon on Catalina. Turns out she's a champ swimmer. He pinches some arsenic from Genter's chamber of horrors and dumps it in Mamie's Scotch. She's a champ here, too. Absolutely no effect on her. Up on the platform, above the chute, where Dick and Smitty spend their time, he loosens a bolt that braces the guard rail. Happens that Mamie is not killed. Sheila is. And the cops grab Dick when he struggles to see her; they say he is trying to escape. If Genter was the o and o–o on the wheel, then surely Sheila was the diamond.

The cops sweat Dick, but he won't crack. The Ecanaanomic Party backs his defense with $3000. It's a murder rap—Sheila not Mamie. The state has everything locked up. "I tell you, all I could think of was Sheila and I hoped they would kill me. I didn't care." The DA's address to the jury "all sounded so perfect," it seemed foolish to go on trial. Recall that at Mannie Gottstein's, Dick had switched suddenly from black to red, hoping to lose. That was his eleventh bet and structurally in the novel we're in the eleventh bet (chapters 43–45). The state convicts him and sentences him to the noose. Winner or loser? Depends on how one reads the story—thus far.

Dick is on Death Row and Genter, more strange and perverted than ever, less a gender than ever, visits him and mumbles, "*Mea maxima culpa*," mumbles that he has never loved anyone. The rest of the world is "a movie." He subsequently commits suicide and leaves "a full confession" of Sheila's murder; in a technical sense, he was guilty, for he had egged on Dick to "remove" Mamie. Dick is given a reprieve, then freed, and at a hearing, Genter is declared guilty. Eleventh bet was a bad one. He's "won" after all. He can't lose. He has one bet left him. He goes to the police and gives himself up for "the murder of Mamie Block." This is his $3200-play, but he gets the same treatment: no one will cover his bet. No one believes his story; everyone laughs. He dredges up the hold-up, bigamy, his desertion from the Marines. Laughter. They simply won't cover him. "All of a sudden I was sick crazy just to see Sheila's face."

And we're back to the frame. He has loved a woman in California and he hits the rods again, this time out of L.A. There is a really fine (granted, specialized) evocation of the city founded, in 1781, as "El Pueblo de Nuestra Señora de Los Angeles de Porciúncula." But running away is no good. "Because Sheila was gone with everything else." I've spoken of Dick's *modus vivendi*. It has been a temporary arrangement, at best, pending a settlement of matters. Dick had tried to settle with his final bet. They weren't having any of it. Very well. He throws himself off the moving freight and kills himself. There's some mystical business in the final pages; however, he's dead, and in the end, he must cross a desert before he can reach his beloved "golden mountains."

"*Vaya con Dios,*" says a very old Mexican peon.

Raymond Chandler
From Bloomsbury to the Jungle —
and Beyond

HERBERT RUHM

RAYMOND CHANDLER, who followed Dashiell Hammett and other *Black Mask* writers in perfecting the hard-boiled mystery, thought that he had only refined the form of the mystery which "had been pretty well exhausted" when he came to it. It was his pride that he had taken this tired old genre, had extended it, and "had made something like literature" out of it. In his fifth book, he had written a realistic novel with a murder or two in it, and in the four chapters of his last one, which he had completed at the time of his death in 1959, he had begun to write the mystery as the novel of manners. It thus seems an ambiguous accolade that in the last year of his life he had been elected President of the Mystery Writers League of America, but one accolade more than any other group in America had given him. Chandler's achievements are impressive: he mastered the American style—a combination (as he defined it) of idiom, slang, wise-crack, hyperbole and tough talk that in the hands of a man of genius can be made to do anything; he had a view of the world more serious and more valid than a good many craftsmen working in a more respected genre; he invented a hero, Philip Marlowe, who has been called a "great creation"; he expressed his vision with wit and vigor, though occasionally with sentimentality; he is indisputably the best writer about urban California, and he wrote the best novel about Hollywood. But all these achievements seem somehow not enough to overcome the fact that he realized them while working in the mystery genre. This fact has kept him out of any serious literary discussion, a silence which even some honorable exceptions (Richard Schickel, George P. Elliott, Auden, Maugham) have not broken.

He came to the form late. He was forty-five when he published his first novel. He died twenty years later, as successful a writer in the form as there had ever been, who had so far perfected and extended it that Somerset Maugham did not see how, or where, beyond Chandler the mystery novel could go. Chandler knew quite well what he had set out to do, and what he had done.

> All I wanted to do when I began writing was to play with a fascinating new language, to see what it could do as a means of expression which might remain on the level of unintellectual thinking and yet acquire the power to say things which are usually only said with a literary air. I didn't really care what kind of story I wrote; I wrote melodrama because when I looked around me it was the only kind of writing I saw that was relatively honest and yet was not trying to put over somebody's party line. So now there are guys talking about prose and other guys telling me I have a social conscience. P. Marlowe has as much social conscience as a horse. He has a personal conscience, which is an entirely different matter.

Notably this master of the American idiom was educated in England. Born on July 23, 1888, in Chicago of parents who were Quakers on both sides—Anglo-Irish and Colonial on his mother's, and of old Pennsylvania stock on his father's—the boy spent his summers with his father's relatives in Nebraska: "I remember the oak trees and the high wooden sidewalks beside the dirt roads and the heat and the fireflies and the 'walkingsticks' and a lot of strange insects and the gathering of wild grapes in the fall to make wine and the dead cattle and once in a while a dead man floating down the muddy river and the dandy little three-hole privy behind the house. I remember the rocking chairs on the edge of the sidewalk in a solid row outside the hotel and the tobacco spit all over the place." Eight years old at his mother's divorce, the boy returned with her to England (he never saw his father again), and entered Dulwich College "not quite on a level with Eton and Harrow" socially, "but very good educationally." He completed both the modern and the classical sides at seventeen, and continued his education the next year in France and Germany. His wealthy uncle, a solicitor, wanted him to study law, but Chandler, though he had shown no particular literary gift in school, wanted to be a writer. As a compromise, Chandler took a Civil Service exam, passed it brilliantly, and received an appointment in the Admiralty. But he found his job so boring that he resigned after six months. He next holed up in Blooms-bury, and for four years contributed sketches, verse, and anonymous paragraphs to highbrow weeklies like the *Spectator* and Lord Alfred Douglas' *The Academy*, and to dailies like the *Westminster Gazette*. He could have become a pretty fair poet, he estimated later, "but that means nothing because I have the type of mind that can become a pretty good second-rate anything." He borrowed five hundred pounds from his uncle—repaid in full with six percent interest—and sailed for the United States. He was twenty-three.

He did not quite know why he chose to return to America. He did not feel American. He did not feel English. He liked Paris but did not like the French; he liked the South Germans but knew that soon England would be at war. But as opposed to the stuffiness of the British, he liked the Americans' liveliness and bounce. In 1912 he arrived in California, and in 1914 enlisted in the Canadian Gordon Highlanders, transferring to the First Canadian Expeditionary Corps because the Corps paid a dependency allowance to his mother, who had remained in England. Chandler served in France. He was taking flight-training in what was to become the R.A.F. when the Armistice came.

Discharged in England, he returned in 1919 to California. This time his mother was with him, and he lived with her until her death in 1924. Chandler was then thirty-seven. He taught himself bookkeeping, completing a three-year course in six weeks. But his rise in business was "as rapid as the growth of a sequoia"; in some ten years, Chandler had become an officer or director in half a dozen independent oil corporations. But by 1932, in the depth of the Depression, "all that was finished," and he now began his second career as a writer. "Wandering up and down the Pacific Coast in an automobile, I began to read pulp magazines. . . . This was in the great days of *Black Mask*, and it struck me that some of the writing was pretty forceful and honest, even though it had its crude aspects." He spent five months on an 18,000 word novelette, "Black-mailers Don't Shoot," sold it to *Black Mask* for $180.00, and thereafter he "never looked back." He wrote *The Big Sleep* (he coined this synonym for death), his first novel, in three months. All told, he published some twenty short stories in *Black Mask*, and its various detective magazine successors, and one slick story. He also wrote one or two tales of fantasy; he wanted to write enough such tales to make a book, for he felt that he had been exhausting the form of the mystery. He also published three essays on Hollywood, based on his experiences as a script-writer from 1943 to 1946. In 1945, he wrote his very important essay on the detective story, "The Simple Art of Murder," which is crucial for his survey of the weaknesses of the traditional detective story—it is weak because it is unrealis-tic—and for his evaluation of the work of Hammett, whom he credits with inventing the hard-boiled mystery, but faults for omitting the element of redemption.

Of his seven novels, two are masterpieces—*Farewell, My Lovely* (1940) and *The Little Sister* (1949); *The High Window* (1942) is a failure. His last completed novel *Playback* (1958) is only as good as a novel can be that is based on a work done in another medium—in this case, an unproduced screen-play Chandler had written in 1947 for Universal. In addition to acquiring the Holly-wood background for his three essays as well as for *The*

Little Sister—the three central chapters are an acknowledged "comic masterpiece"—Chandler also initiated in Hollywood the high-budget hard-boiled mystery by writing with Billy Wilder the screenplay for *Double Indemnity*.

At the death of his mother in 1924, Chandler immediately married Pearl Cecily Bowen Pascal (née Hurlburt, in Perry, Ohio, in 1871). Twice divorced and fifteen years older than he, she was for him, he wrote later, "the beat of my heart, the music heard faintly at the edge of sound." Understandably, her death thirty years later affected his fiction and his life. Chandler's hero, Philip Marlowe, and the characters in popular and literary fiction to whom the detective has been related had hitherto lived their lives alone, in retreat from civilization and women, who exert a corrupting influence on them; but after "Cissy's" death, Chandler married Marlowe off; and he himself attempted suicide. Obviously overdramatizing, and drinking more than usual, he shot off a gun in his bath-tub a few months after "Cissy's" death, and was found still sitting in the tub with the gun in his lap, laughing his fool head off. "I cannot for the life of me tell you whether I intended to go through with it." Within a few months, Chandler had sold their La Jolla home, and for the remaining years of his life, he wandered through New York, California, and England. In England, he was lionized as a serious novelist by the likes of Cyril Connolly and Stephen Spender. He had been seriously reviewed by Elizabeth Bowen, and now he was equally pleased as strangers introduced themselves to him at his hotel, shook his hand, and told him how much they had enjoyed his books. "A writer of the detective story, if he is any good, is as highly regarded here as the good writer of anything else." He died in La Jolla on March 26, 1959. In 1950, he had written to his English publisher, Hamish Hamilton: "I am supposed to be a hard-boiled writer, but that means nothing. It is merely a method of projection. Personally I am sensitive and even diffident. At times I am extremely caustic and pugnacious; at other times very sentimental." This description also fits

Philip Marlowe, whom he has described as a projection of himself, as well as "a fantasy and an exaggeration, but at least an exaggeration of the possible." (Source of material quoted above is *Raymond Chandler Speaking*, ed. Dorothy Gardiner and Kathrine Sorley Walker, Boston: Houghton Mifflin, 1962.)

Philip Marlowe (detective, sleuth, gum-shoe, private eye, private investigator, PI—take your pick) grew out of the pulps, especially *Black Mask*, in which the hard-boiled detective story was being perfected. Chandler has called Marlowe a fantasy, "an exaggeration, but at least an exaggeration of the possible." He's a "great creation," according to Richard Schickel. H. B. Parkes has traced his descent from other figures of popular American and literary culture, heroes who fled into the wilderness to escape the corrupting influences of civilization, figures like the trapper and the cowboy, and heroes such as Leatherstocking, Ishmael, Huck Finn, Nick Adams, who could still associate innocence and Nature. But Marlowe, like Hammett's recurrent hero, the Continental Op, is among the first urban heroes in that tradition. For both, the frontier is closed, the identification of nature and innocence is no longer possible; but while Hammett's Continental Op worked within an organization, and cooperated with the police, Marlowe, a decade later, finds no one to trust; the police are both reflections and victims of a corrupt society, and of the powers within it or without—the man of wealth, or the gangster—who manipulate it. For the Continental Op, his work is no more than a job; but for Marlowe, his work is a defense of people and values that can be related to Chandler's own traditional and orthodox background and education in the Anglo-Irish family and the English public school system. Thus the paradox of the mastery of the American language, with a hero in the tradition of the American folk-hero exposing the corruption of American urban society and defending essentially conservative values.

No other hero—certainly not Hammett's—is so all-knowing and competent as Marlowe, so innately good and contemptuous of sham and of phoniness, or is so alone. Marlowe is a "most wised-up guy," as George P. Elliott put it. In all the novels, Marlowe ranges the gamut of his society, from the poorest to the richest, from flop-houses to millionaire's mansions and the palatial offices of talent agents. He is, in his range, like Inspector Bucket of Dickens's *Bleak House*, who moves from Tom, the crossings-sweeper, to Sir Leicester and Lady Dedlock, the aristocrats; but law and Inspector Bucket, the representative of that law, are one, while in Chandler, the law and its representatives are corrupt, and law and Marlowe are at odds. Cities, Chandler has pointed out, are ruled by gangsters; movie stars are the finger for mobs and the girl friends of mobsters; and the truth in the newspapers is what its millionaire-owners allow to be printed—which is certainly not the truth that Marlowe, and Marlowe alone, finds.

In his search for the truth that solves the crime, Marlowe has to fight corrupt law as well as the corrupt society it reflects. While for the Leatherstocking, society was thought only to be corrupting, for his descendant, society is literally corrupt; while Leatherstocking, like Ishmael and Huck Finn fled to avoid personal corruption, fled to the frontier or past it into the farther, uncorrupted wilderness, Marlowe finds no escape. The frontier is closed. Marlowe remains honest, poor, lonely, single (until Chandler's very last and unfinished book—of which more later); he takes terrific beatings; he is slugged, shot at, doped, strangled; he is tempted; yet he survives because it is in his nature as a catalyst to survive. Like Hemingway's heroes, who think only to write, he prefers to think only in the course of duty, only to solve a crime; he plays chess, but only to solve a puzzle. But while Chandler's hero does not think, he has character, and he responds to character in others. He knows and understands character; he makes distinctions between people; he responds to their moral qualities and is himself moral; he believes in truth, and justice, and honesty and fidelity, and he will go to any length to protect those in whom he sees these qualities, usually the aged (with some important exceptions). Just so, he responds to the qualities of the city; and just so, Chandler gives a richness and fullness to his style. There are all gradations of class and milieu and speech and diction in Chandler's novels. For these reasons, Chandler, through Marlowe, succeeds as no one else has succeeded in portraying Los Angeles, including Hollywood, and it seems at times that it is neither the violence nor the solution of the mystery Chandler is interested in as it is the city and the people, through the whole range of which, in the solution of the crime, Marlowe moves.

Yet Marlowe, though heroic, tough, and wise, is a sad character. For all the personal life he has and the people he can trust, he might as well be in the wilderness. He is a lonely figure, a man without personal life. Marlowe's adventures end in his return to the "blank wall in a meaningless room in a meaningless house," wherever his home may be that year in urban Los Angeles, or to his shabby office (he has no secretary) with his dust and flies and occasional spot of sunshine and telephone, which usually brings him a call for help as misleading to begin with as the mystery he then sets about to investigate. The mail usually brings him nothing, or only appeals from men as lonely as himself. Marlowe stays alone by choice, guarding his incorruptibility by his aloneness, and in part symbolically, as a measure of his uniqueness. His adventures consist of forays and he returns unchanged, his adventures being *pittoresque* images of his corrupt society and time. His reflections are not puerile but neither are they stirring. They express either the anguish of his loneliness, or his disgust with the deterioration of his world. Emphasis is usually placed on the portrayal of Southern California, including Hollywood, and on the interrelation in this society between power and crime, and the unexpected relation of one segment to another, from the bottom (the little, helpless, incompetent, and hurt), to the top (usually, the ruthless, rich, and spoiled). Marlowe's adventures occur in a mean, nasty world, run by legitimate power, most often money power, that suppresses truth, or by gangsters and violence, that threaten Marlowe's search for truth. The tokens which express this world (the gigolo; the gorgeous blonde; the gangster and his number one hood; the corrupt cop and chief of police; the shady doctor; the very rich man and his two spoiled daughters) are fairly constant; they change only in their relation and their function, as emphasis changes among plot, pace, character, wit. In Marlowe's world, disunity, disruption, mobility, immorality, rootlessness and ruthlessness provide the constant motif. Marlowe himself is an old-fashioned character, chivalrous, with an individual sense of conduct and of justice; he judges his world, implicitly at least, from a point of view as conservative as Chandler's upper-class English education and his own cheerful admission that he was a snob would suggest.

Chandler finally resolved the problem of Marlowe's loneliness by marrying him off (in his last, unfinished novel, *The Poodle Springs Story*, the four chapters of which were published posthumously in *Raymond Chandler Speaking*), and by extending his genre into the novel of manners further than he had yet attempted. He turned his catalyst into a character, and set Marlowe in conflict with his millionairess wife, Linda Loring, and with the gangster, Lipshultz—personifications of legitimate and illegitimate powers, hitherto parcelled out in various social manifestations, that had opposed Marlowe in his search for truth and justice. Chandler didn't know to the end whether Marlowe should be married and whether he had picked the right girl—whether, that is, the conflict between her wealth and his integrity could be resolved. By allowing Marlowe to marry, however, Chandler had already gone beyond his hero's traditional solitary existence; and there is at least a suggestion that in this widest extension of his genre Chandler himself pessimistically studied the final improbability of his hero's redemptive capacities, if not of his world. From the stories of fantasy Chandler wanted to do next, Marlowe would in fact have been expunged.

To this situation, the turn from catalyst to character

had led. (Possibly, personal reasons contributed to this change, for Chandler married Marlowe off only after his wife's death.) Marlowe, who had begun as an anonymous narrator-hero in the short stories, had gradually, over the years, been turning into a character. In fact, in his last major novel, and in some ways his most ambitious, *The Long Goodbye* (1953), Chandler had written a novel of character, as well as the sort of novel which he had envisaged in 1949, "ostensibly a mystery and keeping the spice of mystery [which is] actually a novel of character and atmosphere with an overtone of violence and fear." Although it is not a success, this novel is worth looking at in some detail, because of its importance in the development of Marlowe.

In *The Long Goodbye* Chandler came closest to writing the mystery novel that isn't a mystery novel, the realistic novel with a couple of murders in which character is more important than anything, except style. Eileen Wade is as convincing a murderess as ever there was, yet that she commits both murders is relatively unimportant; that is subordinate to the book's study of conflicting loyalties and to the study of a second character, Terry Lennox. The father with the two daughters, one good, one bad, is repeated from Chandler's first novel, *The Big Sleep* (1939); again the younger is a tramp, and again the father has written her off; but while General Sternwood in the earlier novel, is very old, rich, and dying, and Marlowe, having solved the mystery he has been hired to solve, sets out to solve another to protect the general's sense of character and his illusions, Harlan Potter, very much richer, uses his power, which is a consequence of his wealth, only to protect his privacy, which Marlowe from his own sense of character and his loyalty is bound to violate. A couple of gangsters—power outside the law—want the lid kept on the Lennox case for their own reasons and out of their own sense of loyalty. The uses of power are now contrasted—legitimate wealth and its effect on political power, and the effect of that power on the police; and the gangster's wealth and his threat of violence. Both powers are corrupt, though one is outside and one inside the respected community, because both attempt to suppress the truth, which for his own loyalty Marlowe alone is interested in uncovering and does uncover. The only villain presented as a villain is the brutal police captain, Gregorius. As in *The Big Sleep*, the solution of *The Long Goodbye* is not entirely successful, because the solution stems from surprise not development, and because the villainess is ill rather than criminal. Marlowe's major motive is again sentimentality allied to loyalty in one part of the double plot-structure, but there is an improvement in that sentimental loyalty; the motive in the primary and enveloping plot is causally related to the novel's second group of episodes, in which Marlowe is called on to protect a lush who is a writer from homicidal and suicidal impulses. This part of the novel becomes a fairly realistic study of an upper-class L.A. group living in a restricted community called Idle Valley.

This further extension of the form affects the style. The realistic novel does not lend itself to hyperbole, wit, and wise-crack, to the humorous exaggeration of the usual; the style is tame in the more realistic series of episodes. (The problem does not exist in his incomplete novel of manners; on the contrary, as in the Restoration plays from which it derives, the novel of manners has always thrived on exaggeration, on contrast of speech, and style, and attitude.) On the other hand, Chandler is as vivid as usual with the circle of the gangster Menendez, the police, the newspapers. This division of style points to a similar break in the plot, between the story of Lennox, a "moral defeatist," and Roger Wade, a writer and a lush; the parallelism of the different uses of power is carried further: Terry Lennox is the link between the two camps of power, having been married to Harlan Potter's younger daughter, and having been a war-time comrade to Menendez.

The novel begins with the mystery of Terry Lennox, then moves to the mystery of Roger Wade, which is less interesting, though it is by far the longer sequence. It does not work to have a hero who is weak, whom, as one is told again and again, Marlowe does not think he can help, who cannot help himself, and who is not tragic. The connection between the two is Eileen Wade, once wife of one, now wife to the other; when she confesses to both murders and commits suicide, the interest is returned to Lennox, with whom the book ends. Lennox, then, a member of both worlds, is the crux, and Lennox, also a lush, is also weak. The flaw in the novel is that the important characters are either weak or insane (Eileen Wade), and the strong characters, Potter, Menendez, who oppose Marlowe's attempt to do justice to Lennox, are not seen often enough. Marlowe himself, confronted by a sentimental and a medical problem, is also not strong enough, though stronger on the first than on the second problem, which, however, occupies the greater part. The novel's conclusion, which reveals that Marlowe was "had" by Lennox's "beautiful manners," enlarges the character of Marlowe—but only to the point of an anecdote, and diminishes further the stature of the hero, Lennox, and with that the stature of the novel, which was essentially about him.

This is the farthest that Chandler had gotten with the character of Marlowe, as opposed to his catalytic function, until, in the unfinished *The Poodle Springs Story* he was to treat him as character in domestic conflict with wealth and in public conflict with unlawful power, with some suggestion that this conversion of convention into character would undermine the legitimacy of the convention. Marlowe as character would destroy Marlowe as function. With Marlowe's function destroyed, the mystery novel could indeed not go beyond Chandler; Maugham's guess would be confirmed.

But if in his last novel, Chandler had finally begun to question the very idea of his hero, whose validity he had hitherto assumed, in an earlier novel, Chandler had already indicated the limits of the mystery as mystery, by opposing to the ritual of the mystery novel—murder, suspicion, complication, solution—a much older ritual. *The Little Sister*, Chandler's best novel, is the true fruit of his

Hollywood years, and it is by far the most accurate of
Hollywood novels. But that is not all. To Chandler's
devastating view of Los Angeles, which is now focussed on
Hollywood, is added also a view of the Midwest, repre-
sented by Orfamay Quest, the bloody "little sister" from
Manhattan, Kansas.

Having as its heroine a rising starlet, and allowing Marlowe to range as usual over all of L.A. so as to show, also as
usual, the inter-connection and unity of its wickedness,
Chandler begins *The Little Sister* with the periphery of its
action set in the periphery of its locale (the western
outskirts of L.A., close to the ocean). Progressively, action
and setting move inland, ever closer to the center of the
conflict in Hollywood, especially to its three superb comic
scenes there: the scene in the agent's waiting-room; the
scene in the agent's office; and the scene in the studio lot.
The setting and the action gradually move from Santa
Monica, to West L.A., to Hollywood—from the search for
the starlet's brother in a shabby roominghouse in Santa
Monica (first murder); to the search for an all-important
photo in a cheap hotel in West L.A. (second murder); to
the agent's anteroom. In each case, before he can enter a
room, Marlowe has to overcome an obstacle: a hood with
an ice-pick; a corrupt hotel dick with a gun; a tough secretary in the anteroom, and an even tougher assistant to a
Hollywood agent; and, finally, the moral doubts of the
agent concerning Marlowe's integrity. In this way, the
kind of obstacle or danger also changes as Marlowe approaches Hollywood.

Having finally been hired by her agent to guard the
starlet from a blackmail threat (her boyfriend is a hood,
and a photo is the evidence of his identity), Marlowe
moves from the agent's office to the studio lot, meets the
studio boss, moves to the set and finally to the starlet's
dressing-room, and there to her first acknowledgment of
him. In this way, Marlowe has finally penetrated to the
sanctum sanctorum, the heart of Hollywood, the goal of
his quest.

Marlowe's progress has been similar to that other ritual,

wherein the hero, usually a knight (and Marlowe has been called a knight, as his client is called Quest—Orfamay Quest, suggesting both a quest and a fay), goes in search of a treasure (the original grail), or some extraordinary goal, and before he can reach it, must overcome certain obstacles, must pass certain tests, either of temptation or of danger. The tests I have narrated have been of danger; but there are also, as in the other ritual, obstacles of temptation in *The Little Sister*. They are in the form of another starlet, the Gonzales, the sexiest of all sexy women, who, tempting Marlowe, and resisted to the end by his incorruptibility and integrity, sets him on the way to the solution.

The Gonzales, it turns out, is the one who has killed the boyfriend of the starlet, his second client and the little sister's sister, and has killed the gangster's enemy, who is another gangster. But having been tempted, and having resisted all temptation, the path is clear. And as in the other ritual, he, too, is praised by the temptress in acknowledgment of his fortitude, chastity, and integrity. As the Gonzales says, when she does not kill him, too: "You, amigo, I have liked much!"

This inconspicuous redoing of an ancient ritual in criminal dress, with realistic detail, makes of *The Little Sister* the best of Hollywood novels. There is, at any rate, an enormous sense of satisfaction—more, of release—when Marlowe finally penetrates the office of the starlet's agent, an atavistic, ritualistic satisfaction; and in keeping with that identification, there is a self-satisfaction when the agent, acknowledging Marlowe's honesty, hires him to protect the damsel in distress.

That scene, however, and the two other great scenes at the heart of Hollywood are followed by a letdown, a consequence of this early penetration and recognition (we are no further than half way through the novel). The ritual is not carried through to the end; the search—the ritualistic search—is not rewarded at the end. Yet to enable Marlowe to continue to function, this early penetration had to occur, just as the solution had to wait until the end, as the nature of the form dictates. Here, if anywhere at all, the form defeats the art; here is the limit as art of Chandler's detective story, or, as Auden has called his fiction, studies of "the great wrong place."

Thus Chandler's continual experimentation with his genre had led him to study the possibility of the convention of his catalyst and of the strength of his plot. Turning his hero into a character had shown him the improbability of his hero, and counterpointing his ritual to a far older one had shown him the weaknesses of his plot. Beyond this, in his historical view of California—from a kind of paradise to the land of the chiseler, the shyster, the angle-boy—Chandler had also accurately studied (so George P. Elliott again testifies) the last frontier of continental America. He set an end to the fictional coverage of America, and provided America incidentally with a most devastating concluding image.

The Gangster Novel
The Urban Pastoral

GEORGE GRELLA

IN AN AGE when gangsters turn out to be prosperous gentlemen who head corporations, give generously to charity,
patronize the arts, elect politicians, and seldom get their
custom-made suits stained with blood, the professional
hoodlum of the thirties seems ludicrously anachronistic.
After all, the modern hoodlum, who looks pretty much
like everyone else, lives in a wealthy suburb, and sends his
daughter to Vassar, has very little in common with those
small, dark men in pinstriped suits who talk out of the
sides of their mouths, cruise the streets in long black
touring cars, and slay scores with their tommyguns. In
spite of the disparity between the contemporary criminal
and that quaint figure of the thirties, it is the figure of the
past, transformed into an archetype by fiction and films,
not the executive of the present, who strides into the mind
when the average American thinks of gangsters. Even in a
time when dope addiction, mugging, street rioting, and
mass murder seem to form the nocturnal amusement of a
disturbingly large segment of the population, the gangster
of the thirties remains a favorite image of malevolence; for
he—along with his cleancut counterpart, the cowboy—has
left the world of everyday reality and entered the magic
realm of myth. The stereotyped American gangster, fic-
tionalized in books like *Little Caesar* and realized on the
screen by precise and deadly men like Edward G. Robinson and James Cagney, has become yet another American

folk hero and contributed a sizable amount to what is often called the American Dream.

The gangster novel or movie, like the Western, has become a stylized and predictable form; like the Western, it has also influenced foreign fictional and cinematic talents—the French filmmakers of the New Wave, for example, admit their debt to the great American gangster movies. In America, however, the gangster novel reflects some basic cultural truths and speaks more to the American imagination than to the national aesthetic sense; in its own clumsy way, the gangster novel reflects some of the traditions of American fiction. Although one of the great directions in our country's fiction is Westward—escaping from the problems, complexities, and corruptions of civilization—there is also what may be called an Eastward movement too, a fascination not with Huck Finn's "territory," but with the meretricious beauty of the metropolis. The gangster novels, which in large part reflect some of the facts of life in the thirties, also announce the twentieth-century engagement with society and the city. If the Western exists at one subliterary pole of the American Dream, then the gangster novel inhabits the other. The literary currents flowing through the Leatherstocking novels, *Huckleberry Finn, Moby-Dick,* and the Western merge with those of Henry James' novels, *The Great Gatsby, What Makes Sammy Run?* and gangster fiction.

In this century, where the city first becomes a meaningful milieu for literature, the gangster becomes an important literary figure, appropriately symbolic of his environment and his era. Much like the cowboy, he inhabits an oddly pastoral world, and the gangster novel (like many American detective stories) seems a kind of urban pastoral. With his spacious, empty surroundings, his lonely, nomadic life, his close association with animals, his simple physical pleasures, the cowboy is a purely pastoral figure. The gangster, on the other hand, seems at first the direct antithesis of the cowboy—he lives in the crowded, manifold world of the city, never sees a beast larger or wilder than a cockroach, and copes with an unremittingly cruel and corrupt world. Yet the gangster shares some of the cowboy's pastoralism; he, too, is basically individualistic in a society where conformity to rules and traditions is the price for security. Like the cowboy, part of the gangster's appeal lies in his refusal to acknowledge the priority of social regulations. Again like the cowboy, the gangster is admired because he is a "natural," untutored, proud of his ignorance, responsive to the clear call of his instincts. He, too, lives by a code and a gun and inhabits a lower, and fundamentally, more corporeal level of existence. Finally, the gangster novel has a pastoral appeal: all its violence, excitement, and glamor exert their strongest pull on the reader who does not know firsthand the world of crime and corruption; the pastoral is not written, after all, for the shepherds but for those who have the leisure and education to indulge their fantasies in fiction. (The modern cowboy who reads Westerns and patterns himself after Gary Cooper, like the modern criminal who reads gangster fiction and emulates Cagney, represents yet another delightful example of Nature imitating Art.)

Since it is an urban pastoral, gangster fiction quite naturally reverses some of the usual motifs of what we generally expect in the more ordinary manifestations of the genre. Where the Western, for example, requires expanses of lush, uninhabited scenery (the Technicolor imagination seems vital to the form); herds of animals; a taciturn and manly hero; a pure and sexless love; the simple code of the six-gun; delicate, virginal women; and a sense of innate goodness and justice, the urban pastoral depends on almost exactly inverted aspects. Gangster fiction and film use narrow spaces and stark blacks and whites (the bleak chiaroscuro of movies like *Little Caesar* and *Public Enemy* remains vividly appropriate); people rather than beasts congregated in large numbers; a hero who is not only talkative and offensive but also even effeminate; a love which is only lust; a code of intricate betrayal; hardfaced bleached blondes; and an overwhelming sense of the totality of corruption. The gangster novel is yet another example of the reversal of values and symbols which Northrop Frye would call demonic rather than apocalyptic, the nightmare as opposed to the dream, the city and all its sin replacing the virtues of rural life.

One example, of the crudest possible sort, of gangster fiction of the twentieth century is Donald Henderson Clarke's *Louis Beretti* (1929), which contains the raw materials of novels and films which were to follow it in large numbers. The novel details the young manhood of the title character, an Italian-American born in the slums of New York who rises to prominence in the underworld. Louis progresses from petty thievery and hooliganism to hijacking, bootlegging, and murder. He accounts for the deaths of at least a dozen people, mostly other criminals, goes through a period of opium addiction, behaves with the mindless cruelty of an animal in his personal relationships, yet ends up not only a prosperous speakeasy proprietor, but also something of a public hero for gunning down a kidnapping gang (made up mostly of his former associates). Although the book lacks any attempt at structure and reads as if it were written with a trowel, it shows the upward movement towards acceptance which is one possible resolution for any pastoral.

Louis himself is pre-eminently the toughest guy in a world full of tough guys; he likes to fight and kill when he gets liquored up, is respected by all his colleagues, and participates generally in the anarchic rebellion of crime. His toughness, like the toughness of all gangster heroes, is merely an assumption that the world is a sinful place where every man must fight for anything he cares to hold. Yet, since the book is sentimental in all the worst senses of the word, Louis Beretti, a most objectionable person, turns out to be that favorite American hero, the Boor With the Heart of Gold. Like other characters of his type, he has always before him a dream of lost innocence. He and his best friend, Salvatore Perugino (known as Big Italy) witness the death of a third child, Little Italy, who runs off a rooftop while they are flying kites; this incident, and the shared feelings of the two boys, creates a lifelong bond between them and defines the closeness of their criminal relationship—they fight, drink, steal, and kill together.

The author (surely too dignified a word for the kind of writing the book displays) also attempts to account for Louis' behavior with the usual determinism; Louis tells the sister of a wealthy young man who befriends him in the army (a singularly unconvincing episode) that his environment made him the way he is: "I dunno, . . . I was what it was the most regular thing to be where I was born and grew up. And it was a tough spot. I'd probably been a Boy Scout if I'd been born in a Boy Scout neighborhood." To redeem him from his coarseness and mindlessness the author gives Louis a code and some chivalric virtues. As he says, he won't have anything to do with dope: " 'I don't mind killing a guy if I have to, . . . but this coke business ain't for me. Those poor junkies make me sick.' " In perhaps the most incredible part of the book, Louis chivalrously answers the plea of the Whore With a Heart of Gold to protect her sister from the evil advances of a Dirty Old Man, the same one who started her on her downward path; Louis saves the Damsel in Distress, preparing himself for the ritual of redemption which allows him to enter ordinary society. This ritual means breaking with his own friends, especially Big Italy; but the dream of lost innocence fails to work its magic when Louis realizes that Big Italy and his friends have masterminded the kidnapping of a friend's child. To protect his own wife and child Louis turns on his associates and becomes a hero.

Although the novel is atrociously written, with more intrusions than George Eliot would have permitted herself, and a tone I can describe only as illiterate archness, it does contain some of the important elements of gangster fiction: the Italian hero, an unbelievable amount of brutality on the part of both criminal and policeman, quite a bit of very rapid and decidedly unexciting sex, a Robin Hood sort of romanticism, and some fairly knowledgeable accounts of the methods of criminals. It seems to stand midway between the sentimental novel about lower class life and the true gangster novel: though it contains little of the lively argot that gives vitality to writers like Hammett and Chandler, it does attempt to render an approximation of tough patterns of speech, and though it sentimentalizes its characters enormously, it does present a few real pictures of Italian family life (the best-drawn character in the book is Louis' mother, a Neapolitan Earth Mother type). But because it shows its hero unconsciously renouncing his own background and subculture and thereby forsaking anarchy for order, the book fails to make crime and criminals as real and menacing as they should be. Ultimately *Louis Beretti* becomes a novel about bourgeois acceptance of the rebel and ends its potentially violent pastoral with a silly complacency; at the end of the book, Louis' heroics and their outcome can have no sequel but middle class happiness. Louis Beretti is on the road to becoming an Italian Willy Loman.

Although it certainly fails to be a really good novel by any standards, *Little Caesar*, which appeared the same year (1929), remains the classic gangster story. Using the same materials as Clarke, W. R. Burnett turned the gangster novel into a powerful and influential type. *Little Caesar*, and the novels and films it inspired, stamped indelibly the hard-edged outlines of the gangster and his world which still inhabit the American imagination. Despite its date, the book retains its rapid, economical movement and a great deal of its vitality even in this age of rapidity and violence. It is easy to see why *Little Caesar* appealed to movie-makers; the book obviously formed the style, not only of the movie it inspired, but of the other famous gangster movies as well. The novel proceeds in a series of tightly focused scenes, almost blackouts, each of which establishes a character or a situation, hints at an important relationship, or moves the action forward. Nothing is wasted, nothing is repeated, nothing impedes the cinematic immediacy of the story. In contrast to *Louis Beretti*, the novel attempts to show the world of the gangster in his own terms, using his own language and his own peculiar world view.

But aside from its stylistic influence, the novel's greatest achievement lies in the character of Cesare Bandello—Rico—the little Caesar of the title. He inspired all the imitations of the gunman which proliferate in fiction, motion pictures, and television programs. Rico is the tough guy in his purest form, a totally disinterested killer who cares about nothing but power. He doesn't drink, cares little for women, apparently enjoys nothing in common with his fellows; the police, despite their corruption, hate him, and his minions fear him. Little Caesar is not only a new type in American life, but also a new type for the Italian-American underworld of Chicago. His very lack of the ordinary interests of men and his "motiveless malignity" make him a figure of pure menace and evil. He shoots down a fellow gunman because he suspects him of squealing; at the funeral he cannot participate in that grotesque enjoyment mixed with solemnity which makes the gangster funeral a stock scene in fiction: "He was a little uneasy. Not that he felt any remorse. What he had done was merely an act of policy. A man in this game must be a man. If he gets yellow, why there's only one remedy for it . . . It was the massed flowers; their sickly and overpowering odor made him vaguely uneasy."

Despite the apparent prejudices of filmmakers and novelists, there is no justification in *Little Caesar* for blaming Rico's character on his Italian background; the author makes it clear that Rico is totally outside the pale of common humanity. He shares nothing with his cohorts; when a woman offers to play Italian music on the player piano, for instance, he refuses it, showing no interest in his own antecedents. Again, he remains a mystery even to those close to him; no one can account for his success.

> Rico was not understood. He had none of the outward signs of greatness. Neither the great strength and hairiness of Pepi, nor the dash and effrontery of Ottavio Vettori, nor the maniacal temper of Joe Sansone. He was small, pale, and quiet. In spite of his new finery he wasn't much to look at. He did not swagger, he seldom raised his voice, he never bragged. In other words, the general run of Little Italians could find nothing in him to exaggerate; they

could not make a legendary figure of him because the qualities he possessed were qualities they could not comprehend. The only thing that redeemed him in their eyes was his reputation as a killer. . . . Rico was capable of sudden audacity, but even his audacity had a sort of precision . . . Rico's great strength lay in his single-mindedness, his energy, and his self-discipline. The Little Italians could not appreciate qualities so abstract.

Curiously, it is his abstraction which makes Rico the powerful figure who dominates gangster fiction. Apparently without antecedents, relationships, ties of any important kind; a man devoid of love and almost without lust; a gunman who kills without hate or remorse; an Italian with no "Italian" qualities; a gang leader who cares for none of the rewards of leadership except the sense of power: Rico's purely abstract, motiveless proficiency gives him his paradoxical reality. He becomes the prototype of the gangster because he is the pure professional, a mere killing machine, a negative creator with absolutely no redeeming human qualities.

In the anarchic disorder of the underworld, where all values are reversed, Rico is the natural leader; the least human man becomes the most powerful figure. Since killing is his true vocation, Rico enjoys the professional's detachment from his work. His efficiency and cold-bloodedness are only necessary aspects of that professionalism. The only reason for his downfall is the lack of professionalism in others; at the moment of his greatest success, Rico is betrayed by a subordinate who breaks down under police questioning. He declines as rapidly as he rose, ending up dying in an alley in a shootout with the police.

In a world where slaughter and corruption dominate human activity, where cops, judges, and lawmakers can all be fixed, where the criminal lives in a world as intricate and treacherous as the Italy of the Renaissance, the gangster Rico is the perfect symbol of society. He is a product of his world but possesses no real affinity for it; he does best some of the most valued work of his time—

murder—and is therefore marked by greatness. I don't know if it has ever been suggested before, but it seems quite likely that William Faulkner had read *Little Caesar* before he wrote *Sanctuary*; he is the only literary author I know of who used the gangster archetype (and his gangster, Popeye, has a lot in common with Rico) to suggest the breakdown of traditional order and the evil tendencies of anarchic modernism. Faulkner's Popeye is an obviously symbolic, and indeed allegorical, character; in his own way Burnett's Cesare Bandello seems no less symbolic.

Sanctuary is probably the only literarily important gangster novel by a major author, but some other books deserve at least brief comment. Benjamin Appel's *Brain Guy* (1937) shows the unfortunate effects of a more gifted and intelligent writer's attraction to the gangster novel; it is an interesting failure because it is not quite good enough to be a decent novel nor bad enough to be excused as merely another gangster novel. Its hero becomes a tough guy through hard work and by overcoming a great many doubts, fears, and scruples. An intelligent, college-educated young man who loses his job because of the Depression, Bill Trent decides to be a "brain guy," the man who cases likely robbery locations and plans jobs. He succeeds, but not without a great deal of introspection, and some rather tiring repetition. Appel has some literary gifts; therefore, he is compelled to supply motivation, guilt, soulsearching, and all the other tools of ordinary popular fiction. In the process he gives solid novelistic reasons for his hero's progress from punk to gangleader, but fails to make him important in the way that Little Caesar and even Louis Beretti become important. When Bill Trent reaches the acme of his career, he is afflicted with a sure sense of his own doom, but is also guiltily satisfied with his own eagerness to take the pleasures of the moment. Some sense of the decline of the form is apparent in the characters themselves; instead of toughness or flamboyance, Italian cruelty or beefy Irish brutality, the gangster Trent turns out to be that nice Anglo-Saxon man gone wrong for a variety of reasons, none of them interesting. Paradoxically, the book is too lushly written for its milieu and subject matter and too narrow in its treatment to be a literary success. The sex, for example, is well presented—a flaw in any gangster novel, where sex seems merely a bodily function rather than a normal or meaningful human activity; sex for the fictional gangster should merely express his lack of humanity. Because Appel treats sex with some skill and sensitivity, he weakens the toughness and violent neutrality of the gangster.

No Orchids for Miss Blandish (1942), James Hadley Chase's hugely successful novel, represents the ultimate in the decadence of the form. The work of an Englishman who obviously learned all he knew about the United States from gangster fiction, the novel's plot is loosely stolen from Faulkner's *Sanctuary*. In dialogue, action, locale, and character the book is ridiculous; it would be a funny example of American gangster influence in England if it were not an utterly obscene book. Like Faulkner, Chase uses the impotent gunman, another apparently unmotivated killer, and his love for an unattainable girl whom he has kidnapped, as the center of the novel. The book shows a relentless obsession with the most frighteningly sadistic and masochistic cruelty, an appallingly brutal sexuality, and a violence so explicit, so badly presented, and so meaningless as to make Mickey Spillane seem a very reticent, old-maidish type with his nose only pressed against the torture room window. Chase apparently took all the elements he found striking in gangster fiction and magnified them as far as his imagination and the censors would allow; the result is one of the rarest of rare birds, a truly horrible book.

Where *No Orchids for Miss Blandish* and *Brain Guy* both fail is in their magnification of gangster elements; the authors fail to see the mainstream of American literature flowing through subliterature. The gangster hero is, for instance, distantly related to the lovable rogue of the picaresque novel; he has many affinities with American folk heroes (many of them *picaros*) who generally dwell outside the normal scheme of things. Since part of the meaning of toughness lies in the assumption that society is corrupt, there is no need in the gangster novel to dwell on the juicier aspects of that corruption; in the average gangster novel corruption and the need for a disenchanted view of life develop naturally from an objective portrayal of existence in the modern world. Since Mark Twain and even Emily Dickinson (not a gangster writer), understatement has been an important method of literary expression; stylistically the gangster novel makes good use of this understatement—it seems the normal mode of speech for Rico and Louis Beretti. This aspect of American style often functions humorously—in Twain or Hammett or Chandler—but also as a vehicle for serious statement, as in Hemingway or Robert Frost. Most important, for the gangster novel, the tough guy seems to make understatement an essential way of communicating the toughness so important to his character. No gangster seems to speak with color or vivacity; instead, Louis Beretti and Cesare Bandello use the limited vocabulary and simple patterns appropriate to their environment and their world view. Raymond Chandler thought the most effectively understated example of true American slang was a remark by a Chicago gangster; telling a man to beat it, the gangster said "Be missing." This, we feel, is indeed the kind of expression of toughness that the American fictional gangster really uses; his cynicism, his thorough initiation into the rottenness of the world, his self-possession and coolness are all reflected in the understatement of his speech and in the necessary understatement of the form he inhabits.

In this characteristic American mode of speech the gangster once more shows his similarity to the cowboy, his counterpart in wish-fulfillment fantasy; unlike the cowboy, who needs few words because he has a depth beyond mere words or because his audience would never accept anything like eloquence or because he is more attractive as an untutored, inarticulate, physical being, the gangster is not really inarticulate. He uses a similar speech pattern because it is appropriate to him and his world; he does not fumble with words as the cowboy does, but uses them precisely and meaningfully. The spare, terse diction of the gangster reinforces the rapidity of incident and the nervous tension of his existence; to talk at length is to reveal too much, to slow down, to show weakness. Constant activity and watchfulness, self-possession and neutrality, are implied in the gangster's speech and in the artistic presentations of his world: the memorable gangster novels and films display this characteristic terseness.

Gangster fiction represents a kind of nadir in twentieth-century fiction; the tough guy as gangster has gone about as far as he can go. Tough detectives, tough cowboys, tough attitudes of all kinds are familiar to any reader; we read about them in our finest authors, we see them in movies and on television. But the gangster is the tough guy in open rebellion against society; any rebel is attractive, and when he goes as far as the glamorized gangster of the films he seems even admirable. In fact, if toughness is a necessary attitude in the twentieth century (and many books make it seem just that) then the gangster of fiction is the logical end of any tough guy worth his salt: if the world is corrupt (and tough fiction paints it so) why not declare one's independence from the world by violating the social contract? Only a soft dependence on outmoded codes (often ironically derived from the brutal codes of medieval knighthood) redeems the tough hero from total degradation; yet the gangster hero, the Little Caesar, has the commitment to his life to refuse the normal softening of the code which every other tough hero accepts. In a sense, then, Cesare Bandello is the ultimate tough guy, going to his death with absolutely no weakening of his amoral adherence to himself above all. The true tough guy, whose solipsistic faith in his own competency helps to define him, should therefore be the gangster; all others are pulpy at the center. Cesare Bandello's death in an alley results, finally, from his insistence on his own values; in the inverted pastoral, so appropriate to our age, destruction should be the normal end for the rebellious hero. Further, in the inverted pastoral inverted values should be most highly prized: thus, the morality of the gangster, the cosmopolitan complexity of the city, the romantic violence of the battlefield of life, all make the gangster hero somewhat larger than life. Like the cowboy he has entered the mythology of America, half-hated, half-admired, feared and envied, the true professional, the rebel against traditions, the really tough guy brave enough to fight law and order. It is no wonder that, confronted with the realities of Cosa Nostra and the ubiquity of executive-type crime, we turn with relief and pleasure to the simple rebellion of the gangster of the thirties, the symbol of his times, the hero of the urban pastoral; prohibition, gangland warfare, stark brutality, an ugly, strife-ridden city—they're beautifully clear, we can understand them. Now things are complicated and crepuscular; good and evil are difficult to distinguish; but the gangster's world is full of violent contrasts and easy distinctions. We choose it gladly, with all its violence. We can feel simultaneously involved and dissociated from it; we are physically and culturally beyond it; and we are, in our innermost beings, fulfilling some of our aboriginal desires in it. It is, finally, a pastoral world, a resurrection of the past, a romanticization of fact and legend, an expression of contemporary horror; the gangster, in short, has entered the plane of myth. There he can speak to the American imagination.

The Hollywood Novel
The American Dream Cheat

CAROLYN SEE

WE HAVE FOUND out to our edification in this century that literature has become the "bone locker" of philosophy, perhaps because with all our other troubles, straight philosophy is just too hard to read. But apart from the general contemporary novel, another set of "literature," both more popular and more formalized, has carried the ideas of our time. These popular manifestations are generally ignored until twenty years after the fact, then if there still remain any copies which have not been read to death, critics study them. Western pulps eulogized a dying brand of hero—they felt rather than thought their nostalgia for a dead age. Magazines like the *Black Mask* made a cult of reality as much as of violence; a generation who "smelt fear" in their world read Raoul Whitfield when it couldn't tough out the more refined anxieties. The Fifties' preoccupation with outer space brought an epidemic of science fiction. This decade, weary of the cold war, has produced its disillusioned, formalized, popular tales of unheroic espionage.

Another sub-genre not usually recognized as this kind of popular, formalized fiction is the Hollywood novel, which takes the whole American history and the American dream as its province. As the hard-boiled novel has its Hammetts and Chandlers, Hollywood has had its Wests, its Fitzgeralds. Yet in spite of the stature of some of its authors, the (accurate) critical axiom is that they rarely turn out more than "another Hollywood novel," or "the best Hollywood novel." This is because the form—like the western, the novel of violence, the spy story—speaks over the heads of its creators. It is the property of the public, a popular form which can be mastered by its authors but hardly ever transcended.

What makes the Hollywood novel a distinctive genre? A great deal has been written about Hollywood as a microcosm, not just of America but of the American dream: "Everything that is wrong with the United States is to be found there in rare purity." (Everything that is right, too, perhaps.) Either way, Hollywood is the place where people have a chance to be—somehow—their ideal selves.

In the beginning, the American dream promised that by working hard everyone could *be* somebody. The Puritan sermon, The Way of Life, preached that to find one's own best occupation and work unfailingly at it was the surest way to salvation. From all that hard work, prosperity came to be seen as a secondary characteristic of being saved. Money was the raw material; a man could have a home, family, and make a down payment on tangible beauty in his own life. Ideally, the boss's daughter was not only rich but beautiful; and a collateral part of the dream, as Gatsby knew, has been to possess the most beautiful girl in the world, a woman commensurate with man's new vision of himself as a youthful, handsome prince.

In the 1920's Freud and the movies added a theoretical freedom of sexuality to the goals of the standard American dream, and pleasure became one of man's inalienable rights. But always, the central element of the dream was to make something of one's self—to climb from rags to riches. Each one came naked to the new world, leaving his old identity behind, and then constructed—tragically, expediently, triumphantly—an identity of his own. If he were lucky and smart, the identity was what he wanted it to be. If he were stupid or venal, the dream turned to nightmare.

Thus certain themes turn up repeatedly in Hollywood novels which mirror typically American concerns. To illustrate these themes the authors have used devices so repeatedly that they form a tradition of their own, a set of stereotypes from which even the most ambitious or original Hollywood novel cannot escape.

Artificiality is perhaps the most pervasive device, and points to the most dominant theme: that the whole American world is a cheat, that there is something wrong with the dream, that after you get what you want, it was not what you wanted at all. The artificiality of *things* so prevalent in Hollywood, and movie sets, the houses that look like Zulu huts or Tudor cottages, reflect the puerility of the dream itself, the discrepancy between what America leads us to expect and what it has to give.

Another theme is the *distortion of time,* which leads to *sterility* and *decay.* Both past and future are discarded; characters find themselves living in a never-ending present tense. The protagonist typically leaves his home, his past, his real position in society, and sets out to make his ideal place in the world. Since no one knows for sure how old he is (he is no one's little boy, no one's older brother), he does not have to get old at any particular rate; he may sustain youth to the brink of old age. But without time there is no growth; things and people find themselves in a state of either sterility or decay. Like the Valley of Ashes in *The Great Gatsby,* Hollywood is a dead land. "Real" geography contributes to this set of symbols; since Easterners have trouble recognizing seasons as they think of them, most of these novels take place in never-ending sun, with flowers which don't smell, fruit which doesn't taste, etc.

Sexual freedom was early associated with Hollywood because so many of the public's erotic fantasies were voyeuristically dependent upon the movies. This freedom was celebrated with exuberance in the Twenties and early Thirties; in fiction and reality, California was a rake's paradise. But the effect of this generosity of flesh was that by the middle Thirties, a major theme in almost every Hollywood novel was the *failure of sexuality.* Protagonists craved a little sentiment with their sensuality, and, denied it, became impotent. The typical attitude toward sex in the later Hollywood novel is at worst one of revulsion, at best a polite reluctance.

Another theme in these Hollywood novels which makes a mockery of the whole American dream is the *meaninglessness of work*. Early on, the American *raison d'être* was to work hard and make money; in Hollywood, the money flows in incredible sums for little if any work, or work which is seen as either pernicious or silly. The novels are filled with examples, say, of writers put in rooms with typewriters but told not to type because the noise will disturb Rin Tin Tin who lives next door. The archetypic (perhaps apocryphal) real-life example is P. G. Wodehouse, who took an unexpected six week trip to England without telling the administration, and returned to find six two-thousand dollar checks pushed under his office door. Money come by in this way is not *real*; it does not contribute to the identity of its earner in the accepted Puritan way; it is truly an embarrassment of riches.

All these combine to form—in the minds of the writers at least—a last preoccupation; what Edmund Wilson has called "goofy unreality." California is the place where crazy things happen, its novelists are "poets of the tabloid murder." While this attitude superficially denies the relationship of California to the rest of the U. S. A., it intensifies it by reinforcing the whole of the Hollywood myth. It is so crazy out on the coast, dozens of writers have intimated, why try to deal with it seriously?

The life of a typical Hollywood novel character goes like this: He comes West, meets some friends on the spur of the moment. Since his old society is not watching him, he becomes involved sexually in any number of depressing intrigues. When not working he goes to endless rounds of premieres and parties; to pick up extra money, he is apt to make pornographic movies, or sell his sex in other ways. Finally he gets depressed enough either to go insane, kill himself, or kill someone else. Then he either attends a funeral or is the star of one. It is a meaningless life, filled with triviality, leading to a violent end. To keep the nightmare at bay, he clings to his dream: more youth, more sex, more money, more *fun*. This *can't* be the American way—but it is. And what the "hard-boiled" novel and the Hollywood have most in common is that they each offer an excellent set of concrete objects, a perfect form—popular enough to appeal to the general public—for telling it as it is.

This is not to say that all hard-boiled novels set west of the Mojave Desert must necessarily share the two sets of formal characteristics. In Paul Cain's *Fast One* (1933), Hollywood myths are operative only in the sense of providing a kind of open city where conventional ways of behavior mean little. The protagonist, Jerry Kells, is an American (therefore Hollywood?) hero in that he makes his own destiny—but many another "existential" hero can say the same. In fact, Jerry Kells, or Tod Hackett of *The Day of the Locust* (1939), or even Jake Barnes of *The Sun Also Rises* (1926), are all modern, alienated characters who choose stoic endurance or wry objectivity as a method of controlling a crazy world. Their stories share many presumed attitudes on the part of reader and writer; what they don't share are the devices.

Fast One and, say, *The Day of the Locust* are written in comparatively strict forms, with recognizable persona and situations particular to their sub-genre. Kells's drama in *Fast One*, a story of one man's attempt to take over L.A.'s organized underworld, could be acted out in any city. Hollywood could as easily be Hammett's Poisonville. The characteristic Hollywood descriptions are missing; there are no flowers, fruits, clear skies, movie stars. For reasons of his own, Paul Cain shows us his hero against a background of dirty downtown buildings, ordinary city streets. Kells himself is hardly a Hollywood hero: he is forever "grinning mirthlessly," saying things like "Dave is cold with an egg over his ear, and Ruth Perry says that a little queen with glasses shot Doc and sapped Dave." Kells can also sustain an incredible amount of injuries; literally riddled with bullets and with an ice pick between his ribs, he survives for an extra chapter to work out his destiny; the formal strictures of the genre require that he do so. Tod Hackett is in temperament much the same as Kells, but his first experience with death is limited to a dead rubber horse, and he learns about violence as he is mauled by a mob in front of a movie theatre rather than treacherously gunned down in a gambling den. The thematic content of these two novels (and many more modern novels of funk and alienation) is much the same; the forms are different. It is where these superficially dissimilar forms closely overlap that they become interesting. With the exception of *Fast One*, novels of violence set in Los Angeles / Hollywood—and there are an extraordinary number of them—partake of both genres, and the characteristics of each reinforce the other.

Raoul Whitfield's *Death in a Bowl* (1930) uses Hollywood in its most simple, general application; it is incongruous that such a pleasant place as this still pastoral town should breed crime and chaos, yet it is so; it is incongruous that the same town which houses naively ostentatious movie stars and taciturn citrus farmers should shelter either criminals or their hard-boiled pursuers, yet it is so. The novel features a detective, Ben Jardinn, who is morose, tough, and cynical. During those cryptic conversations which fill the novel, Ben preaches that you cannot trust anybody. He himself trusts neither his best girl nor his best friend, and inspires them in turn with distrust for each other. They then spend the better part of their time spying alternately on other suspects, and on each other, and reporting back to Jardinn. But they also spy upon Jardinn and report back to each other.

Hollywood is, from Jardinn's point of view, a grotesque mixture of tranquillity and shocking violence. On either side of its main boulevard, the little city declines into flowery residential areas; when Jardinn attends a Hollywood Bowl concert, he walks to it, and as he observes the clouds and stars, someone kills the guest conductor. Later, when Jardinn investigates the bungalow of his missing secretary, he almost persuades himself in the neat domesticity of kitchen and porch that she is safe, but returns home to find her brutally murdered on his own living room couch—and thinks at first that she is asleep. It is no wonder that he has learned not to trust appearances.

When he discovers his "sleeping" secretary, he experiences anguish, perhaps the only emotion of which he is capable.

> He got his right hand fingers against the skin over her heart. Then he went over to the window that faced down the canyon and stood staring out. His face was colorless; the tears in his eyes made a blur of the road. Several minutes passed.
>
> . . . he went into the small dining-room and poured himself a drink . . . he sat on the edge of a chair and downed the liquor. He felt broken up inside. He said in a puzzled tone:
>
> "Christ—maybe I thought more of her—"

By the time the police arrive Jardinn is again in control of himself. He tells the photographers, "if you shoot the house from the outside don't miss that rosebush back of the patio. . . ." and even the police are shocked. "You're hard-boiled, Jardinn," one of them says. But the reader knows that this toughness, too, is only appearance, an individual's defense against an intolerably meaningless world.

This world, as in most Hollywood novels, exaggerates all things American; rural pastoralism, together with astonishing opportunities for success, to be found only in the most sophisticated Eastern cities. But success is usually obtained by using the tactics of Chicago, against an atmosphere of unfulfilled cheap dreams typical of Hollywood itself. The established "right" in this world, the police, only hinder Jardinn, for he is the only man here who is honorable, who has any idea, no matter how obscure, of what really is right. He cannot trust his clients, his enemies or his friends, and his doctrine of distrust is given validity by the fact that his best friend is guilty. Jardinn's tragedy is that though he mourns his dead secretary, were she alive, he could not love or even trust her. The nature of his world dictates that the guilt—or *some* guilt—could have easily been hers.

The problems of corruption in what started out to be such a brave society, a "fresh, green breast of the new world," is more explicitly dealt with in Richard Sales' *Lazarus #7* (1942). The book is a true hybrid, borrowing heavily from the sub-genre of the comic-detective tale as well as the Hollywood novel, yet it is also both hard-boiled and a novel of violence, since it deals with the effect of violence upon a set of vulnerable human-beings who apply varying modes of control to a chaotic world. *Lazarus #7* uses several Hollywood themes and devices to dramatize this corruption—particularly *artificiality* and *decay*.

The hero, Steven Mason, a doctor fresh from several years in the Orient, visits an old friend, Joss Henry, who now makes his living as a Hollywood writer, cannily adding to his reputation as an artistic genius by acting deliberately bizarre. Stereotypes come and go, crimes are committed, and Steven investigates, becoming for the duration, a brilliant amateur detective. Superficially the tone resembles something by Craig Rice rather than Hammett or Chandler. But the fact that Steven Mason is a bacteriologist specializing in rare diseases is no coincidence. He functions in Hollywood as he did in the Orient, not only as a fighter of moral infection, but as a researcher for the germs which have caused it. On the surface, the Hollywood way of life which he examines is healthy; everything looks fine, but then crimes begin to be committed, symptoms of a sick society. While wise-cracks are recited, bodies hidden and alibis checked, Steven Mason meets a professional colleague, the studio doctor, Max Lekro. This sinister figure confides that although he is employed by the studio, his real interest is in experiments which he carries on at home; he wishes, more than anything, to resurrect the dead. Doctor Lekro's grisly projects are carried on throughout the course of the novel, and he himself, though murdered, is brought back to life long enough to name his own killer.

Some few of Doctor Lekro's subjects—dogs labeled

Lazarus 1, 2, 3, etc.—have been brought back to some semblance of life. They eat, sleep, may even respond to command, but *they are not alive.* Hollywood, too, looks all right, but since its values are greed and self-indulgence, as a community it is bestial, comatose, not really alive.

The murderess is discovered to be a beautiful actress, who has killed in order to cover up the fact that she is suffering from leprosy. This woman is of course emblematic of Hollywood. Her external appearances have been carefully constructed and reinforced to keep her beautiful and appealing. Though her eyebrows have fallen out, they are penciled back in, and her nose-septum scars are passed off as plastic self-improvement surgery. The star remains beautiful, but to make love to her is to wallow in infection.

Steven Mason, as diagnostician, recognizes that the germ which has caused the real disease is greed. It has deprived Joss of the writing talent he formerly possessed; it has driven the idolized star to degradation and finally to murder. It has in fact turned the entire community into something more dead than alive. The agent of this destructive greed is Al Roche, a producer whose entire concern is the money which his film company accrues. Knowing his most beautiful star is a leper—and by implication that his whole business is sick—he keeps her in bondage to him, working to turn out more tainted, phony Hollywood products. "Well, by Jesus, what did you expect me to do, go out and shout it to the world? For Crysake, I had a lot of dough tied up in that girl, and a lot more pictures for her to make. She grossed. She had the stuff." By using his money specifically to corrupt, Roche becomes a kind of Typhoid Mary spreading the Hollywood infection—even to people not in the industry. The supreme ignorance of his dialogue would indicate that like a disease carrier, he is not even particularly conscious of the harm he is doing.

What makes this a novel of social criticism, different from and "better" than the ordinary detective puzzle, is the assumption of a real corruption within the world of the book. Hollywood is here a sick society; those infected cannot even remember what the old standards were like, what it was like to be well. But somehow it has managed to effect a "one-hundred per cent cosmetic cure." "I particularly should have been able to tell," says the detective-diagnostician, "but the very artificial halo over this town tricked me."

Generally speaking, Raymond Chandler's Philip Marlowe is a Los Angeles detective. He operates closer to Wilshire than Hollywood Boulevard; he is more concerned with the civic indignities of Bay City than the movie colony. But as a disaffected screen writer, Chandler was not averse to biting the hand that fed, and his one Hollywood novel, *The Little Sister* (1949), presents a far from favorable report on the community. Chandler's Hollywood world combines the deceptive health of *Lazarus #7* with the sporadic domesticity of *Death in a Bowl*. On the surface it is no more than an innocuous collection of pretty places and relatively tame amusements. Violence hardly seems rampant; a few women timorously gamble away their grocery money, weak-chinned men accomplish routine seductions in their well-furnished flats, helped along by bottles of Vat 69 and artistically placed flower arrangements just on the edge of wilt. Like Whitfield, Chandler deliberately juxtaposes climatological and domestic tranquillity with senseless violence; within this world the old values mean nothing, and the rules of evil are not necessarily consistent.

It is in these set-piece descriptions of a corrupt community that Chandler excels. When he turns to explicit social criticism of the film world, his voice turns specific, cranky, un-hard-boiled, and all too typical of those writers imported to Hollywood who suffer from a strong sense of rejection or annoyance or both. *The Little Sister* includes what one recent critic has called "undoubtedly one of the most vicious and pointed satires of the movie industry ever written," which, if nothing else, proves that the critic has not read many Hollywood novels. In this scene, Marlowe meets the head of a studio, who is watching his dogs as they "pee in order—question of seniority." The executive, who has no place as a regular character in the novel, and whom Marlowe has met by the merest coincidence, pours out his heart to the detective, confiding that movies are "the only business in the world in which you can make all the mistakes there are and still make money," that all one needs is to own fifteen hundred theatres. This "satire" is at best a so-what proposition; everyone knows—and certainly knew by 1949—that Hollywood had a lot of goofy people in it, and that as an industry it dealt in volume and was more interested in making money than art. This "satirizing" of certain elements of the movie industry to death, and resuscitating them only to do them in again, is in a grand old tradition of Hollywood writers, especially those from somewhere else.

In this obvious sense, *The Little Sister* is an ordinary, not very original Hollywood effort. But there is another theme, the *failure of sexuality*, which is treated less directly, more interestingly, and which places the novel still more securely in the Hollywood genre. It also compares surprisingly to Norman Mailer's *The Deer Park*, which whatever else it did, set out to catalog the various effects which the Hollywood myth has had upon American sexual mores.

I have already mentioned that since the middle Thirties, the sexual familiarities to be found in the Hollywood scene has bred the strongest contempt in countless fictional heroes. Women sell their sex to the movies, and boorish men take advantage of this bargain basement full of beauties, but the effect on sensitive men is a virulent hatred of the flesh as such. There exist as well recurring themes of voyeuristic as opposed to physical passions, of protagonists safely in love with women on the screen or of the screen world. The minute these mythical women become real, they are once again mere slabs of beef, and the men once again impotent.

Something of this rather peculiar frame of mind and body may be seen in *The Little Sister*. One of Marlowe's so-called "knightly" qualities is that he is traditionally celibate, that he cannot be hero and lover at the same time. Critics have treated this celibacy kindly; and Chandler's own quote about Marlowe, "I think he might seduce a duchess and I am quite sure he would not spoil a virgin," sounds nice. But as far as his novel-reading public is concerned, Marlowe, until *The Long Goodbye*, never seduces anyone at all, and his statements reveal an attitude far from chivalric but medieval none the less, a practical detestation for things of the flesh (presently in the Hollywood tradition, because the women are so available). Earlier, in *The Big Sleep*, Marlowe has spurned with a tirade of wise cracks a lady who offered herself to him, and thrown a naked girl out of his apartment to protect the sanctity of his home—perhaps an odd attitude for a bachelor. Later, in *The Little Sister*, he is profoundly American, profoundly adolescent; he kisses the girls and is repelled when they respond. One woman who particularly earns his dislike is a pseudo-latin movie star who "must have men." The honor of the chivalric hero evidently doesn't extend to good manners; he not only refuses, but says he would rather cut his throat.

A certain sort of critic might justifiably make much of the fact that Marlowe's famous objective attitude, his sardonic dandyism, functions only in the face of violence or death; he is interested in dead bodies, shocked by amorous ones. This monkish hatred of the flesh is amplified in *The Little Sister* to include the whole world of human beings who live physical, ordinary lives. In his famous ride through the new Los Angeles, Marlowe departs from objectivity to fulminate for pages against the neon, the artificiality, the vice, but also the quality of L.A. hamburgers, and the fate of men who are driving home to spoiled children and the "gabble of silly wives." Interestingly, the only children mentioned in *The Little Sister* are seen as ankle-kicking monsters, an appropriate attitude for W. C. Fields, but hardly becoming for a knightly protector of helpless humanity.

Marlowe saves his enthusiasm and amorousness for an admittedly puerile dream—for the movie star Mavis Weld. He flirts with her in engagingly boyish, junior-high-school ways, he allows himself to day-dream a future with her, but settles for being her fan: "I could sit in the dark with her and hold hands, but for how long? In a little while she will drift off into a haze of glamour and expensive clothes and froth and unreality and muted sex. She won't be a real person anymore. Just a voice from a sound track, and a face on a screen. I'd want more than that." But his abortive encounters with "real" women suggest that he wants just that or less; his disgust on the one hand for unmarried sex, on the other hand for family life, would indicate that far from being willing to seduce a duchess or anyone else, he shares that Hollywood failure of sexuality, a psychical if not physical impotence. In this respect, Marlowe compares to Sergius O'Shaugnessy in *The Deer Park*, who after a harrowing war experience, is temporarily impotent, seeing each woman as another manifestation of the flesh and thus a reminder of napalm atrocities, a kind of living putrescent corpse. O'Shaugnessy regains his virility in an affair with a Tuesday Weld-type starlet where the sex is somehow not real; they "do the mime on clouds of myth," pretending to be everyone but themselves. After this convalescence, O'Shaugnessy is able to rejoin the "normal" world, but Marlowe, like many others in the fictional Hollywood pantheon, prefers the romanticism of a voyeuristic dream.

The *failure of work*—man's loss of his "way of life"—is seen in John O'Hara's *Hope of Heaven* (1938). Jim Malloy, a genuine writer on the east coast, is made richer than ever before when he comes to Hollywood, and is rendered more helpless than he has ever been. Like many of these protagonists, he wants nothing more than a "normal" life; he is in love with a young girl and wants, decently, to marry her. But in this environment nothing could be less possible.

In *Hope of Heaven* as in these others, the Hollywood and hard-boiled genres combine. Malloy is conventionally hard-boiled, a tough in a world of toughs. He has a gift-giving relationship with at least one crook; he has been a fugitive from justice and gives expert advice on how to take it on the lam. But he is also incurably romantic. He is a "sucker for Christmas," he thinks his girl would make a wonderful mother. He was even in love with his first wife, and now he subscribes to that most sanguine illusion of the cynic—that second marriages are made in Heaven.

Malloy has left his real work in New York, but, like the sentimentalist he is, he doesn't worry about finding himself in work as much as in love. He is a *family* man, he wants a place in the real world. One reason he is attracted to his girl, Peggy, is that though she is still very young, she has formed, very precariously, a working family unit. She and her brother live together in a one generation, present-tense family, typically Hollywood. The mother is dead. The father, a drifter, has been missing for years. When he turns up unexpectedly to claim a place as part of Peggy's family, he is revealed as a warped product of the American way of life, a piece of human waste who lives by the externals of the corrupted American dream; good clothes, youthful appearance, plenty of women. Peggy's father is also a typically Hollywood figure, a parent who refuses to become old, whose platonic idea of himself cuts danger-ously in on the lives of his children. He destroys the fragile family life of his children by the falseness of his fatherly attitudes; he murders his own son during an argument which is really the quarrel of two would-be lovers over a beautiful woman—Peggy's best friend.

But this is only the last event in a steadily worsening set of circumstances. Most of the novel is devoted to es-tablishing an ominous atmosphere of corruption and vice and nothing but apathy to counteract it. Malloy is acutely aware of Peggy's father as a threat to their own happiness, but deprived of his own identity, he is as rootless and helpless as the rest of the characters. As he watches Peggy become progressively more menaced by her father, he can think of nothing more to do than ask *one* convict if he has ever seen this "wronggo" (as if there were one big prison where everyone were sent, along with one foreign language to learn, or one supermarket to patronize). He doesn't check this man's police record or hire a detective. In fact, he socially accepts the status-quo, goes nightclubbing with his fiancée and her father, watches dispassionately while this lecherous gent spends his time snapping the garter of his daughter's best friend.

Malloy's only weapon against this corruption (which will eventually rob Peggy of all belief in any values, leaving her, like her father, part of the west coast waste) is to buy things. He spends vast quantities of money in a kind of embarrassment, but there is always more to spend. In an effort to win Peggy over to his vision of normal domesticity, he rents a Beverly Hills home for five hundred a month. He even pretends to have bought it, but the entire spread is a kind of movie set, good for a few love scenes, profoundly impermanent.

After the murder, Jim again tries to "save" Peggy, to make her his wife. But he lacks the personal strength to do it. He might have been capable in the east, but is reduced to a consumer / observer in the west, castrated by too little work, too many rewards. His and Peggy's roles have in fact been reversed; while she leaves for work each morning to put in eight hours, he, a kind of hairy-chested harem queen, is left figuratively on a sofa with a box of bonbons; he has nothing to do but shop, and while away whole mornings picking out expensive neck ties.

O'Hara's Hollywood shows an America gone wrong. The old days when a man had his work and his place in society no longer exist. In this city love is not stronger than death; it does not admit of children or a future. Death is the true operative—violent, absurd, demoralizing. Against this world, all Jim Malloy's expensive socks and ties, his rented homes and ostentatious engagement rings, avail nothing. He can only insist in a limited way upon the amenities.

It is interesting that the theme of *goofy unreality* is most explicitly dealt with in *You Play the Black and the Red Comes Up* (1938), which is admittedly a "made book," a literary exercise. Its central assumption—as a diabolical director repeatedly explains to the dull-witted but honest protagonist—is that people lose their brains directly they come over the mountains, that Hollywood, as someone once said of United Artists, is an asylum with the lunatics in charge. The worker-hero's sad, sordid story is acted out against a background of legalized insanity. One of his spur-of-the-moment acquaintances, an aging divorcee, drunkenly remarks in a second rate saloon that if everyone paid a little money each week, then everyone could be subsidized with a minimum income, and thus keep the economy going. This is of course a vulgarization of Upton Sinclair's plans if he had become governor; a basically socialist scheme made mindlessly utopian. The director to whom the lady confides maliciously urges her on, just to see what will happen. What does happen is that this beery vision of a new Canaan becomes, with true Californian élan, the Ecanaamic Society. The divorcee rises from a thick-legged alimony collector to a prophet of a new religion. There is nothing new in eccentricity or insanity as fictional devices. But Hollywood's insanity, in the novels, is made horrible by its power, by the fact that it is not recognized as madness but accepted as reality. The lunatics really do take over the asylum. Dick, the working-class hero, sees society as crazy, but is surrounded by people who really do believe in this lunacy, by paying customers who believe in this middle-aged lady dressed up in a bed sheet. After some plot complications, Dick is sprung from a bum murder rap by an excellent lawyer who is paid good money, Ecanaamic money. If insanity becomes majority rule, the sane have to be careful. Dick intuits this; his normalcy makes him a freak, particularly vulnerable to his environment. His only defense, again, is a "hard-boiled" stoicism which is part inarticulateness, part shyness, and quite inadequate to conceal his bewilderment and fear.

The point of the hard-boiled attitude, certainly, is that the toughest exterior is apt to cover a three minute egg. Dick mourns for his lost child and cries like a baby over his dead sweetheart. Jim Malloy is "a sucker for Christmas." To be hard-boiled is necessary as a defense because offense is impossible. A few men cannot change the world;

Tod Hackett cannot prevent "the burning of Los Angeles," he can only prophesy it, paint it, indulge himself in useless wit, distract himself with the prospect of pleasureless lust.

Where the attitude differs in the Hollywood novel is in the bleak sense of transcience, the relative helplessness of the protagonist. The detective, even though he realizes that it is an absurd posture, has elected to make some kind of battle against the establishment, be it only a gesture, one criminal taken in out of a whole population. We have already seen that some of the best examples of the Hollywood hard-boiled novel do not have detectives for protagonists. The "heroes" of Horace McCoy's *They Shoot Horses, Don't They?* (1935) and *I Should Have Stayed Home* (1937) are both naive, would-be actor-directors. Richard Hallas' hero is an unemployed restaurant owner. Jim Malloy is an alienated Hollywood writer. These men do not put up much of a fight. Their attitude is typically a bewilderment which leaves them weak to the point of mental incompetence. Once one comes over the mountains to California, it doesn't matter what one is—or logically—what one does. *No one cares;* the present world is without meaning. When Dick in *You Play the Black and the Red Comes Up* discovers that his wife and child have left him, he dramatically switches from the world of established reality into a kind of Hollywood state of mind. He literally walks away from his factory job and away from the restaurant upon which he has lavished his money, his art-work, his time. He jumps a freight and begins an aimless trek to nowhere, to California. All the outward signs of his identity have been shed; his family, his job, his "project." He is alienated; he is bereft: "I lay there and it was cold, but I couldn't think about it. The way I felt, I didn't care if school kept or not. That's the way I felt." The drama of these helpless heroes is that while they have already been deprived of so much, they can still lose more. If, spiritually speaking, alienation turns men to stone, then these are stories of how it is still possible to get blood from them. The common heroism of these men is that, like their detective counterparts, they consciously or unconsciously follow the ancient stoic values; whatever happens, they feel bad but try to say nothing.

A genuinely hard-boiled hero is in fact hard to come by in all these novels. Jardinn weeps, Marlowe fulminates, and even outside Hollywood, Hammett's Ned Beaumont pales, blushes, trembles. The useful division might be made not between people who don't mind killing and people who do, but between people who try not to be shocked and those who continually are. A novel may erroneously be called hard-boiled by the critics simply because violent, undesirable things happen in it—as *Madame Bovary* was first called a novel of adultery. A final glance at two "straight" Hollywood novels will make this distinction clear.

What Makes Sammy Run? (1941) has been called hard-boiled by several critics because Sammy Glick does socially unacceptable things. But Sammy himself is not at all hard-boiled, he is incurably enthusiastic, even about his third rate acts of "creation." He may not love his ladies, but he unabashedly enjoys them. Al Manheim, who observes Sammy, is the very antithesis of hard-boiled. He is shocked when Sammy deserts his nice Jewish girl. He is shocked when Sammy sleeps with other women, when Sammy makes up a stupid scenario, when Sammy buys a new item of tasteless clothing. But he does not gun Sammy down, or punch him, or even leave him, because he rather *likes* to be shocked, to live vicariously in Sammy's vices. (For this reason, the reader is sneakily apt to like Sammy better than Al.) To put it another way, Manheim is a Robert Cohn rather than a Jake Barnes, a square, living in a morally outdated world.

But the hard-boiled attitude as an ethic is implicit throughout *The Day of the Locust*. Claude Estee, the successful director who is Tod Hackett's mentor, lives by it as a defense against Hollywood's dehumanizing artificiality. Estee controls the artificiality by parodying it; he is thin and pretends to be fat, calls his Chinese servant a "black rascal," labels his scotch and soda a mint julip, orders a rubber dead horse for his swimming pool. (The irony of these pranks is that he is "understood too easily." The worst people laugh at his jokes, even as Marlowe and Ned Beaumont are continually being beaten up by clods who are hard because they never had a sensitive thought in their lives.) Tod wants nothing more than to gain the sardonic control which Estee has imposed upon his life. (And West himself was so taken by the character and the posture that he first wrote part of the novel in Estee's first person.) Together Tod and Estee glumly, glibly discuss (and control) their one remaining weakness, love, which has been so debased by the movies — before an excursion to a whorehouse. Estee observes, "love is like a vending machine, eh? Not bad. You insert a coin and press home the lever. There's some mechanical activity inside the bowels of the device. You receive a small sweet, frown at yourself in the dirty mirror, adjust your hat, take a firm grip on your umbrella and walk away, trying to look as though nothing had happened. It's good, but it's not for pictures." The assumption is that Estee, like Tod Hackett, Ben Jardinn, Philip Marlowe (or Jake Barnes), has a "code" in which manners come first, then philosophy. *You are what you pretend to be*, and enough flippancies, put-ons, sight-gags, and trash-talking will build the armored mechanism that a good man needs to be in order to live in a bad world.

Focus on Three Descendants

Nightmare Alley:
Geeks, Cons, Tips, and Marks

CHARLES SHAPIRO

> "Towners just don't like us away from the troop."—
> Humphrey Bogart to Eddie Albert in *The Wagons Roll
> at Night* (1941)

WILLIAM LINDSAY GRESHAM, bard of the carnivals and the
Homer of the freaks, first became fascinated with the
side-show world when, as a boy, he would visit the ten-
in-one show at Coney Island. He was, by his own admission, obsessed by one attraction in particular, "a dignified
Italian with beautifully trained mustaches and a calm,
kingly look in his eyes." This man was one of the top
oddities in the business. "Hanging from the front of his
abdomen was the body of a vestigial twin, the size of a
two-year-old child." To add to the horror, the vestige was
dressed in a suit with garish black and white checks, "with
tiny patent leather shoes and red socks on its feet." It was
headless, joined to its owner by a cord of flesh.

Gresham's mother became ill, but her son kept staring,
intrigued by the Italian's grace and charm, "his noble
face," and the fact that the human exhibit was making
money by simply displaying himself. And when young
Gresham learned that the freak was happily married and

the father of five normal children, he was downright envious. He contrasted the Italian with his own father, constantly bothered about factory affairs, and he was certain, that, unlike his mother, the Italian's wife probably never worried herself to sleep brooding about money. Unfortunately, Gresham knew he had little to offer in this line, but perhaps he might get himself tattooed from head to foot.

Many years later, Gresham, while serving with the Republicans in the Spanish Civil War, met up with a medic, an old time carnival worker who loved to reminisce about the lives and adventures of those associated with the carnival business. Rejected by society because of their strange bodies or rebellious natures, these men and women evolved an insulated culture of their own, with their own code of ethics and their own contempt for outsiders. Gresham learned, for the first time, about the geek, the lowest form of carnival life, a chronic dope addict or alcoholic who, placed in a cage, posed as a wild man, and bit the heads off chickens and snakes. Geeks, Gresham's friend carefully explained, were never born—they were always made. The geek is brought to his final degradation through the careful and systematic planning of the carnival boss who slowly reduces an alcoholic to an animal. For the carnies, the geek seems almost a living parable of the big world outside; for the tips (customers) he is a frightening and amusing savage from Borneo. The truth, of course, lies between.

Gresham tells us that after listening to the carny spin his yarns he immediately conceived the plot for a story. "A man learns, from working in a carnival side show, that a geek is made by exploiting another person's desperate need. Taking this as his guiding principle in life, he rises higher and higher, finally meets someone who works the same process on him, and tumbles back literally into the pit—biting the heads off chickens for a bottle a day." Thus came *Nightmare Alley* (1946), a tough, relentless, colorful novel that exposes the private world of the freaks in order to comment on a sick, degrading society. Each individual freak in the Ackerman-Zorbaugh Monster Shows represents, by the peculiar nature of his performance and his life, an attitude toward American life. The grifter hero's rise and fall from con-man to geek becomes a meaningful, personal horror that somehow could happen to us all, and in some sense, perhaps does. And, above all, the constant conflict between the entertainers and their gaping audiences reinforces the tough guy theme that in a tough guy world dreams can be manipulated for profit. For Stanley Carlisle, incapable of love, caught in a series of sado-masochistic relationships, the carnival is the perfect background against which to play out his fantasy life, a perfect place to reinforce his belief that "nothing matters in this goddamned lunatic asylum of a world but dough." His life, as he readily admits, was "a torment of scheming," and, though we gradually come to understand the forces operating on Stan, he never does and thus is one of the doomed.

One of the epigraphs to *Nightmare Alley* is a quotation from *The Waste Land*, and much of Gresham's novel is too obviously salted with references to Eliot's lengthy poem. More important, the dry despairing tone of the poem is an influence on Gresham, who uses such images as Tarot cards to reinforce the action and particularize attitudes of hostility, despair, and false arrogance. Outsiders, those who stay in one place, are rejected, taunted, fooled, and envied.

But it is the carnival itself, specifically the carefully and lovingly delineated freaks, that reflects the action of the novel and places the tough guy hero in context. As Gresham's nonfiction work *Monster Midway* shows, the author knows his subject first hand and, in a strange way, is committed to the carnival mystique, an adolescent commitment at best. He has learned, from his association with the carnival life, of a world "where eccentricity is not punished as it is in the anthill life of the big corporations. In fact, if your eccentricity is colorful enough . . . you can make it pay off." Gresham believed that an answer to Thoreau's lament that most of us live lives of quiet desper-

ation is found in the carnival "where steady rain or continued bad business may produce moments of desperation
but no one has to be quiet about it." The midway, then, is
one of the last stands of rugged individualism and, during
the depression years after 1929, the glitter "lifted people
into wonderland for an hour, only to drop them again,
when it was over, back into a world of worn clothes and
worried hearts." The man who fought the good fight
against Franco is finally reduced to using freaks and grif-
ters as spokesmen for a freer life. That, in itself, tells us a
good deal about the failure of the radical imagination of
America.

Besides Stan and the geek (who eventually and inevitably become the same person) Gresham's small-time carnival featured a number of significant characters, each
with his own set of attitudes toward himself and the
marks. The strong man, Hercules (Bruno Hertz) is almost
a parody of the big man who is all soft inside. He understands Stan and watches, with fear and helplessness, as the
young and slick operator seduces the most decent girl in
the show, a girl Hercules cares for. Hercules has many
good instincts, but his isolation and shame render him all
but useless.

Hercules' physical antithesis, Major Mosquite (Kenneth Horsefield), boasting inaccurately of "twenty inches,
twenty pounds, and twenty years," is evil squeezed into its
essence. He delights in exposing private shames and harm-
ing all those of normal size. His few inches are an accurate
representation of his emotional development. Hercules
and the Major provide the extremes within the freak
show, extremes against which we can measure Stan and
his attempts to dominate.

The other human exhibits make shrewder adjustments.
Joe Plasky, billed as "the half-man acrobat," is unable to
use his crippled legs but has more than compensated for
his handicap by walking on his hands and developing the
agility of the rest of his body. When trouble arises, Hercules stands by, the Major becomes actively sadistic, but
Joe acts, and acts quickly, out of decent motives and to

good effect. Stan, who studies Joe closely, picks up Joe's tricks but fails to grasp Joe's motivation, Joe's dedication. Toward the end of *Nightmare Alley*, when Stan, like so many of the tough guy heroes, is on the run, headed toward what we feel is his inevitable geekdom, Joe offers him hope and a risky last chance for survival which Stan is, by now, incapable of understanding, much less accepting. The only thing Stan has learned from the half-man that he utilizes is a judo hold, which he uses to kill a policeman and further insure his doom.

The saddest freaks, of course, are those who are self-made, such as Sailor Martin (Francis Xavier Martin), a vulgar man who lusts after women but gets very little action. The woman Martin desires, most of all, is the one Stan seduces and finally is forced to marry. Mary Margaret Cahill, father fixated, simple, all-trusting, serves the carnival as "the electric chair lady," pretending to let killing amounts of current pass through her unusual body. Her passive role in the carnival, her beauty, and her willingness to submit to Stan's brutality bring them together and allow Stan to exploit her. They leave the carnival together, and embark on careers as con artists, working their way up to eminence as quack faith healers. Only when Stan meets a woman who can handle him as he has handled Mary does his pattern of success begin to change. Mary, the most innocent of all the carnies, is, quite simply, unable to cope with the evil that Stan represents. Only with Stan's destruction can there be hope for her.

Stan studies them all and bides his time. He is especially impressed by the lessons taught him by his mistress, Zeena, whose drunken husband Stan manages to kill. Zeena, who has worked with her husband to perfect a mentalist act, gives Stan the secret code that is the heart of the mystery. She shows Stan how the code operates, but more important, she impresses on him that the trick to all of life is deception. "I've always let on that a man that will spend his time learning misdirection can just reach in his pocket and put something in a hat and then go ahead and take it out again and everybody will sit back and gasp, wondering where it came from."

In his biography, *Houdini: The Man Who Walked Through Walls*, Gresham describes his ambitious subject as "eager to possess any kind of key—to any kind of door." This same ambition drives Stan Carlisle, who, lacking Houdini's innate honor, is capable of all crimes from blackmail to murder. Unlike most of the performers and freaks, however, he obviously cannot simply be explained away with references to a country in poverty or a series of unlucky breaks. Gresham does try to explain Stan's behavior, and it is at this point, where the tough guy is placed on the analyst's couch, that the novel itself turns sour. Gresham's half-baked Freudian bromides too often turn the hard, brutal, and evocative study of carnival life into a case of special pleading for the existence of evil.

Stan, when we first meet him as a carny, states his philosophy, a code of behavior ably summarized by his knowledge that "one in five is a born chump." It is up to the sharp operator to locate and fleece these suckers. What is more, Stan feels he has a certain honor, which is mixed up with his ambiguous feelings toward the stern father he has rejected and the mother who was unfaithful. "My old man and his deals. Church vestry-man on Sundays, con man the rest of the week. Damn him, the bible spouting louse." Terrorized by his father, the witness to his mother's adultery, Stan is explained away in terms having to do primarily with an unhappy, almost archetypal childhood. We are left to believe that this unhappiness leads to his cleverness as well as his cynicism. "There's a rat buried deep in everybody and they'll rat on you if they get pushed far enough."

After leaving the carnival and falling the victim of a woman who easily outmaneuvers him, Stan's life is saved by a Negro who is riding the boxcars North to help in the union movement. The Negro and Stan exchange attitudes, and the colored man tells Stan, with a good deal of justice, that he should relax and hate a bit less. But it is too late for any last minute proletarian heroics. Stan turns savagely to his possible savior. "Listen, kid, you got everything figured out so close. What sense does it all make? What sort of God would put us here in this goddamned, stinking slaughterhouse of a world? Some guy that likes to tear the wings off flies? What use is there in living and starving and fighting the next guy for a full belly? It's a nut house. And the biggest loonies are at the top."

As hero of *Nightmare Alley*, Stan is its crucial weakness. Gresham's admiration for carny life never quite flows with his attempts to explore Stan. If, as Stan believes, "fear is the key to human nature," if mankind exists to be used, if having roots is a disaster, then how does one explain away Gresham's worshipful approach to the carnival life? "The speech fascinated him. . . . It was the talk of the soil and its drawl covered the agility of the brains that poured it out. It was a soothing, earthy language." If the Ackerman-Zorbaugh Monster Shows is to serve as a representation of a possible answer to the horrors of American society, it cannot also be Stan's moral training ground. It is only in a later carny novel, Herbert Gold's *The Man Who Was Not With It*, that a possible reconciliation is reached which makes a meaningful analogy between the carnival world and ours. As Gold puts it: "There's a good and with it way to be not with it, too."

The Damned:
Good Intentions: The Tough Guy
as Hero and Villain

CHARLES ALVA HOYT

I DON'T THINK we need puzzle ourselves greatly over the popularity of the tough guy novel. It has long been noted that ordinary people who wage a generally successful struggle with their impulses to violence tend to indulge themselves in admiration for the extraordinary people who do not. From this admiration to identification is only a short step, made possible by convincing one's self that the violence in question is necessary, or at least justified. It is this process which has produced the enormous gallery of good criminals of the popular imagination—the merry men of Sherwood; housebreakers in dinner jackets like the Saint and Raffles; and all those gallant and genteel pirate bands over at Twentieth Century Fox.

This process has often been called sentimentalism, but I prefer to think of it as the super-ego's inevitable call for equilibrium. The id demands approval for acts of violence: the seizure of other people's property, the rape of a woman who pleases us, the murder of him who stands in our way. In ordinary living, the super-ego is bound to choke off these impulses, and even in vicarious experience, life in books, it moves to correct them. The property in question was not seized unlawfully: it was the hero's true inheritance, stolen from him by a Yankee carpetbagger. As for the woman, she is in fact more guilty than her attacker, to whom she sobs out her acquiescence every second line; and the man murdered—he has dishonored our house; he is Claudius, whose death is hallowed by every decent impulse.

Whatever origins you care to give it, this process has been in our country richly productive of popular heroes. That force must not be underestimated which can create of an unassimilable border-ruffian a knight like Jesse James, or make of a treacherous saloon brawler that pillar of the law Bill Hickok, to say nothing of—perhaps its greatest feat—turn an undernourished paranoid like William Bonney into that ideal of rebellious youth, Billy the Kid. It is this same force which in a different but no less congenial sphere has made a great man of an overworked, plodding, rather seedy figure—the private detective.

Of course the basic charm of the private eye is that he is aggressively outside the law. That is, like all tough guys, he despises convention, proper conduct, due process, search warrants, *habeas corpus*—in short, decent behavior as it is codified. On the other hand, he is presumed to subscribe to a rigid code of his own, which, though elastic enough at its periphery, is at its center as fixed as society's own—protect the weak, honor property, oppose tyranny, treat women as they wish to be treated (there is plenty of elasticity there). And so the shabby dealings of a rather dubious occupation are made to order for the ritual practices of a cult which we may call latronolatry.

We all know about the little peccadilloes of Sam Spade and Mike Hammer, but must perhaps be reminded that Sherlock Holmes himself was usually happier working outside the law, or even at cross-purposes with it—surely the source of much of his charm, for he was not in himself a particularly likable man. No one *can* be who is right as much of the time. Was Sherlock Holmes a tough guy? Well, it has been pointed out that his most famous case, "The Speckled Band," owes little of its celebrity to his powers of deduction. It is in that adventure, it may be recalled, that Holmes bends a poker with his bare hands.

An even better example, and to my way of thinking a much better story, is "The Adventure of the Illustrious Client." There Holmes finds himself completely balked by a murderous adversary whom Due Process cannot touch. So like any tough dick he breaks into the fellow's apartment, having first provided a smokescreen in the person of the amiable Watson, and steals the evidence. Archie Goodwin never did a prettier piece of work. I think we may identify Holmes, for all his savoir faire, with the popular avenger who lurks just at the outer limits of the law, making fools of the police, playing his own game for high stakes, and wreaking a rough justice upon those who otherwise might never have been touched.

And that brings us to the critical factor in the Cult of the Tough Guy: intention. Actually the distinction between the "good" tough guy (Mike Hammer) and the "bad" tough guy (Frank Nitti, say, in his televised, fictional self) is rather delicate. It certainly does not rest upon the means they employ, but rather on the ends they seek. A better way of distinguishing between them is by the words "Successful" and "Unsuccessful," because any tough guy, good or bad, has a certain magnetism about him. Whether he sustains this magnetism and becomes a hero, or loses it to become a villain is a question solely of *intention*.

I first came across *The Damned* (1952) by John D. MacDonald in my undergraduate days, when it seemed one of the most powerful and dazzling works imaginable. Indeed it was not only my fraternity brothers and I who found it so; I believe it has sold several million copies. Time has effected certain changes, however, and today it seems only the grossest imitation Hemingway, with every one of the master's punches telegraphed, and all his delicate little notes amplified as on an electric guitar. It is, on the other hand, of particular value for our purposes because it presents a rare confrontation of the successful tough guy and the unsuccessful tough guy, both in the same story.

We meet the unsuccessful one first. He is bad, to be sure, bad clear through, but none the less attractive for that. The plot mechanism of *The Damned* is provided by a stalled ferry boat, which brings up all the characters on the Mexican side of the border, in various stages of exasperation and despair. Del Bennicke, tough guy number one, is in particularly bad shape; he is running from the law. He has seduced a bullfighter's woman (not much of a job, in fact) and then killed the bullfighter, although in self-defense. Notice that his intentions in both these acts were not bad; the reader warms to him immediately. The girl came and got into bed with *him*; actually it was not his fault. And it is false Mexican justice that would throw a man in jail for trying to save his own life.

> Bennicke was a short, compact man with thick shoulders, a wise and worldly tough-nut face, brisk tilted eyes, and a black brush cut, wiry as horsehair. Wars and rumors of wars in the earth's far corners had nurtured him. He had the strut of the soldier of fortune, but too fond a regard for his own skin to wish to hear any shots fired in anger. A brisk line of patter and more brass than a dozen temple gongs had enabled him to worm his way into the homes of the weirder variants of the international set, and be adopted as mascot, drinking partner, or bed companion, depending on the circumstances.

He was a professional guest, and between times he had smuggled gold, worked on oil crews in Venezuela, pimped in Japan. Fists and tongue and knife had got him out of nearly every variety of trouble. He had an ungrammatical flair for languages, came from New Jersey, and thought of all other races as gooks.

A masterful introduction. Note interspersed among the many authentic attributes of the successful tough guy—the physique, the opportunism, the odd jobs—the suggestions that Bennicke is not in fact going to be the hero of the novel: the suggestion of cowardice, for example ("regard for his own skin"), the use of the knife, so unbecoming to a man, and the crude racial prejudice. MacDonald is rather adroit at this sort of thing; a little later he daringly confirms our suspicions of Bennicke by allowing him to beat up a couple of fairies. Now this is really a *coup de main*; homosexuals occupy a rather uneasy position in tough guy literature for obvious if complex reasons. Normally they are fair game for every sort of violence. But these two are singularly inoffensive, somewhat funny young boys, quite incidental to the main plot. Bennicke's attack on them is entirely gratuitous, as all the other characters in the book realize; his intentions in the matter are thoroughly bad. Moreover, the homosexuals are defended from his cruelty by the other tough guy, who now appears on perfect cue.

The effect of MacDonald's arrangements is somewhat spoiled, by the way, by a characteristic explanatory burst; one homosexual, comforting the other, says, "They have to humiliate us to get even with themselves, you know. It's because they have the same . . . slant on life and won't admit it. So they have to go around being terribly 'he,' strutting and making women." But the second tough guy is now on stage. He is Bill Danton, also a pretty rough customer: "He and his father owned and ran, as partners, a big place near Mante. Cotton and rice. Work on the place had baked him dark. When he stood up, however, there was a rawboned Texan looseness about his big frame that differentiated him from the others." He is a Texan, a good sign, and a thorough Anglo-Saxon, although on intimate terms with the Mexican laborers with whom he is travelling and from whom he is practically indistinguishable. The author emphasizes Danton's free, unprejudiced attitude. Danton and his father have settled south of the border to avoid persecution because of his stepmother, who is Mexican. But Bill himself went to "private school in Houston" and has a college degree. With this fellow it is very much a case of the reader's having his cake and eating it.

Danton's intentions are pure. He defends the fairies as he would any of God's creatures: "They aren't doing you any harm. They're just different from you, man." No masculinity doubts there. Danton can be tough enough; he "came up onto his feet, reached Benson [Bennicke's alias] in three long strides, deftly caught the arm, twisted it, and brought it up between the man's shoulder blades, holding him helpless." And like all tough guys, he is a man of few words: "One more time you use that word, man, I'm going to pound on you a little."

Of course a full-dress fight between these two is on the program. By the time it comes, we have confirmed our early impressions: Bennicke is not going to succeed because his violence is not justifiable, whereas Danton's is, and so he will win. There is an incident when a powerful politician and his bodyguards shoulder to the front of the line, ahead of a desperately ill American woman. Danton almost loses his life disputing the way, while Bennicke hides in a ditch. Finally comes the fight which is resolved thus: "from somewhere out of the night there came a vast, hard-knuckled fist, swung like a bag of rocks at the end of a rope." One punch is all Danton needs, as is traditional.

Each tough guy ends up with his woman. Danton will marry his, who is well-nigh perfect: beautiful, intelligent, perky but serious, sensual but respectable. Bennicke gets a blowsy tramp whom he knocks around with the heel of his hand—nothing wrong with that of course. But if he had been the successful tough guy, she would have been a debutante who had been asking in vain for that beating all of her eighteen years. *This* girl cries broken-heartedly, a bad sign.

The ferry is put to rights, and the characters go off to their various fates. It is strongly suggested that Bennicke will be taken by the police, who by now have his name. But most readers will hope that he makes it, I venture to say, because as contemptible as he has become, he still represents opposition to law and order, and *that* is the tough guy's last resource; even Al Capone had that much going for him.

Recent years have brought a resurgence of "sophisticated" fiction and television shows featuring the rank and file policeman. He is an excellent fellow to be sure and the sort one would want to have living next door in real life, but no threat to the eminence of the tough guy. Stolen fruits are sweetest; the policeman after all has a *right* to shoot people, or even, as some suppose, to beat them up. That takes most of the fun out of it. In fact the whole business becomes tedious and rather sordid. So although Joe Friday had his day, it was not quite as splendid as James Bond's day, which is full of cars, women, drinks, and clothes. Poor old Joe was like the rest of us: all he got were the facts, ma'am.

The Killer Inside Me:

Fear, Purgation, and the Sophoclean Light

R. V. CASSILL

TOLSTOY GAVE US a starting point by declaring of a younger "tough" Russian novelist, "He says 'Boo' but he doesn't scare me." (Did Tolstoy *want* to be scared? Well, he felt seriousness only in confrontations with existential anxiety, and he hungered and thirsted after seriousness.)

In the trade of the American Boo-sayers there are low-brow, middle-brow, and high-brow conventions for saying Boo. We tend to take these conventions seriously and, in academic company at least, admit our fear or concern only according to the caste lines manifest by the externals of a book. And since most of us middle-brows need to believe we are high-brow and therefore affect a taste for conventions not really in harmony with our native concerns, we are generally pretty well insulated against a literary experience that provides more than an immunizing shock or tonic jolt for tired blood. As has often been noted, democratic man uses the fiction of violence for its purgative effect. What needs to be noted is that whatever his brow level, he doesn't really want to be purged very hard. Not really scoured. . . .

Through various levels of sophistication (which, in shorthand, we can label according to the publishing format: pulp, paperback original, hardcover, and little magazine) the neutralizing variation of the "crime does not pay" formula is detectable in astonishingly consistent proportion. It wheezes through such simple-minded "classics" of the tough guy novel as W. R. Burnett's *Little Caesar*. (You and I wouldn't want to be gangsters, though they're kind of interesting.) James Baldwin's fictional confections proclaim that discrimination against Negroes and addicts doesn't pay. And that great scarecrow of our decade, William Burroughs, said (no doubt sincerely!) that *Naked Lunch* was written as "a protest against capital punishment." Protest, as Mr. Burroughs' cunning reminded him, can be a slightly more sophisticated variant of the crime-doesn't-pay formula, merely substituting "society" for the individual who is unrewarded for transgression. So from top to bottom of the brow scale, we find novels of protest and violence affirming the indissoluble contiguity of the democratic mass, the adequacy of received ideas, and the justice of our aspirations toward a Better World.

But there is something else to be said about local crime and violence besides that they don't pay; and the writer who chooses them for his theme and subject matter may use them on a journey outward from the comfort of consensus. They may be followed as the tract of that American devil which is with us in affluence as in poverty, in sickness as in health, and unto death. This is the devil predicated, I suppose, by Robert Penn Warren in *Brother to Dragons*, hinted by Auden in a poem "Gold in the North came the blizzard to say" (with its unequivocal line, "America will break your heart."), pointed at by Hawthorne's fear of desert places, and—no use going on with this list. Readers of serious American literature, like readers of American pulp, have heard our peculiar devil cough or snap a twig beyond the campfire. We have an idea of where the big scare awaits us—so mostly we prefer to look at paper devils painted in fiction: at social injustice, shocking crime rates, sexual deviation, addiction to narcotics, whiskey, cigarettes and wild, wild women, or, as academic jargon has it, at EEE-VILL.

My experience in recommending *The Killer Inside Me* (1952) has convinced me that most readers will try to have done with it by assigning it a place in the multitudinous ranks of painted devils by which our eyes are decoyed away from the thicket where the Old Fellow hides and pants and laughs and waits for us. Among caste-minded readers this misprision can be ridiculously easy if not automatic; for this novel bears considerable internal and external evidence of its origin among "paperback originals."

It was hastily written. (According to Arnold Hano, the editor of Lion Books who commissioned it, it was written in two weeks. Hano also told me once, not very convincingly, that the "plot" of the whole thing was his contribution, implying that Thompson merely "wrote it up." The truth of that confidence seems to me irrelevant in view of the way the plot has been integrated and caught up to serve the unified vision and statement of the novel as a whole. Nevertheless, some of the text does have the mangy discoloration that shows haste, some of it is pocked with the formular, hard-breathing clichés of literature for the working man, and a few of the episodes have the stale cigar smell of editor-author collaboration—"I think you could clarify it on page 80, Jim, if you. . . .") I see no more point in denying the irrelevant warts than in affirming them. We know the novel is an impure art, and we had better be guided by Ransom's axiom that we "remember literature by its noblest moments." One needs a goat's stomach to hold out long enough for the noblest moments in Balzac and probably Dostoevsky, too.

The reader of *The Killer Inside Me* will have some obligation to spit out the indigestible bones and husks that are part of the literary mode in which this novel was born. Whoever wishes to can give it up at the first token of low birth and retire to the comfort of the notion that only a "hardcover author" who takes a lot of time with his work and has been authenticated by the reviewing and critical media can successfully "paint EEE-VILL."

But what I would like to declare is that in Thompson's hands, the mode of the paperback original, husks and all, turns out to be excellently suited to the objectives of the novel of ideas. (See Balzac on Stendhal for definition thereof.) Using the given idiom—and for all I can be sure of, a given plot as well—Thompson makes a hard, scarey, Sophoclean statement on American success.

That statement can be tentatively paraphrased thus: Even if you are a rotten, murderous piece of astral excrement and know it, you're supposed to go on and succeed.

Succeed at what?

Well, the society expects you to succeed at something socially valuable, of course, but it gives you the momentum toward success in any case. And your nature splits between this momentum and the inertia of the heart, however vile or sublime that heart may be. The American dream (conscious, unconscious or merely fatal as it may be) makes no provision for an asylum for failures. Among a decent, godless people those who are—and that which is—hopeless from the start find no repose in the bosom of the author of their inadequacy.

The central character (the light bearer of this idea) is Lou Ford, a deputy sheriff in a small, booming Oklahoma city. Ford is a social success. People like him and count on him. He shows heart. He doesn't carry a gun. His talk is cheerful and optimistic. He laughs. Quite a lot.

And there is the flaw already—presented masterfully on the first pages as character trait and novelistic *effect*; the laughter is the "crack in the china cup that leads on to the land of the dead." (Read it as, roughly, the equivalent of Leverkuhn's laughter in Mann's *Dr. Faustus* if you really want to cross the line out of the paperback original as briskly as you can.) Ford's cheerful talk is, when he doesn't "watch it," a putting on. He puts people on with sayings like, "I mean, if we didn't have the rain we wouldn't have the rainbows, now would we?" And what this putting on will lead to, by a dazzlingly managed *progression d'effet*, is the dramatized revelation that Ford puts himself on in a somewhat different sense—that is, he wears himself as a disguise, his other self tragically invisible. . . . *free* in that catastrophic sense of the word which was vainly ignored by our founding fathers.

In the book, this clear split, between the social person playing his social role and the invisible person admitting with horrid resignation that there is no role for it to play except to superintend the irreparable disjunction, is called paranoiac schizophrenia. (Or, in the rather dismal vocabulary of the paperback medium, *the sickness*. Italicized for those who read with their finger.) But Mr. Thompson is not out to give us a cheap scare by sketching the bloody course of *a* criminal schizophrenic. Alas, he is out to show us the meaning of the sort we search for when we ask for the meaning of a crucifixion or of the massacre of innocents.

The mental illness (which serves as a manifestation in which the spiritual torture and dismemberment are immanent) breaks loose early in the story when Ford discovers that a lovely hustler whom he is supposed to get out of town will fall in love with him when, without premeditation, he beats her black and blue with his belt. (A sadomasochistic relationship? All right. It is that, if you like. You will not like it so well when the novel shows you that this beating is an image of a *free* man *liberating* a woman.

I asked a friend of mine—who is neither a professional critic nor a psychiatric social worker—if the passage describing the beating made her hot. "Well . . . ," she answered thoughtfully. Some of us will, however timidly, take peeps through our reading at the mouth of hell and concede that the "hard Sophoclean light," like any other, breaks into a spectrum dusky red at one end.)

In Ford's relation with the whore lies immanent the murder of the girl who loves him. For some years he has carried on an affair with Amy Stanton, a pretty school teacher who is a neighbor of his. Being a compromised school teacher, Amy naturally wants to marry him. Ford has postponed this ingeniously because he knows what is wrong with him. Though he knows, vaguely at least, that a day of judgment must come when he will show himself without the disguise of his other personality, he dreads it. For the Ford who is helpless to control the life situation that has been handed him has a heart—while the successful, optimistic good samaritan in whom he hides has none.

After he has decided he must kill Amy to prevent her finding out or inadvertently helping to expose his other murders, he agrees to marry her and a period of superficial tenderness and harmony follows. (Complicated, be it said, by their discovery that she too responds womanly to the belt.) In this period, Ford tries (with what justification? why?—the absence of answers is part of the horror) to feel kindly toward her. "Amy came to see me every day. . . . She always brought some cake or pie or something, stuff I reckon their dog wouldn't eat (and that hound wasn't high-toned—he'd snatch horseturds on the fly), and she hardly nagged about anything." Obviously, this attempt to be charitable is broken into something ghastly by the joke he *can't help* making of it. Here is a progression of the habit of laughter enunciated in his previous formulas for putting people on.

There is another turn of the screw yet to come. After Ford has killed Amy (with his fist and foot, naturally—this extraordinarily brutal murder is the logical extension of their pain-tinged sexual passages, the end to which a *free* man will come, given the momentum toward it by the consenting invitation of the female), he tries to formulate his remorse. "I guess that stuff she'd brought to me when I was sick wasn't really crap. It was as good as she knew how to fix. I guess that dog of theirs didn't have to chase horses unless'n he wanted the exercise." The joke is still there at the end. Its being there does not merely mean that the heartless deputy is still making jokes—but that Ford has heard and is echoing the joke that lies at the still center of the turning world, in the heart of light, in the silence. It is the laughter of nothingness. The ridiculousness of the spaces between the stars, given tongue by the criminal human.

For a novel of ideas, like this one, to work as fiction, it is necessary that there be a series of developing correspondences between the condensed flashes of meaning (whether epigrammatic language or significant effect) and the extended movements of action in which the relations of characters change and the pattern begins to emerge. Obviously my space is too limited to account for all, or even many of these correspondences.

But, as an example of the formal synthesis, we might consider the relation between one of Ford's definitions of his own situation and the progress of recognition and incrimination going on among the townspeople around him. The hidden Ford is, quite credibly, an intellectual—even something of a theologian perforce, formed parthenogenetically by the sheer dynamics of the condition into which he has been born. Now and again in the course of the first person narration he speaks in a language very different in tone at least from the folksy crudeness of the deputy. Ford says of his disease: "We might have . . . the condition: or we might just be cold-blooded and smart as hell; or we might be innocent of what we're supposed to have done."

This is a very peculiar set of similarities indeed. Puzzle on it for a while and you will realize that something *very tenuous but absolutely crucial* must be present to make any difference at all among these three alternatives. Inwardly it is a theological puzzle; outwardly it is a riddle for which no society has more than the crudest of answers.

Then note in Thompson's novel how he has concretely represented, in the developing action of the novel, the way the people entrusted with the law and the power in this Oklahoma city grope slowly through the mazes of this riddle. Astonishingly (ah, but not really!) they know from the beginning that the deputy is the one who has done the series of murders culminating in Amy's death. Yet, they *never* know until they *choose to believe* that he is the one who must be punished for them. They must, in a word, enter the theological maze into which Ford's misfortune has decoyed them. They must choose the killer because they can find him no other way. The slow mustering of townspeople to this choice is shaped to flesh out the intellectual paradox which I have quoted.

There is an eerie sort of suspense in the movements by which the law closes in on Ford. He has to lead his pursuers to himself, and that means that he must choose to make real one of the three alternatives in his ambiguous condition so that the others will ultimately have something to find. And in choosing a reality of guilt for himself—by this alone—he comes to know the reasons for what he has done. These are not the reasons that he gave himself for each successive murder, but rather a set of fatalities that both transcend and fall short of the operations of the rational mind. He identifies himself at last as a murderous monster dying for the sins of mankind, a guilty scapegoat—which is not really so near to anomaly as we might like to believe.

The technique which builds and fuses effects that permit these hard and subtle definitions seems to me worthy of being read as we read the very best modern novels. The representation of that universal disjunction which *is* laughter appears no less serious or scarey than Kurtz's "Exterminate the brutes" (which is heated and sharpened by a very different technique and context, to be sure, but which finally scares or doesn't by its conformity to our religious intuitions).

The Killer Inside Me doesn't end—I suppose a novel can not end—with a purely nihilistic pessimism. Since novels probably can't produce any ultimate wisdom of hope or despair—we are left at the end with a synthesis compounded of despair and the human inability to accept it. Here is the note.

> "What are you going to say when you're drowning in your own dung and they keep booting you back into it . . . when you're at the bottom of the pit and the whole world's at the top, when it has but one face, a face without eyes or ears, and yet it watches and listens . . . ?
>
> "What are you going to do and say? Why, pardner, that's simple. It's easy as nailing your balls to a stump and falling off backwards. Snow again, pardner, and drift me hard, because that's an easy one.
>
> "You're gonna say, they can't keep a good man down. You're gonna say, a winner never quits and a quitter never wins. . . . And then you're gonna get out there and hit 'em hard and fast and low, an'—an' Fight!
>
> "Rah."

This is not quite Kurtz "pronouncing on the adventures of his soul on this earth" and winning, by the pronouncement itself, some measure of remission from their horror. One will not find here much trace of the great Conradian resonance which builds the luminous haze of meaning around the events in a Conrad novel. For those readers who depend heavily on the element of evocative language for their reception of a novel's meaning, Thompson's limited idiom may remain an obstacle to reading.

But it's worth being as clear as one can about what language Thompson *is* using here. Read the American cadences in the passage above and ask, Is this any less effective than that of Sartre's Goetz, who says "*Il y a la guerre, et je la ferai.*"

Focus on *To Have and Have Not:*

To Have Not: Tough Luck   YOUNG

1. No great hit at the time, the first movie version of *To Have and Have Not,* Humphrey Bogart in the lead, script by William Faulkner, has become a minor classic, much in demand.

2. "Funny we didn't get no boys," Harry says. His wife replies, "That's because you're such a man. That way it always comes out girls." Oddly enough, the author got only boys.

3. Apparently, Hemingway refers here to yet another source of his overdetermined protagonist: Joe Russell, owner of a charter-boat out of Key West from which Hemingway often fished in the days before he had his own boat built, and before Russell settled into the operation of his Key West bar. It was here that many war veterans, temporarily employed by FERA depression projects, came on pay days to get drunk and fight.

4. Hemingway pointed out to *his* then wife, Pauline, that "Jane was flattered when people took her for Mrs. Macomber in that story" ("The Short Happy Life of Francis Macomber"). "Well," Mrs. Hemingway replied, "I can't imagine that her husband would exactly feel set up about that." Mr. Gingrich told the story in the December, 1966, issue of his magazine. As he himself points out, Jane Mason is now Mrs. Gingrich.

Focus on *Appointment in Samarra:*

The Importance of Knowing What You Are Talking About   BRUCCOLI

1. "Special Report," *Newsweek*, LXI (June 13, 1963), 57.
2. *New York Times Book Review* (September 10, 1950), 1. I do not extend the rest of his sentence to O'Hara: ". . . the most outstanding author since the death of Shakespeare." This review has occasioned a good deal of jibing at O'Hara for hyperbolic misjudgment of a poor novel; but the review is clearly not a rave notice of *Across the River and Into the Trees*, which he obviously considered weak Hemingway. It is a defense of Hemingway's career.
3. "Don't Say It Never Happened," *New York Herald Tribune Books* (April 18, 1962), 3. Surprisingly, it is "a store."

Horace McCoy's Objective Lyricism   STURAK

1. Allene Talmey, "Paris Quick Notes / About Sartre, Gide, Cocteau, Politics, / The Theatre, and Inflation," *Vogue*, CIX (January 15, 1947), 92. Miss Talmey recalls that among others Sartre and Claude-Edmonde Magny were astonished that she had never heard of McCoy (letter to the author, April 6, 1966).
2. Unidentified source quoted by Roger Bourne Linscott, "On the Books," *New York Herald Tribune Weekly Book Review*, February 9, 1947 (loose clipping, held by author).
3. "Writer Tells / Success Way" (loose clipping, held by author). This news report is datelined Mesa, Arizona, April 21. McCoy was on location for the Paramount picture, *The Texas Rangers Ride Again*, which was released in 1940. According to this account, the book, then called "Approach With Caution," would soon be released by Knopf.
4. See the unpubl. diss. (Northwestern University, 1949) by Philip Calvin Durham, "The Objective Treatment of the 'Hard-Boiled' Hero in American Fiction: A Study in the Frontier Background of Modern American Literature," p. 259.
5. Quoted in Philip Durham, *Down These Mean Streets a Man Must Go: Raymond Chandler's Knight* (Chapel Hill: University of North Carolina Press, 1963), p. 121.

6. Albert Van Nostrand, *The Denatured Novel* (New York: Charter Books, 1962), see especially pp. 29–47.

7. Joseph T. Shaw, editor, "Introduction," *The Hard-Boiled Omnibus, Early Stories from Black Mask* (New York: Simon and Schuster, 1946), p. vii.

8. In a letter to Charles W. Morton, May 2, 1949; in *Raymond Chandler Speaking*, ed. Dorothy Gardiner and Kathrine Sorley Walker (Boston: Houghton Mifflin, 1962), p. 83.

INDEX